New

ELVIS
Costello

ELVIS
Costello

a biography

TONY CLAYTON-LEA

FROMM INTERNATIONAL
NEW YORK

First Fromm International Edition, 1999

Copyright © 1998 by Tony Clayton-Lea

All rights reserved under International and Pan-American Copyright Conventions. Published in the United States by Fromm International Publishing Corporation, New York. First published in Great Britain by Andre Deutsch Limited, London, 1998.

LIBRARY OF CONGRESS CATALOGING-IN-PUBLICATION DATA

    Elvis Costello : a biography / Tony Clayton-Lea. — 1st Fromm International ed.
       p.   cm.
    Includes bibliographical references and discography.
    ISBN 0-88064-235-1
    1. Costello, Elvis.   2. Rock musicians—Biography.
    ML420.C685C6 1999
    782.42166'092—dc21
    [B]   99-12714
                                                CIP

10 9 8 7 6 5 4 3 2 1

Manufactured in the United States of America

Contents

Acknowledgements

Despite rumours to the contrary, no author ever writes a book on their own. This book would never have been written if it hadn't been for the following:

My agent Chelsey Fox, who worked diligently and with extreme kindness and patience to get this book off the ground; Commissioning Editor at André Deutsch, Hannah MacDonald, whose sympathetic reading of various deadline problems made this book a relative joy to start and to finish; my researcher, Linda Higgins, whose ready response and dedication to any job I asked her to do went way beyond the call of duty; my two families, who, unwittingly or not, assisted in giving me the time to work without interruption; my children, Paul and Sarah, who quite unknowingly and guilelessly kept my feet on the ground when all I wanted to do was fly; and last but not least, my wife Angela, who managed to hold everything together when it could so easily have fallen apart.

Aside from the above – all of whom played such a pivotal part in the book that if any one had not been in place, it wouldn't have been written – the following were also instrumental in playing their part. Even if they were totally unaware of it ...

My various editors in Ireland: Victoria White, Arts Editor of the *Irish Times*, whose rigour in wanting to get things right for her own pages inspired in part the way this book was written; Vincent De Veau and Paul Whitington of *Cara* magazine, whose good humour, solid comradeship, and continual commissions helped me focus on matters other than the book – no bad thing; Annette O'Meara, Lucy Taylor and Aine O'Connor of *U* magazine, whose constant good humour alleviated the occasional difficulties of deadline fever; and John Ryan, Editor of the *Sunday Times* Culture Ireland section, whose suave and urbane mateship over the past couple of years has strengthened my belief in quality journalism.

Other people that more than spring to mind: my close (despite distance) and irreplaceable friends from the late 1970s onwards – Ria and Arthur Mathews (brother and sister), and Peter and Gillian Murphy (husband and wife). In many ways, some of which they know only too well, this book is as much their experience as mine.

Of course, because the subject of this book could not be persuaded to talk to me (a decision I utterly respect) I had to look elsewhere for his words. To all the writers and journalists whose work I quote, many thanks (a full list of names can be found at the end of the book). Also, a word of thanks to Clive Wichelow, of *Back Numbers*, who provided crucial back issues of various magazines, Martin C. Strong, who kindly gave permission to use his superbly-researched discography, and David Clynch of MCPS who shed light on the more arcane songs Elvis Costello chose to cover. I also doff the hat to Paul Du Noyer, who clarified certain matters of which I had scant appreciation.

While I'm on the subject of the subject: Elvis Costello was contacted and requested through his management company, By Eleven, to contribute to this book. Firmly, but politely, he refused. Neither he nor his management used any tactics of any kind whatsoever to prevent me from writing the book. For this I am extremely grateful – my life wasn't made any easier by his refusal to co-operate, but neither was it made any more difficult.

The hardline fan and observant critic will notice that throughout the book I have not quoted from any songs written or performed by Elvis Costello/D.P.A. MacManus. There is a reason for this: I was informed by his management that copyright of his lyrics would be protected to the utmost.

However, anyone with even a casual interest in Costello will need no reminding as to just how good a lyricist he is.

Finally, with no facetiousness or provocation whatsoever, this book is dedicated to Elvis Costello. Simply, thank you for the music ...

Tony Clayton-Lea, March 1998

CHAPTER 1

'The only two things that matter to me, the only motiva-
tion points for me writing all these songs, are revenge and
guilt. Those are the only emotions I know about, that I
know I can feel. Love? I dunno what it means, really, and
it doesn't exist in my songs.'
  Elvis Costello, talking to Nick Kent, NME, *August 1977*

'I said that more for effect. When you're confronted by a
35-year old hippie asking you what the difference is
between Punk and New Wave you tend to say things like
that. I was just trying to irritate, you know?'
  Elvis Costello talking to Paul Rambali, The Face,
  August 1983

'Most of the punk bands couldn't play in time. So it was
just cacophony that didn't mean anything. Whereas The
Attractions could actually get on with the thing and make
it musical. Plus we were really horrible to people . . . In
fact, we were much nastier than any of those groups. In
fact, all of them put together.'
  Interview with David Wild, Rolling Stone, *June 1989*

At the time few could have guessed that Elvis Costello, one
of the finest songwriters in the history of rock music, would
have been spawned in the miasma of punk rock. In retrospect, of course, the natural evolution from pigeon-toed punk
to the embodiment of musical eclecticism makes perfect
sense, but in 1976 it would have made no sense at all.

1

While the musical influence of punk rock is negligible, the individualistic attitude that informed it has inspired millions. The word soon spread from the cities to the suburbs – from London to Whitton in Middlesex, where a songwriter called Declan Patrick MacManus sat in his bedroom writing songs of biting hurt and bitter humour. Contacting record companies. Being humiliated. Biding his time . . .

1976 was unkind to traditional singer/songwriters, especially in the UK. Sensitive, bedsit-angst merchants like Joan Armatrading, Clifford T Ward, Cat Stevens and Al Stewart were looked upon by the rock music press and its readers with as much indifference, antipathy even, as those at the opposite musical extreme, Yes, ELO and Pink Floyd. The London-based cognoscenti, the self-appointed arbitrators of taste, had new fish to fry and new ways in which to dish up the lip-smacking morsels.

This indifference was distinctly English, even though the musical influences behind it were American. The diehards of the more commercially-oriented North American branch of the singer/songwriters' union (notably old hand Bob Dylan, new kid Bruce Springsteen, Paul Simon, Joni Mitchell, Leonard Cohen and Neil Young) still reigned supreme, with their credibility intact. Dylan had released *Blood On The Tracks*, *The Basement Tapes* and *Desire* in an eleven-month period from February 1975 to January the following year, and so at the time was critically unassailable. In 1975, Springsteen released *Born To Run*, Simon *Still Crazy After All These Years*, Mitchell *The Hissing Of Summer Lawns* and Young both *Tonight's The Night* and *Zuma*. Leonard Cohen was, as usual, missing in action, practising Zen and the art of making records whenever the mood took him. Other US singer/songwriters, either in solo capacity or within the structure of a band (John Prine, James Taylor, JJ Cale, Carole King, the Band, Little Feat's Lowell George among them) continued to make records.

The literacy of the US hierarchy, occasionally surreal but more often than not purely commercial in its aim, was further smoothed out by the music itself. By and large this was dominated by session players, and therefore lacked a certain spontaneity. Dylan and Young were honourable exceptions. Although influenced by the Americans, the new British breed of singer/songwriter turned away from the pursuit of perfect sound, preferring instead to make their point with a fistful of acoustic strums and a headful of cynicism.

The catalyst was 'pub rock' – a phrase credited by some to *Time Out*'s then music editor, John Collis. One of the scene's mainstays, Kokomo, was actually drafted in by Dylan – who at the time could tell which way the tide was turning – for the initial *Desire* sessions. In his view, though, the English band seemed to lack the right spirit for the job in hand.

Ironically, the pub-rock scene was initiated by an American band called Eggs Over Easy. At the fag end of Spring 1971, they had arrived in London from New York's Greenwich Village to make a record with Chas Chandler, former Animals bassist and ex-Jimi Hendrix manager. Following contractual difficulties, the band grew tired of studio-bound work and, eager to flex their musical muscles, walked into a pub near their house in Kentish Town, The Tally Ho, and secured a Monday-night residency. This grew to four nights a week by the end of the year.

'We were basically a trio,' Austin de Lone told *Mojo* magazine. 'I guess you could say we were a loose rockin' unit, with a countryish tinge.'[1] Joined by a colleague of Chandler's – Animals drummer John Steel – the band's set comprised original songs and a judicious selection of crowd-pleasing cover versions. Aside from appearing at The Tally Ho, Eggs Over Easy also played at more established venues such as The Marquee. It was here that they met Irishman Dave Robinson, who managed Brinsley Schwarz. This band had endured an initial hype that fell apart hilariously – Robinson secured them a down-the-bill spot at Fillmore East, and flew a planeload of journalists out to see them. By the time the party arrived at the gig, after endless delays, they were too late to see the band. The Brinsleys were now living in a communal set-up in Northwood, Middlesex, more out of lack of finances than domestic emulation of The Monkees.

Inspired by the Eggs Over Easy one-take human-jukebox approach to songs, Brinsley Schwarz member Nick Lowe quickly began to write rough'n'ready songs. Soon, Eggs Over Easy were influencing more than Lowe. 'At first it was a groovy little thing,' Lowe recalled in *Mojo*, 'rather Hogarthian, with snotty-nosed urchins hanging around the door and a Sikh bus driver doing a wild frug-a-gogo routine. But within a few weeks it was getting discovered by the clique, the beautiful people.'[2]

The Tally Ho was descended on by throngs of people eager to hear the American band. People would shout out the names of songs they wanted to hear and the band would play them. So it was that Brinsley Schwarz began to play at the pub, happy in the knowledge that their abortive attempt at premier league success was forgotten, and that 'a bit of credibility started to come our way'.[3]

As Eggs Over Easy flew back to the US, new groups began to filter through. Consisting of working musicians (regularly comprising a smattering of Irishmen, due to Dave Robinson's Murphia connections), eager for the dosh and free beer for the night, the bands included Bees Make Honey, Ducks Deluxe, Kilburn And The High Roads, Roogalator, Help Yourself, Clancy, Chilli Willi and the Red Hot Peppers, Ace and The Winkies.

The new bands needed more places to play, however, and gradually other pub venues were made available to them, creating a gig circuit that enabled them to move around London on a nightly basis. Previously playing host to jazz, folk, and country & western outfits, the likes of the Hope & Anchor, The Kensington, The Cock Tavern and The Lord Nelson became the breeding ground for a motley assortment of jobbing musicians with an anything-goes attitude and an unpretentious approach to stagecraft.

Every scene needs some kind of glue to bond it together for more than the requisite few months, though. In this instance, it was Charlie Gillett's *Honky Tonk* radio programme. Broadcast each Sunday morning on BBC Radio London, the show's gig guide acted as a rallying call for denizens of the pub-rock scene, and by mid-1973 the pubs could hardly cope with the demand. As the scene grew, so did its fanbase – generally speaking, ordinary music lovers who had become increasingly weary of the musical and on-stage excesses of the current rock bands. Glam rock was too poncy for them, Krautrock was too avant-garde, and US rock was too smooth. In pub rock (and in its genuine offspring, punk rock), the punter was in cahoots with the music, eyeballing the lead singer and the guitarists, smelling the body odour, stepping on the butt ends, and wiping the spilt lager from his jacket. 'The regrouping of a bunch of middle-class ex-mods who'd been through the hippy underground scene and realised it wasn't their cup of tea,'[4] is how Nick Lowe described the scene.

It didn't last, needless to say. With a few exceptions (Dr Feelgood, Ace, Kokomo, Eddie and the Hot Rods), the record companies weren't biting, and even with these bands commercial success was short-lived. The rest of the groups carried on for a couple of years, but with Ducks Deluxe, The Winkies, Kilburn and the High Roads and Brinsley Schwarz splitting up, an era had come to an end. However, it was not without its benefits. The seeds were sown for a musical aesthetic that would have endless repercussions for many generations of (especially) British musicians. A large number of band members were, as Nick Lowe testified, people who had all but forgotten how to rock, but who were swiftly energised by the no-nonsense spirit of the genre. As the musicians picked up on the energy, so did the audience, who saw in the music a vitality that their erstwhile lumbering rock heroes and pouting pop stars sorely lacked.

While a number of the musicians drifted about, picking up gig work and sessions along the way, three participants in the 'demo section' of Charlie Gillett's programme were soon to reap benefits from the fragmentation of pub rock – Graham Parker, Dire Straits and Declan Costello's Flip City.

Once described by his father, Birkenhead-born Ronnie 'Ross' MacManus, as a 'left-of-centre anarchist'[5] in a *Sunday Times* interview, Declan Patrick MacManus was born in Paddington, London on 25 August 1955. An only child, he lived with his parents in Olympia, West Kensington until he was seven, and then Twickenham until he was sixteen when, following his parents' separation, he and his mother (born on Merseyside) moved to Liverpool for two years. His father subsequently re-married, providing him with four half-brothers, all of whom play music in both rock and folk bands.

There's as strong an Irish dimension as a musical one to Costello's background. His grandfather, Patrick MacManus, born in Dungannon, Northern Ireland, was an Ulster Catholic orphan who attended the Military School of Music in Twickenham. He was thus formally trained in music – unlike Costello's father, who could in fact read music but who felt that a good musical ear was just as important as an ability to follow the rule book.

Invalided out of the First World War, Patrick was stationed in Dublin once he was removed from combat. Although he wasn't in active service he still nevertheless wore a uniform. Some Irish friends advised him, quite literally, to keep his head down – there were people who would gladly kill a member of the King's forces.

In the political climate of Ireland at that time one was never too sure exactly who your real friends were, so Patrick left Ireland after the 1916 rebellion, and travelled to New York. There he became entangled in the Prohibition world of boxers, musicians, gangsters and bootleggers. At one time, he shared a house with the infamous gangster Legs Diamond. He later got work as a musician on the cruise liners that worked out of Birkenhead, the place where his family had moved to. His last semi-professional job was in the theatre pits.

Declan's mother, Lillian, held a number of jobs, including one as part-time usherette for the Liverpool Philharmonic, where she occasionally took her son to concerts, but perhaps more significantly she worked in Brian Epstein's NEMS store and as manager of the record department in Selfridges, Oxford Street. She had a broad interest in classical and contemporary popular music, numbering Mel Tormé, Frank Sinatra, Peggy Lee and Ella Fitzgerald among her favourites. When Costello was eight, his mother took him to see Tony Bennett, who, at that time, was singing with the Buddy Rich Orchestra. Costello had no time for the frantic drummer, but liked Bennett. Since Bennett was a singer, and so was his dad, singing was okay in Declan's book.

For as long as Costello can remember, his father worked with the Joe Loss Orchestra. This was a job out of the ordinary in comparison with those of his schoolmates' nine-to-five dads. When he was a kid, during the school summer holidays, Declan would travel around England with his father, meeting up with British jazz stars such as Ronnie Scott, Phil Seaman, Bill McGuffie and Tubby Hayes. Later, Joe Loss would play a residency at the Hammersmith Palais, where Declan would regularly go to watch. Occasionally, the orchestra featured a guest group or pop star, a lottery effort that included (if you were lucky) The Hollies or (if you weren't) Engelbert Humperdinck. The fact that Costello saw his father at work demystified the process of creating pop music, and made it a normal thing for him to listen to.

Ross MacManus was probably the most versatile of the three singers with the Joe Loss Orchestra, and was given songs that were more difficult to sing, interpretatively if not technically. The band was a huge strict-tempo attraction from the mid-1930s onwards with all levels of society, and aristocratic dances and Royal Family get-togethers were a speciality. The orchestra survived as a popular dance band in an era when many competitors were being drowned out by the noise of The Beatles. It didn't just restrict itself to ballads in waltz time. The orchestra – through its arranger, a man with the most unlikely name of Leslie Vinyl – had to learn the hits of the day, which included everything from The Beatles, The Beach Boys, Dusty Springfield and Trini Lopez to Pink Floyd, The Kinks, The Who and Bob Dylan.

In order for Ross MacManus to learn the songs, he rigged up a repeating device on the trusty MacManus Decca Decalion, and it tricked the record player into thinking it had another record to play. Playing the song ad infinitum, Ross would sing along loudly. Referring to himself as a musical pawnshop, he would bring home acetates of new songs to learn for both gigs and radio programmes.

'I take anything in,' he recalled in the *Sunday Times*, 'but Elvis was very specific, even then . . . When he was three, he'd say 'Siameses' – he wanted the Siamese cat song by Peggy Lee.'[6] Inevitably, Irish folk music was played and sung while he was growing up.

School education was of the regular kind, although Declan didn't appear to like it very much. He attended Catholic schools in Twickenham, was taught by nuns for the first few years and then by lay teachers until he was eleven, by which time he was a member of the Beatles' Fan Club. From then until sixteen he attended a secondary-modern school in Hounslow. And from there (with his mother, who had by this time separated from his father) to Liverpool, a move he regarded as more a return to home than an unwanted wrench from the pleasures of Swinging London. His education record wasn't particularly exemplary, with only a single 'A' level to his name – English, inevitably – but he read voraciously, including newspapers and magazines from start to finish, particularly on topics of political theory. He had faith in the Labour Party, but possibly due more to his somewhat naive and fanciful notions about socialism than anything else.

He was somewhat of a loner, and friends didn't figure too much on his priority list. A strong sense of independence had developed in the wake of his parents' divorce and his father's regular absences. From an early age music was always his main interest, a lasting preoccupation that stemmed as much from his parents' tastes and lifestyles as his own specific ambitions. Too young to be a mod, too individualistic to want to be a skinhead, and too wary of the more farcical elements of glam rock, Declan listened initially to American singer/songwriters such as James Taylor, but eventually tired of the persistently confessional aspect of the songs. Party records in London consisted of Tamla Motown and reggae, the staple Sta-Prest diet of the discerning teenager, but when he moved to Liverpool he discovered that people there preferred either the calming sounds of US West Coast groups or British progressive rock bands such as Deep Purple, Uriah Heep and Black Sabbath.

Unable to come to terms with either, he slowly drifted back to soul, though he did respond to peer pressure in forcing himself to like The Grateful Dead. Although he couldn't play any sport well he was fanatical about football, in particular Liverpool and Roger Hunt.

Already the mode! of a typical teenage social outcast was taking shape – someone who didn't want to join in on just anything, or to kick a ball around when there was Tamla Motown and ska music to be listened to on the radio. The glasses more or less completed the picture. Elvis had quite good eyesight until he was fifteen, but when he left school at sixteen to work in a computerized office, the artificial lighting and paperwork began to give him serious headaches. Suffering from a condition known as astigmatism, he can go about normal daily life without wearing spectacles, but if he tries to watch television or films, or read for any length of time, the headaches keep on coming.

Declan left school in the same year that one million people signed on the unemployment register. Scarcity of work, particularly in the North of England, created an urgency about securing a job, irrespective of its suitability. He had neither the qualifications nor the inclination to go to college, and at sixteen was already too old for jobs that required apprenticeship entry-age levels. He once went for a job as a tea boy, only to be informed that he was over-qualified. Another job he applied for was as an Admiralty chart corrector, a Dickensian job requiring a high boredom threshold and precision handwriting, two things he didn't have.

He then applied for a job as a computer operator in a large banking centre, which he clinched despite his scant knowledge of computers and his virtual incompetence at mathematics. He decided this made him a perfect candidate. Didn't computers make all of that obsolete? Realizing that the (then) technological status of the job far outweighed the actual brainwork involved – his work consisted of placing tapes on the machines, feeding cards, and lining up paper in printers – Declan was content to push buttons while songs were beginning to ferment in his under-occupied mind. Costello was an IBM 360 operator, working on either an ICL or a Honeywell computer – a gigantic billion-dollar brain with banks of whirring tapes and printers. The staff worked in shifts because the computer could never be switched off, giving Costello enough time to formulate his ambitions for international success.

His debut appearance on stage was at a folk club in Liverpool, just before he reached sixteen, in an attempt to try out his own songs, no matter what shape they were in. He had already harboured keen ambitions to be a professional musician, and knew that the only way to get better was to play his songs in public, performing them almost religiously, despite the abject humiliation he felt when audience response was indifferent.

In Liverpool, he played several folk club dates on his own, and a handful with a small group called Rusty, but he came to feel restricted by folk music's narrow and rigid boundaries. It's also likely that he was put off by the fact that at one of his folk dates Ewan McColl – sitting in the first row – fell asleep during his brief set!

'They weren't very interesting,' was how he described the songs in Q magazine. 'It was quite funny, like anybody's first steps at doing anything, but you wouldn't want them put under the microscope ten years later . . . I can't even remember a lot of it . . . I used to play in those clubs, or the British Legion in Birkenhead, or in libraries, anywhere where they'd put something on for the night . . . So I'd be up there with my little sensitive teenage songs, which I don't know now 'cos I don't remember any of them. But I wrote from the start, from fifteen onwards.'[7]

A minor turning point arrived in the form of an appearance by Brinsley Schwarz at a Liverpool pub called The Grapes in 1972. In contrast to the soothing sounds of American West Coast music, he heard soul and R&B played

10

by white guys, and Costello's eyes were opened. Brinsley Schwarz reminded him of The Band, one of his favourite groups: 'The Band were it for me,' he told *The Face*. 'I thought they were the best. I liked them because they had beards . . . It appealed to me that they looked really ugly. And they weren't boys. They were men, and all their songs seemed to be about olden days, but they weren't dressing up as cowboys . . . It wasn't phoney.'[8]

Declan saw Nick Lowe relaxing at the bar prior to the gig at the pub, and walked up to him. 'There was a barrier at first,' Costello recalled in *Mojo*, 'because although I'd been around music people often with my dad in the 1960s, I was just an amateur musician . . . That night Brinsley broke a string and the gig just stopped. I think I liked that, together with the self-deprecating way they talked.'[9]

By this time, Costello's singing voice and style were beginning to evolve from being merely copyist and were becoming extremely distinctive. The style was initially described as odd and unusual, an American with a sneer. This had evolved from the music he liked and listened to at the time – either R&B acts or white musicians influenced by R&B. Suspicious of the way in which some white UK 'soul' singers appropriated the vocal mannerisms of the black soul greats, he perfected a style that reflected his love of the work of people like Van Morrison, Doug Sahm, and, most importantly, The Band's Rick Danko.

'He was my absolute hero,' Costello admitted in *The Face* interview. 'He had a unique style that was kind of nasal, and it had a little bit of what I now realize is country in it . . . It was just so unusual to me, such a lovely relaxed falsetto.'[10]

Eager to make his mark in the centre of the UK music industry, an increasingly cynical Costello moved back to London when he was eighteen, working in a small factory with a compact mainframe computer system that he was able to operate by himself.

'I read the papers all day long because . . . no one realized that the computer did all the thinking,' he told *Q*. 'I wore a white coat and people thought I was a rocket scientist

11

because I was the only person in the building who could work this machine. That's how specialist it was . . . Everyone thought I was a genius. It was brilliant. I just skived all the time . . . I took my guitar in. I used to work evenings when it was the end of the month and the payroll stuff was due. I'd stay late, sometimes work thirty-six hours just on coffee and write two or three songs and read the music press.'[11]

He played solo gigs for a while, preferring the immediacy and intimacy of the stripped-down tune, finding the prevailing mood of big rock bands playing 'big' music distasteful. He liked the fact that nascent pub-rock bands were playing short songs that had no hidden, supposedly profound or unintelligible messages. And he respected the fact that these bands chose to have no virtuoso musicians peddling long-winded solos. Likewise, he loathed the likes of Yes, Caravan, and the heavy metal/progressive rock groups of the day.

His musical ambitions were such that a daily 9–5 job could not maintain his interest. There was solid support from his parents who, because of their own backgrounds, were not particularly distressed when their only son wanted to become a professional musician. 'My parents were aware of the dangers and pitfalls and disappointments of it, but they never discouraged me,' he recounted in *The Face*. 'On the other hand, sometimes when you get families in a career like that, they tend to be over-encouraging. My parents were never really insistent . . . I think they were very conscious of not putting me off.'[12]

1973 was pick-me-up time for a certain number of UK-based musicians who felt uncomfortable with the inanities of glam rock, and as he became more and more involved in the scene, Costello decided to develop his songs in a group setting. Flip City was Costello's pub-rock venture, a band in the vaguest sense of the word. Poorly organized, they played gigs (the Newlands Tavern, south of the Thames, being a fairly regular venue) but rarely saw a profit entered into their accounts ledger. With little shame and very few reference points, Flip City imitated the executive elements of Brinsley Schwarz.

'The Brinsleys switched instruments,' remarked Costello, who once roadied for the band, in *Mojo*. 'A bit like The Band. I thought that was pretty hip. Also, they played pretty quietly, a club dynamic, and did unexpected covers . . . Flip City ended up sharing a house, just like the Brinsleys. We thought if it worked for them, maybe it could work for us. We stayed there for a couple of years, mainly copying the Brinsleys' blueprint.'[13]

Replicating the 'Brinsleys' blueprint', however, wasn't one of Costello's more astute moves. Flip City turned out to be as much a commercial failure as the Brinsleys' own farcical attempt at achieving international success on their 1970 jaunt to New York.

By this time, the real name of Declan MacManus had been replaced by DP Costello (the surname taken from his paternal great-grandmother) and with a demo tape of his songs taking up air space on Charlie Gillett's *Honky Tonk* programme, the time had come to break up Flip City. Claiming later in *Rolling Stone* that this particular band format 'trapped me in mediocrity',[14] the closest Costello got to anything beyond that mediocrity was supporting Dr Feelgood at The Marquee, where they were resident house support act for a spell. The Feelgoods were pub rock's biggest UK success story, an exciting live act that featured the masturbatory beer-swilling gestures of Lee Brilleaux and the amphetamine-fuelled marionette antics of their William Wordsworth-loving, bug-eyed guitarist, Wilko Johnson.

By the end of 1975, Costello was both solo and in partnership. Now living in Whitton, Middlesex, with Mary (whom he married in 1974), with one young son, Matthew, and working as a computer operator at the Elizabeth Arden cosmetics factory, he began in earnest the long, often debasing trail as he hawked his songs around to various record companies. It was all to no avail, however. To the record company executives and A&R people, the rough and ready songs (some of which would end up on his acclaimed debut album) smelled of stale pub rock. If they'd listened, they might have heard songs that were, even then, different from the run of the mill. A different sound, however, is exactly what the record companies didn't want. If Costello had been a closet Queen fan, instead of trying to write songs to beat The Band, the reactions might have been more sympathetic.

'I'd say it was down to lack of imagination on the part of the people at most of the [record] labels,' he said of his well-worn and travelled demo tapes in an interview with *Trouser Press*. 'They can't hear something unless it's put on a plate for them. I didn't think it was all that different; maybe they did. I think it was their ears at fault, not mine, and fortunately that's the way I kept thinking about it. I did sometimes wonder whether I wasn't mad and that maybe it wasn't any good, but I kept on thinking it was they who were wrong and not me. It turned out to be the best way to think about it.'[15]

Experiences such as these didn't exactly enamour Costello to the often mindnumbing logic of the music industry. The responses from the industry 'experts' were invariably the same: they couldn't make out the lyrics, the songs weren't commercial enough, and – the rallying call of A&R divisions worldwide – there was no hit single.

'Those tapes were just voice and guitar demos,' Costello recalled in *Melody Maker*. 'I didn't have enough money to do anything with a band. I felt as if I was bashing my head against a brick wall, those people just weren't prepared to listen to the songs. It's a terrible position to be in. You start thinking you're mad. You listen to the radio and you watch the TV and you hear a lot of fucking rubbish. You rarely turn on the radio or TV and hear anything exciting, right? And, all the time, you know that you're capable of producing something infinitely better. But I never lost faith . . . I wasn't going up to these people meekly and saying "Look, with your help and a bit of polishing up, and with all your expertise and knowledge of the world of music we might have a moderate success on our hands." I was going in thinking, "You're a bunch of fucking idiots who don't know what you're doing. I'm bringing you a lot of good songs, why don't you go ahead and fucking well record them." They didn't seem to under-stand that kind of approach.'[16]

Eventually, after being turned down and shunted about by too many record companies to mention (he would either send demo tapes or carry his acoustic guitar into their offices to be offered advice he didn't want or record deals he knew he'd be mad to accept), Costello handed his standard demo tape, which included the likes of 'Blame It On Cain' and 'Mystery Dance', to Dave Robinson and Andrew Jakeman, at London-based Stiff records in August 1976. The new record company had placed an ad in the music press inviting new acts to submit tapes. Ironically, a previous demo tape that Costello recorded under a different name had been rejected by Robinson. 'He was quite surprised when I turned out to be the same person,' said Costello of the incident. 'When I submitted the tapes to Stiff, he didn't realise that it was the same person who'd done the earlier tape . . . It turned out he already had over an hour of me on tape and didn't know it.'[17]

Costello already knew Robinson from the pub-rock days – the Irishman was now managing rapidly-rising rock wordsmith Graham Parker. A former advertising executive from Pinner who had decided to change career direction, Jakeman was the former manager of Chilli Willi and the Red Hot Peppers who now styled himself as Jake Riviera – the shit-hot manager with sharp jackets and a tongue to match. The other constituent parts of Stiff were the label's in-house producer Nick Lowe (by now a Costello chum), Riviera's assistant Cynthia Cole, general manager Paul Conroy and designer Barney Bubbles, formerly the director of Hawkwind's light shows.

When they heard the songs on the demo tape (which emerged on the bootleg album *5,000,000 Costello Fans Can't Be Wrong*) both Riviera and Robinson instinctively knew that a talent was in the making. 'The tape was actually the very first tape we received at Stiff,' Jake Riviera told *NME*. 'I immediately put it on and thought, "God, this is fuckin' good" – but at the same time I was hesitating because after all it was the first tape and I wanted to get a better perspective.'[18] Riviera contacted Costello, saying he liked it and was interested in signing him, but wondered if he could wait for a week while he listened to other demo tapes. Costello agreed. Riviera received 'a load of real dross in the mail'[19] and promptly signed Costello to the label.

The label purchased a tape recorder and an amplifier for their potential superstar, who still lived out in the suburbs. He was aware of the change in musical direction that was taking place in the capital, but had little chance to view the proceedings up close. Costello had neither the freedom nor the money to wander up to London every night to check out the so-called opposition. With a wife and child and a full-time job to demand his attention, he checked out the burgeoning punk-rock scene through the pages of *NME*, *Sounds* and *Melody Maker*.

As 1976 wound its way into 1977, the album that would be *My Aim Is True* was being pieced together in Pathway Studios, Islington, the same studios that gave birth to the early demo recordings that had earned Costello his lifeline at Stiff. Nick Lowe was assigned as producer for the sessions. Recorded on holidays and 'sick' days off from his computer job, Costello rewrote many of the songs that had appeared on earlier demo tapes and live Flip City/DP Costello performances. Some he scrapped completely, others he held over for inclusion on later albums, such as *This Year's Model*'s 'Hand In Hand', which was specifically written for (and rejected by) Nick Lowe, who at the time was experiencing mixed record-company fortunes with his band, Rockpile. In the main, *My Aim Is True* was written in two weeks.

The exhilaration of working on his debut album counterbalanced the frustrations of his increasingly irrelevant day job. At Pathway, the sessions went by in a flash, with Costello's acoustic-based songs given an ad hoc country-rock feel by American band Clover (who were jokingly renamed The Shamrocks for contractual reasons). Lowe and Costello's ambition was to create a collection of songs that were not only of their time, but which were also rooted in classic songwriting values. Having been thoroughly seasoned by the wait for his stab at success, Costello wholeheartedly

16

embraced the directness, tension, and simplicity of his current material.

While the songs were being arranged, shaped and crafted by Costello and Lowe, the image of Costello was slowly being altered by Robinson and manager-in-waiting, Riviera. Up until the release of his first single for Stiff, 'Less Than Zero', Costello (still more widely known as Declan MacManus) was your average ordinary-looking computer operator geek – rake-thin, bespectacled, with a high forehead. His live performances until then, according to Graham Parker in *Mojo*, had 'neither aggression nor energy. I'd go and see Ian Dury and the Kilburns and Costello with Flip City . . . They didn't have what I was putting out, which was, I'm going to show you fuckers that you don't sit cross-legged on the floor! A year later everyone was on stage giving it stick. Costello was knees bent and screaming . . .'[20]

The change in approach was brought about by a confluence of circumstances, of which punk rock was the primary motivating force. While the words to the songs Costello was writing were streets ahead of his contemporaries, what he had in eloquence he lacked in visual appeal. The style of the day was punk rock – three chords, a guitar, and the boot. The job in hand at Stiff was subtly to alter Costello from what he really was – a singer/songwriter – and transform him into an alternative version. The sensibilities and sympathies within his songwriting that would bubble to the top in later years were, for the moment, submerged in sputum. For now, Costello would have to endure a style change.

Slowly, the core Stiff philosophy of songwriting values wrapped up in bags full of style was being applied to Costello. 'We're not the same – you're not the same' was the tag line of the independent record label who wanted 'the kids' to identify with their underlying work ethic. Declan and Patrick were two Christian names decidedly Irish and therefore unswinging, so in a swift stroke of iconoclasm, Riviera bestowed the first name of Elvis on his charge. Naturally, die-hard Presley fans were infuriated, citing the name change as yet another reason to despise punk rock, but it was chosen by Jake Riviera solely as a another witty Stiff marketing scam. The company was famed for its non-sequitur media adverts – 'You can lead a horse to water but you can't make it float' and 'Contains no hit single whatsoever' were two of the label's more direct marketing absurdities. Some critics questioned the name change, and Costello reckoned Riviera's choice of name to be irrational, but he went with the flow. His father joked in the *NME* that Costello had already used the name himself for a while, possibly influenced by the album *Ross McManus Sings Elvis Presley's Greatest Hits*!

If anything, 1977 in London was the time to be risky, at least to attempt to be outrageous. With The Sex Pistols and The Clash as their louder and somewhat more socially anarchic peers, Costello and company realised that if he didn't sharpen his stance, his social and sexual politics and his stagecraft then he would be swallowed up by the style gurus and spat out with the rest of the hopefuls. Having the songs was only half the battle – if you didn't fit even the loosest portrait of the identikit skinny punk rocker, then the front cover of the *NME* was not for you. The concept, then, was for Elvis Costello to look dangerously close to the nervous edge, a singer/songwriter born out of the bedsit years, blinkered by bitterness. Sweet as a nut, the plan worked.

In April 1977, Elvis Costello's debut single, 'Less Than Zero', was released. A statement of definite and distinctive intent, it focused on Oswald Mosley, the British fascist leader of the 1930s. Not exactly the stuff pop dreams are made of – the single, almost inevitably, failed to chart. 'They [the fascists] are really sick people,' Costello averred in *Rolling Stone*, having written the song after seeing a reflective BBC appearance by Mosley. 'If there wasn't a danger that some people of limited intelligence would take them seriously, they'd be sad and you could feel sorry for them. But you can't.'[21]

Reviews across the board were positive. *NME* – like most English magazines then and now, very much a champion of Costello's – misprinted the song's title as 'Half Past Zero'.

The reviewer got it right, though, when he described the song as a 'great record' while simultaneously acknowledging the fact that it had a 'snowball's chance in hell' of cracking the Top Twenty.[22]

The single's release was a suck-it-and-see venture on Stiff's part. A month later, a second single was released. 'Alison' is a breathtakingly tender but candid ballad on a topic that the writer was to return to with alarming frequency – love and betrayal. It too failed to chart, but a line from the song provided his imminent debut album with its title.

On 27 May, Elvis Costello (the Stiff signing, as opposed to Declan Patrick MacManus) made his live debut at The Nashville, in London's North End Road. Now known as The Three Kings, The Nashville in 1977 was a large pub venue that started out as a country & western haunt, but which soon became inextricably linked with the emergence of London punk. The Sex Pistols and The Stranglers made notable early appearances there, as did pre-Clash Joe Strummer with The 101ers, pub/punk-rock crossovers Eddie and the Hot Rods, and Dave Edmunds' Rockpile. By this time *My Aim Is True* was ready to go, but its release was complicated by a distribution problem between Stiff and Island Records that threatened to undermine the steady buzz generated by the two singles and the rare live performances.

Costello on stage had made the transformation from suburban bibliophile and computer operator to a Buddy Holly lookalike from Generation X. The gauche awkwardness of the superficial image belied the surgical precision of the words he snarled through his spittle-flecked lips. He made no effort to hide the invective that lay behind the lyrics, which were a triumph over pop's preference for meaningless phrases and inane soundbites. It came as no surprise to industry onlookers and assembled media pundits that a mere six weeks later Costello resigned from his day job.

And so the search was on for a band to back him at gigs. While the American musicians who accompanied him on the album sessions were fine for that purpose (Clover, whose lead singer was Huey Lewis, were the initially uncredited musicians who in turn delicately and assertively underpinned Costello's songs), they lacked a certain dynamic tenacity that was sorely needed on stage.

Enter The Attractions, a seasoned trio of musicians culled from the ranks of dear departed pub rock and the more refined environs of the Royal College of Music. When the auditioning began for the backing band, Pete Thomas, former drummer with Chilli Willi and the Red Hot Peppers, was already slotted into position. Following the break-up of pub rock, Thomas had been much in demand as a session drummer, and had received a call from ex-Dr Feelgood man Wilko Johnson while he was in America working with cult folk and country artist John Stewart, best known as writer of The Monkees' hit 'Daydream Believer'. Johnson brought Thomas back to England to form a trio but the rehearsals didn't work out, and the Riviera connection kicked in. The remaining positions of bassist and keyboard player still had to be filled, with Costello using Steve Goulding and Andrew Bodnar from Graham Parker's Rumour as the sounding-board musicians for the auditions.

One of the songs used to try out the prospective candidates was the reggae-influenced 'Watching The Detectives'. Despite a steady stream of willing participants, two musicians in particular stood out from the crowd – bassist Bruce Thomas, who had previously worked with Al Stewart and Sutherland Brothers and Quiver, and keyboard player Steve Nason, who was quickly landed with the rhyming but misspelt 'Nieve' as his band surname, in recognition of his languid innocence.

Bruce Thomas's credentials were arguably the most impressive. Becoming disillusioned with the Sutherland Brothers and Quiver format, he applied to Stiff for the job after seeing an advert seeking musicians. He was initially turned down by Costello, but the decision was quickly reversed through word-of-mouth recommendations (including that of his namesake, Pete), and Bruce joined the club after rehearsals.

Steve Nason was studying composition at the Royal College of Music, and so was ostensibly an unlikely bedfellow, but curiously they clicked straight away – not so much, noted Costello in *The Face*, because of their innate musicianly sympathy but because of their styles. 'Steve was very fond of the reggae style . . . Bruce is a very melodic bass player and Pete is a very rhythmic drummer. That meant we could almost get away with being a trio, because an awful lot of the time I didn't play – and also a lot of what I did play, particularly early on, was just like white noise! I had no idea. I wasn't very experienced at all. Rather than making a bad job of trying to play well, I was quite happy to exploit the simple things I could do.'[23]

Five days after he quit Elizabeth Arden, on 14 July, Elvis Costello and The Attractions played their first gig together as support to Wayne (later to be Jayne) County at The Garden, Penzance, Cornwall, having rehearsed in a village hall next to an army base. Proving that directness and simplicity outshines virtuosity within the confines of a three-minute pop song, the band were gearing up for the release of *My Aim Is True*, which was now less than two weeks away. A third single was released prior to the album – '(The Angels Wanna Wear My) Red Shoes' – but it also failed to chart.

The relationship between Costello and The Attractions seemed always to be founded on dynamics and tension. They played tough and lived hard, and while over the years they have attempted to reconcile their differences it hasn't always been possible: 'That lot had a very strange relationship,' stated Nick Lowe in *Rolling Stone*. His words confirmed many people's suspicions. 'It was very abrasive. There was never any real warmth between them. But you don't have to be in love with the bass player to make great records. They certainly respected each other. But they were never really pals.'[24]

Not that Costello and Stiff weren't trying their respective best. On 26 July, prompted by a bona fide and shameless ambition to secure an American record deal – though it could also have been seen as an inept marketing scam – Elvis performed outside London's Hilton Hotel, where CBS Records was holding its yearly international conference.

21

Costello and The Attractions were playing a gig that night in Dingwalls, and wanted to let some of the Stateside company suits in on the fact. Graham Parker roadies walked around with sandwich boards advertising the gig. Costello played through the battery-powered amplifier that he had received as part of his advance. During 'Welcome To The Working Week' a crowd gathered, including several CBS bigwigs and a tourist who requested a Neil Diamond song.

'All these guys were actually standing there and applauding,' Costello told *Trouser Press*, 'but the Hilton didn't see the humour in the situation and called the police. The police didn't see the humour in the situation and arrested me. It wasn't a big deal . . . just a crazy stunt.'[25] Even so, the cheeky tactic proved to be a decisive factor in Costello being signed by CBS/Columbia before the end of the year. CBS President Walter Yetnikoff had liked the attitude as much as the songs.

The Dingwalls gig coincided with the release of *My Aim Is True*, an event in Costello's life that must surely have been worth the frustrating wait. The twenty-two year old – whose life up until then revolved around punching in computer data, being as good a husband and father as time would allow, music, and harbouring resentment in the form of a possibly-apocryphal black book – was dipping his toes into waters he would never draw back from. As for the famed black book – well, suffice to say that Costello took rejection harshly and harboured an unhealthy fascination with a form of revenge that seemed to focus on whether or not a record company A&R man returned his call.

The imminent release of *My Aim Is True* proved to him what idiots these people were (difficult to argue with that), but it also highlighted the fact that Costello bore grudges – in general with intensity, and specifically with a laser-like tracking beam of pure hatred. True, no one had wanted to know him eighteen months previously, but most people can live with the humiliation of rejection. Costello lived with it, but allowed himself to wallow in thoughts of retaliation. In a couple of paragraphs published in *NME*, the extent of Costello's then apoplectic retribution is revealed. '[He] took the eight-page-long guest list for the night and mercilessly scythed off half the names, including . . . Richard Williams who, as A&R man for Island Records, personally turned down [his] demo tape . . . Also, Elvis personally vets all guest lists making sure that anyone whose name was down but who didn't turn up the last time his name was included is struck off the list for ever more.'[26]

Clearly, here was a man not to be dismissed lightly. For more reasons than the blindingly obvious ones.

CHAPTER 2

'My ultimate vocation in life is to be an irritant! Not something actively destructive, just someone who irritates, who disorientates. Someone who disrupts the daily drag of life just enough to leave the victim thinking there's maybe more to it all than the mere humdrum quality of existence.'
Elvis Costello in conversation with Nick Kent, NME, *March 1978*

'Don't tell them your dad's a band singer. They'll think you share my philosophy that we should all be at home with our families, eating and washing regularly. You're supposed to be an evil being. To have any success you have to come from a housing estate in Liverpool or Sheffield. I haven't murdered anyone much recently and it's really no good for your image.'
Ross MacManus, Sunday Times Magazine, *March 1994*

'Jake's just a little thug. His commercial strategy has always been "We don't need you".'
Greil Marcus, New West *magazine, May 1979*

Released at the beginning of August 1977, *My Aim Is True* took many people by surprise. To all intents and purposes, both album and artist had been turned around in double-quick time. Outside the London-based music industry cognoscenti, not many people had heard of Costello, and those who were aware of him obviously hadn't taken to the three singles issued prior to the record's release, nor to his idiosyncratic brand of charisma. Nine months previously, he had been a full-time computer operator and part-time songwriter, his demeanour and songwriting style such that he was given the old heave-ho from virtually every major record company in London. Once looked upon as a loser (although he never doubted himself) he was now a genuine recording artist, a man with a record deal and a zealous mission to show those who doubted him just how good he was.

While this change in Costello's life could be endlessly analysed, there are several indisputable factors that attributed to his reversal of fortune. Firstly, Stiff knew exactly what to do with him – or at least appeared to. While the majors viewed Costello's truculent, runt-like ambition with no small degree of doubt, Robinson and Riviera focused the singer's talent and arrogance into something that was simultaneously inspiring and irritating – two opposite sides of the public-appeal coin. Insiders, however, knew of the strengths of the songwriting and cast aside any aspersions relating to the antics of Riviera and the considerable contempt towards the industry displayed by Costello. Longevity in the music industry is firmly based on songs, and Costello had them in spades.

Another factor is that Costello was competing for attention at the same time as the punks. The Sex Pistols, The Jam, The Clash, The Stranglers, and The Damned were all (despite varying age differences) looked upon as members of punk rock's premier league. Each had seen single and album chart action by the time *My Aim Is True* was released. The public were, by now, very much aware of the tenets of punk rock and even more so when the inevitable caricature of the genre arose: get pissed, destroy, and spit to the soundtrack of buzzsaw guitars.

As punk almost indivisibly blended into New Wave, so the barriers between what was guitar-driven and song-driven were being torn down. A core element in Stiff's growing importance was its ability to pinpoint the value of songs over the deceptions of image. So whilst Costello had some of the trappings of punk (okay, no safety pins, but he was skinny, he dressed in thriftshop chic, and looked like he wanted to spit into the eyes of children) he also had an innate understanding of song structure. He connected his own inherent songwriting classicism with the tenacity of punk rock, thereby making a subtle crossover from one to the other and vice versa: the under-twenties could empathize with the stance, while an older audience could appreciate the melodies and influences. Those unfashionably caught in between would soon have to make a cultural decision as to whether to stick with Yes, Genesis and Rainbow.

His arrest outside the CBS convention at the Hilton Hotel helped matters along, too, as a publicity stunt to pave the way for the debut album's release. Word of mouth over the past seven months had also begun to reach the London music-press editors, which led to Costello being on the covers of both *Sounds* and *Melody Maker*. The anti-rock star had arrived, and everybody wanted to shake his hand.

My Aim Is True was lauded from every quarter, and justifiably so. In 1977, it landed amidst the barrage of punk, and while it had some attitudes in common with punk, it still stuck out like a sore thumb. It showed musicianship and lyricism that were never out of control, superficially a touch more gentle than the cartoon nihilism of punk rock, but underlined with a unique savagery all its own. Songs ranged from the complex and surreal ('Waiting For The End Of The World') to the unsympathetic ('Less Than Zero') and misogynistic ('I'm Not Angry'), and while critics lathered praise on the record, they also wondered what real pain could be involved that enabled Costello to write such songs, ones that crossed the borders of human emotions so strikingly.

Certainly, while the music brilliantly celebrates a whole musical spectrum, there is little joy in the lyrics. All emotional sentiments expressed are either pessimistic or negative: deceit, sarcasm, bitterness, disdain, scorn, disgust. References to violence, duplicitous sex and death abound in an array of melodramatic vignettes. Costello's voice is a perfect if unsettling mixture of spite ('I'm Not Angry') and rare tenderness ('Alison'). The overall quality and sound of the record astonished many people. Those expecting just a Gatling-gun sensibility were disappointed, though he could probably have got away with it.

But *My Aim Is True* wasn't really punk rock. Punk was probably the only genre that someone like Costello could have emerged from and survived, since the DIY ethic of the genre allowed his maverick, fit-to-bursting talents to break through. More or less the same age as Johnny Rotten, Joe Strummer and Paul Weller, the lyric as a wall scrawl was not for Costello, whose multi-faceted literacy shone through the songs with clarity and purpose. As for the bitterness, was that born out of inner frustration and self-contempt, or simply a burning rage against the population at large?

'I'm an extraordinarily bitter person,' Costello informed *Trouser Press* shortly after the album's release. 'I don't like to sound as if I'm too obsessed and can't feel any other way, but it just happens that those songs evince that kind of feeling and, therefore, the album is like that. The next one could be very, very different, although I don't think it's necessarily going to be any kinder. In fact, if anything, the way I feel at the moment, it's going to be a lot crueller . . . People have noticed that a lot of the album is about being rejected . . . I don't want it thought that I'm totally obsessed with one theme because I'm not. Just like everyone else I have good days and bad days.'[1]

With his debut album in the charts, it was obvious that Costello, despite his ordinary looks and rancorous musings, was doing something right. He'd hit a nerve with people who were on the lookout for an articulate lyricist who was allied to a current musical movement. The fact remained that Costello was hip. Praise from the media had sent out ripples of interest, and the songs were sugar-coated enough to garner radio play, even if beneath the surface they were bilious and voyeuristic. It was time to tour, something that Costello was actively looking forward to.

With the exception of a support slot for Santana at the Crystal Palace Garden Party on 10 September, where Costello faced his largest audience to date (12,000), he bided his onstage time for the forthcoming Stiff's Greatest Stiffs Live Tour. 'There was to be absolutely no compromise,' said *NME*, 'His obvious ploy would have been to play his album and ensure a positive response. No way . . .'[2]

Up until this time, Stiff had more credibility and kudos than cash. Formed at the start of punk but with a more mature (albeit no less quirky) spirit, the independent record label had a roster of closet hitmakers that drew on punk rock's facility to amuse and arouse in equal fashion. Aside from Costello, other members included diehards from the pub-rock scene: Nick Lowe and Ian Dury, both songwriters of note – Lowe a superb structural songwriter and melodicist, Dury a canny cockney showman rooted in a warped vaudevillian dimension; The Damned, the first punk rock band to appear on television, the first to release an album, and the first UK punk band to tour America; veteran music-hall comedian Max Wall (don't ask); Liverpool's The Yachts; Larry Wallis, former member of psych-out protohippies The Pink Fairies, and Motorhead. Perhaps the label's other great songwriting find after Costello was Wreckless Eric, a diminutive man who wrote some of the best unrecognised pop songs of the era.

Both Dave Robinson and Jake Riviera were old hands at the music game, shrewd enough to know how to make and break deals but passionate enough to populate their label with some of the best emerging talent around. (They also inexplicably signed the likes of Max Wall and Larry Wallis, however. With the relative success of *My Aim Is True* under the belt, and the imminent release of Costello's 'Watching The Detectives' (as well as a new US record contract with Columbia in the offing), Dury's album, *New Boots And Panties*, and Lowe's single, 'Halfway To Paradise', it was decided to send out the troops on a reconnaissance mission to the public.

Five Stiff acts (Costello, Dury, Eric, Wallis and Lowe) were to take part in a revue-style package tour playing two dozen dates around the UK. Starting at High Wycombe Town Hall on 3 October and finishing at Lancaster University over four weeks later on 5 November, the five acts would, the music papers informed us, each play roughly half-an-hour in a rotating order. The opening gig at High Wycombe was to be recorded, the resulting live album pressed and made available from 7 October at Bath University. Oh, how the major labels must have shuddered at that one.

The tour promised a lot: variety from a number of excellent songsmiths and performers, with the added *frisson* of internal tensions and egos as competition to be the final band on stage raged. Rehearsals were underway in Fulham where the concept of a rotating bill began 'to look somewhat idealistic'.[3]

The future of Stiff was viewed in a similar light, with Jake Riviera and Dave Robinson falling out one day amidst broken window panes and empty beer bottles. The resulting row, initially thought to be yet another Stiff publicity stunt, left Robinson holding the fort while Riviera took Costello and Lowe with him to the soon-to-be-formed Radar label. This was founded by ex-United Artists staff Martin Davis and Andrew Lauder, and Riviera signed a long-term deal with them to release Costello and Lowe material worldwide, except in countries with existing licensing rights via Riviera. Lowe renewed a relationship with Davis and Lauder that had commenced when Brinsley Schwarz was signed to UA in 1970.

'Jake and Dave were a good double act for a while,' recalled Costello in *Mojo*. 'They could play good cop bad cop with promoters and distributors. Even when they were caught blatantly in the wrong over something, they were so righteous, you couldn't argue with them.'[4]

Notwithstanding this minor glitch, the tour went ahead. The opening night was similar in musical stance to Costello's support slot for Santana: a refusal to please by largely not playing from the audience's primary reference point, *My Aim Is True*. 'If you wanna hear the old songs,' Elvis roared, 'buy the fucking record.'[5] This provocative stance, even amidst a partisan audience who, theoretically, should have empathized with Costello's narky logic, was soon widened to accommodate his own onstage rivalry with Ian Dury, whose act was so tight and full of East End swagger that it threatened to upstage that of Costello's at each subsequent gig. Not that Costello forced unfamiliar material down the audience's collective throat. Along with several choice cuts from *My Aim Is True* and new songs (most of which would feature on his second album) he would run through Richard Hell's 'Love Comes In Spurts', The Damned's 'Neat Neat Neat', Bacharach & David's 'I Just Don't Know What To Do With Myself', Lovin' Spoonful's 'Six O'Clock' and, ironically given the rivalry, Ian Dury's 'Roadette Song'.

Quickly, the idea of the rotating bill was shelved: Larry Wallis and Wreckless Eric proved to have too few songs of any real substance to hold the attention at the close of the night. Nick Lowe preferred to go on early because he wanted to beat last orders at the pub. The competition was now set between Dury and Costello. According to band veteran and music writer Will Birch, though, Elvis 'had his own private agenda. The heavily-publicized tour presented the perfect opportunity for a spot of legend building. With tough new songs like 'Night Rally' and 'You Belong To Me' peppering his set . . . Costello oozed confidence.'[6]

As the ramshackle tour continued so did the rivalry, the drinking, the 'white line fever' and the no-holds-barred hostility. Because of the label split, relationships between Jake Riviera and Dave Robinson were not smooth. Tension between Dury and Costello backstage was high, and while Elvis was whiling away the hours minting new songs ('Sunday's Best' was offered to Dury, 'Pump It Up' was written on the fire escape of a Newcastle hotel) Ian was shoe-shining his act to perfection, ultimately winning the audience vote for best act on the tour and ensuring that *New Boots And Panties* remained in the charts for almost two years.' It was anti-boring stab-you-in-the-back stuff,' explained Costello of the tour in general. 'But it's impossible to look into the mind of someone who was out of his mind on vodka and amphetamines.'[7]

Although Dury was the most obvious success of the tour, Costello also made it happen in a live setting. An electrifying performer backed by an intuitive band of musicians, he still didn't think Dury beat him and the Attractions on stage: 'There was no one that could follow us, really.'[8] While the tour gained plaudits and respect from the music media and the public, the participants themselves (some friendly, others not) were relieved when they each went their separate ways. 'The Stiff tour was a failure as far as I was concerned . . .' said Elvis in *Creem*. 'Like every night the encore would be "Sex and Drugs and Rock And Roll", right, and . . . it quickly reaches a point where the tour started to take on the manifestations of the song. And, like, it was getting so ugly I was compelled to write "Pump It Up" . . . Well, just how much can you fuck, how many drugs can you do before you get so numb you can't really feel anything?'[9]

With songs being written on the run for the follow-up album, Elvis Costello commenced his debut American tour in mid-November. Now away from the often chaotic Stiff empire, and ensconced in Radar with manager Riviera and Nick Lowe, the month-long coast-to-coast stay started in San Francisco (a shrewd place to begin – it was home to Clover), and finished in New York in mid-December. The gigs sated the hungry American music press, who had heard much about Costello through reading the likes of *NME* and *Melody Maker*, and who had heard his music through American FM stations. While *éminence grise* rock writer Greil Marcus wondered what all the hype was about (or words to that effect), a large number of music critics took quite a shine to *My Aim Is True*. As did FM radio stations – despite the album's sparse production, the songs had a patent listenability to them. The American stations placed songs such as '(The Angels Wanna Wear My) Red Shoes' and 'Alison' straight on to the playlist. The album became the biggest-selling import of the decade in America, and would later be the first New Wave LP to enter the American Top Fifty.

Costello had learned a few tricks from the Stiffs tour – assertive stagecraft and internecine politics a speciality. He realised that as far as the American music industry was concerned, a certain amount of compromise had to be applied. For instance, he rewrote 'Less Than Zero', substituting Lee Harvey Oswald for the song's original protagonist, Oswald Mosley (now known as the 'Dallas' version). Critics and public alike grooved on the bespectacled one's fiery disposition on and off stage, but quickly the US press seized critically upon Costello's obvious disdain for Americana.

Much of the credit for such a stance has been placed at the feet of Jake Riviera, a man whose no-nonsense approach reportedly bordered on the fascistic – 'A serious candidate for most despicable character of the decade,' said *Creem;*[10] 'A man possessed. Everybody lived in fear. He was so hot, you didn't want to touch him,' noted *Mojo.*[11] While it's difficult to authenticate, it's quite likely that Costello himself was willing to allow Riviera to use such tactics in order to advance his career. While self-loathing was not high on Costello's personal agenda (he was too busy loathing other people), it's a moot point as to whether he actually liked himself for what Riviera got up to in these early years.

In the context of America, however, it seems that Riviera got it wrong, clamping the lid on press interviews when his charge needed them the most, and even going so far as to 'rough up'[12] several music writers during the tour. Riviera also believed that playing high schools and not standard rock venues would be a strategy for success, something about which Costello's US label, CBS, had strong doubts. Besides, Costello's then sound was distinctly based on rock-'n'roll and R&B jukebox principles. The fact that he appropriated his stage Christian name from Presley and his initial appearance from Buddy Holly, and that his lyrical regret and resignation was inspired by the likes of The Band, George Jones and Gram Parsons, seemed to have been forgotten.

The day following his final date in New York, he appeared on *Saturday Night Live*, filling in as a last-minute replacement for The Sex Pistols. Ostensibly he was to sing 'Watching The Detectives' and 'Less Than Zero', but halfway through the second song he ditched his diatribe on Mosley ('I'm sorry, ladies and gentlemen, there's no reason to do this song') and reverted to the scathing 'Radio Radio', a song he had been specifically requested not to sing.

'It's disgusting that you have so many radio stations and they're all so terrible,'[13] he complained, as quoted in *Creem*, surely not oblivious to the fact that BBC radio didn't bother to play 'Less Than Zero' on its release, and that he himself randomly refused to play his most radio-friendly song, 'Alison', at concerts. Costello's confrontation with the American media was symptomatic of an urgently-felt need to make a stand. Desperate not to be viewed with indifference, he struck an imperfect balance between calculated confidence and manhandling assertiveness.

'It's much better to have a more defined attitude even if it's somewhat negative,' he said of his behaviour, with some justification, when later talking to *The Face*. 'It works up to a point, then you just become a bit pathetic. You're yelling and screaming like an idiot after a while. It wasn't quite that calculated but, looking back on it, it had a good point.'[14]

Costello analysed his self-confessed confrontational approach in two areas: professional and personal. In a professional capacity, he never wished to be looked upon as either one- or two-dimensional. He knew he had to take and make an extreme stand, if only to counteract what he saw as the unwholesome mediocrity of the music scene in general. If he hadn't done that, he would surely have been lumped in with the rest of the timid hopefuls. In his personal life, he was as unsure as he ever was: 'There's certainly a lot of strange things going on in my head,' he said cryptically to *NME*, 'a lot of strange things still happening.'[15]

Underlying his recurrent antagonism was his incessant feeling of bitterness towards the music industry. Despite his swift promotion through the ranks, he still hadn't either forgotten or forgiven the business for its slights when he was attempting to secure a record deal. While sensibly realizing that no one was out to deliberately scupper his chances of further success, he nevertheless refused point blank to play the game in any other way except his own. 'I still haven't forgiven them,' he said in the same *NME* interview, 'and I see no reason why I ever should. That's why I don't want to go to lunch with the *Top Of The Pops* producer. People in this fuckin' business just don't understand that I don't want to join their little club. I don't want to go down to the Roxy and hang out with Linda Ronstadt! [She turned 'Alison' into a moderate UK hit in May 1979, in a version that Costello predictably disliked]. See, the music biz as a whole, the crass-ness of it all, still actively disgusts me and any degree of success I may attain will not weigh against all that crap I went through initially.'[16] This was borne out some time later when Virgin Records offered him a lucrative deal. Costello turned the company down on the basis that it had previously rejected his material. 'I asked Richard Branson to name two songs off of my last album, and he couldn't. So I told him to fuck off.'[17]

Elvis left the States before Christmas, returning to England to see 'Watching The Detectives' enter the UK Top Twenty. This marked the first of his singles releases to chart, begin-ning a hit-making career that, while not exactly of Michael Jackson or Madonna proportions, has continued ever since. In January 1978, having completed the recording of his second album, Costello returned to North America for a three-month tour with Mink De Ville and Dave Edmunds' Rockpile. By the tour's end, *My Aim Is True* was in the US Top Forty, any misgivings on the part of the public about his widely-reported alleged anti-Americanism seemingly assuaged by the resonant strengths of the record. The Attractions, meanwhile, had transformed into a fighting unit of thoroughly-focused musicians. This became all the more apparent at the tour's two final sell-out dates in the El Mocambo Club, in Toronto, Canada, where the gigs were recorded for a North America only live album release. Here, as on the rest of the tour, Costello eschewed his rigorous dressing-down of the audience, treating them to a package of new songs and old favourites. Playing with a rocketing inten-sity, Costello and The Attractions' claims to be the best new act of 1978 rang true.

Released in the UK at the end of March, the new album

was titled *This Year's Model* (the apostrophe was missing on both the original vinyl and CD re-issue covers). Costello initially intended to call the record *Little Hitler*, but his friend Nick Lowe stole the title for one of his own songs, a 'favour' repaid by Costello who wrote a song titled 'Two Little Hitlers'. Another mooted album title was *Girls, Girls, Girls,* an exact steal from a film title track of Presley's. It was used later for a double album of 'hits, misses and personal favourites'.

Preceded by the first single from the album, '(I Don't Want To Go To) Chelsea', described by *NME* as 'a veritable blinder . . . So good that the very act of releasing it amounts to bragging on a colossal scale,'[18] *This Year's Model* was everything the recent Costello convert could have hoped for, and proof positive that the quality and talent displayed on his debut album was by no means a fluke. In addition, the new songs had the advantage of having The Attractions play on them. While *My Aim Is True* encouraged a new attitude towards 'alternative' singer/songwriters, the superb backing by Clover was, in essence, soft rock. The Attractions, however, were especially formed for the punk-rock wars. While the barrage of emotions emanating from the audience undoubtedly spurred the band on, they also responded to the intense emotional commitment of Costello. This was also the case on *This Year's Model.*

There were a number of people in the industry hoping that Costello would falter with his follow-up album. Traditionally, 'the difficult second album' is simply a collection of songs written on the hoof, borne of little thought and quickly-noted theories, released soon after the debut in the hope of capitalizing on whatever fanbase loyalty is left. Often viewed as a burning bridge to the third album (where, ideally, more time can be taken over songwriting, arranging, instrumentation, and production) the second record is the poor relation to be sympathized with, coddled, and told to go away and not come back until it's a lot better.

This Year's Model broke the mould with a collection of songs that focused as much on Costello's recent success as on his by now patented emotional self-lacerations. Musically it seethed with tension, and this fitted the obsessive elements of the majority of the songs. Unlike *My Aim Is True*, there was no obvious nor, indeed, subtle reference to rockabilly, country, or the Dylan/Morrison axis. This was straight-ahead pop music as influenced by punk rock, a gut reaction to the power of tautly-played electric guitars, and an emotive instinct as to the content of the songs. Through the music, twitching and stuttering in a series of drum bursts, rents of organ and guitar arcs, the songs breathed as if through a gas mask – tight, controlled, afraid to splutter, claustrophobic, yet with a clear view of what was happening. The wounding lyrics once again mostly concentrated on how Costello failed to get the girl. When he wasn't singing of refusing to go to Chelsea, a fashionable London area that represented not only the meaning of success but also its in-built faults, he was remarking acerbically (of himself as well as others; he never spared the lash from his own back) of romances that were about to begin or were finished.

Each lyrical and musical detail of *This Year's Model* was bang on the money. It is a remarkably self-contained and thematic record, with more than a hint of menace seeping through it. Costello once again caustically pin-points precisely how downtrodden a fragile ego feels in the debris of a failed love affair. Yet it sounds both terrific and terrifying, the singer/songwriter's facility for articulating the true meaning of dark emotions rarely undermining the actual songs, making them instead both scary and comforting.

'There is less humour on it than on the last [record] . . .' he confirmed in *Creem*. 'It's more vicious overall but far less personal, though. But then, my sense of humour is very, very bleak.'[19] Of course, the inherent danger for Costello in writing songs that people give only cursory ear service to is that he can be casually misrepresented by them. While there is little point in denying that the many lyrical images of his early songs attest to a barely-contained contempt for women, it is also true that songwriters project themselves through other people in order to write their songs. Through the analysis of music critics – 'That's the problem with you music critics, you try to make everything so complicated when it's not'[20] – Costello's personality was described as that of an extreme person, a bitter and twisted man without either tenderness or maturity.

'I don't necessarily think I'm going to become a "nicer person" or a more "complete" person,' he said of the criticisms. 'Because this job is not designed to make you nicer, or more mature, even. You can say, "Oh you're just immature, you'll soften up", but I fuckin' won't . . . Tenderness, I can feel tenderness and I'm not afraid of it, and it isn't entirely absent from either of my albums. It's just that everybody with their typical lack of imagination chose to ignore any signs of that completely and plump for the other extremities instead.'[21]

By now Costello was fast becoming a proper pop star. Indisputably credible in the eyes of the music media, he was both fashionable and newsworthy. Just as *This Year's Model* had a title that referred directly to his own status as a pop star and to the mechanical, emotionally devoid world of the fashion/music industry, so he shirked responsibility for what it made him. A pop star was the last thing he wanted to be. He resolutely defined himself then as a songwriter, and not as an 'artist' nor indeed, as a product of the music industry. In this light, an invitation to Nashville to sing on a George Jones duets album (*My Special Friends*) was a boon to Costello, and quite likely his highlight of the year. 'Stranger in the House', a song on a free 7" single with *This Year's Model* (it was written around the time of the *My Aim Is True* sessions, but considered to be not 'right' for the time), had been heard by a record company executive who deemed it perfect for the project. It was also chosen by famed country-music producer Billy Sherrill as a good vehicle for Jones to try. Joining country greats such as Dolly Parton, Willie Nelson and, er, Linda Ronstadt, Costello didn't get the opportunity to meet Jones at this point. Jones was suffering from the effects of alcoholism, but they later met up and recorded the song. Nevertheless, along with meeting both Bob Dylan and Bruce

Springsteen, this was the kind of thing that inspired the fan ethic in Costello, knocking the star-making machinery into a cocked hat. Never one for the airbrushing proclivities of the style department, either, Costello could not imagine himself as a spokesman for a generation. Or, indeed, as a celebrity.

'Bollocks', was the single-word response he used when asked about the 'complications' of being a celebrity. 'I'm no celebrity,' he told *Creem*. 'That's the problem with being a star. You always let people down in the end. I'm not a bloody arbitrator of public opinion. There's no mass following waiting for my next word off the mountain. People should be waiting for their own next word, not mine.'[22] As for the money that supposedly comes with success: 'Even the money's irrelevant. It's all a matter of whether you own the money or whether the money owns you.'[23]

Describing his vocation not as a singer/songwriter, but as a person who wanted to wilfully disrupt other people's lives (presumably in a meaningful way), Costello defined his public persona as much as the music media did. Irrespective of his anger towards the music industry, he was nevertheless actively eager to explain to journalists his creative *raison d'être*, if not details of his personal life (which then, as now, was closely guarded).

He commenced a twenty-eight-date British tour in support of *This Year's Model* with a public image of both a vengeful and obsessional personality hanging around his neck. He dispensed with the theory that someone who is obsessed with a single idea might be deemed clinically insane, stating that he was, in fact, obsessed with more than one idea. He told *NME*: 'I know I'm not [obsessive], or else I would be completely happy to play up to the image of me as a one-dimensional revengeful character all the time . . . Actually, I think I'm more devious than obsessive.'[24]

As was now usual the live shows generated huge positive response. The tour received a setback, however, in the first week of April. Bassist Bruce Thomas cut his hand in the dressing room of the Manchester venue, The Rafters Club. In a *Spinal Tap* moment, he was unwisely demonstrating how to smash a bottle during a bar-room brawl. He was unused to the intricacies of such an art form, so sharp glass sliced soft skin, and Thomas was driven to hospital where he received eighteen stitches. Nick Lowe deputised for The Attractions' bassist at some concerts, and on one occasion (an encore of 'Mystery Dance' at London's Roundhouse), Thin Lizzy bassist and leader Phil Lynott did the honours. At the same gig, Costello dedicated 'Accidents Will Happen' to his hapless bassist.

By the end of the tour, *This Year's Model* had reached No. 4 in the UK Album charts. Another US tour was in the offing, and with Bruce Thomas still out it was decided to use Clover bassist John Ciambotti, who at least had the advantage of knowing both Costello and some of the songs. By the end of May, Costello told anyone who cared to listen that he was in the US 'to corrupt America's youth. But my visa will probably run out before I have a chance to do it.'[25] The album had reached the US Top Fifty. The tour had done its work, and all was happy in the land of opportunity. Or at least that was the theory.

Unusually for a successful rock star, he and his wife Mary were rarely seen at receptions, since Costello, at least, disliked them. There seems to be little doubt that while he himself was growing in stature, and his son Matthew was growing from infant to toddler, the MacManus marriage was weakening. In a fractured domestic situation poignantly echoing that of his own parents, it was inevitable that his self-obsessed, virtually predestined need to be a successful songwriter, would only add to the pressure. He was touring most of the time, and when he wasn't on the road he was either in the studio or writing songs, feverishly catching up on what he perceived to be lost time. Something had to give.

Something did, but it had to be a joke, surely? Elvis Costello, the man whose latest album was titled *This Year's Model*, and who wrote 'This Year's Girl', 'Lipstick Vogue', '(I Don't Want To Go To) Chelsea' – the titles alone signified one big sneer at the fashion industry – was appearing in the gossip pages with Bebe Buell, a former *Playboy* pin-up and a moderately famous fashion model. Somewhat more infamously, she was a top-notch feminine accessory to the stars. Her world was rock music, and her friends were Mick Jagger, Keith Richards, Ron Wood, Jimmy Page, Iggy Pop, Todd Rundgren and Rod Stewart. Steve Tyler, another of Buell's paramours, fathered Liv, at this time a one-year-old baby girl. And now to her list of friends she added Elvis Costello, the creative antithesis to someone like Stewart or Jagger, and the literate, scornful punk rocker's revenge on the likes of The Rolling Stones, Aerosmith, Led Zeppelin and others.

In truth, something like this was bound to happen, and if it hadn't been Bebe Buell, it would probably have been a woman as equally resourceful and intelligent. Costello was now very much in the rock world's twilight zone, a cocooned and cosseted play area for adults where pretty much everything was easy to come by, especially if you happened to be one of the newest and hottest rock'n'roll properties around. A lifestyle imbued by emotional pornography, endless yes people and hedonism to order, weakened his sensitivity to others. While it's easy to see what Bebe Buell saw in Costello, it's far easier to see what he saw in her: an escape valve from the regular stultification of domestic life, and someone who fully embraced and epitomized the lifestyle of which he was now a part.

Yet Buell and Costello's affair was no inconsequential rock star–model dalliance. Ironically, although they met for the first time in the summer of 1978 in Los Angeles, Buell had actually also seen Costello less than two years previously while in London. She was on a modelling assignment, taking part in a photo shoot, when an employee of Elizabeth Arden, a skinny guy in overalls and glasses entered the studio, left a package there and walked out. Bebe enquired as to his identity. The response 'Declan, married with a kid, plays in a dull pub band' didn't dim her view of him.

Fast forward to LA where Elvis Costello and the Attractions, now a hot property on record and a particular favourite of American hipsters coast-to-coast, was headlining a New Wave concert. Supported by Mink De Ville and Nick

Lowe, to Bebe Buell Costello was a blue-suited figure of magnetic charm. She obtained a backstage pass and, seamlessly, an introduction. By the time several hours had passed the duo were winging their way down Sunset Boulevard oblivious to everything except each other. By the next morning, hungover yet virtuous (they had drunk too much alcohol to make love), Costello flew to San Francisco, leaving Buell possibly to ponder upon what exactly this guy in the suit meant to her, and she to him.

Immediately, correspondence was entered into, with Costello initially posting what Buell remembered as 'some kind of a poem',[26] but which in fact was a couple of (prophetic?) lines from the sardonic 'Wednesday Week' (a song on a free limited edition 7" single that came with Costello's third album, *Armed Forces*). The letter was followed by a flurry of phone calls, letters, postcards and other missives, so naturally eloquent and lyrical that they made Buell wonder whether he hadn't engaged in this kind of communication before. The situation was exciting, fuelled as it was by a romantic notion of star-crossed lovers separated by air miles, their passion existing of sweet nothings written on even sweeter writing paper. It was not, however, ideal.

'I was miserable in Los Angeles,' Buell told *Mojo*. 'He kept telling me that if God's burning fire didn't get me, the earthquake would and he suggested that I fly to London to be with him. Liv was a year old and I didn't want to drag her over there with me to uncharted territories, so I took her to Maine to be with my family. I also thought I would do a bunch of work in London, too, make money and come home. I never expected that I would end up staying because I had never made love to him. I was like a mail order bride.'[27]

So Bebe came to London around mid-August, the proverbial cat being let out of the bag in terms of public knowledge when she appeared with Elvis at a performance by the 'punk' poet John Cooper Clarke, a human stick insect Bob Dylan lookalike. It was public, and therefore personally painful to Costello and his family. The music press were bemused, and reported the pairing with snide asides. The tabloids, who were slowly waking up to the mileage achieved by reporting on the goings, and particularly the comings, of pop stars (they'd had a field day with Sex Pistols' shenanigans) took to the unlikely couple with lip-smacking relish. While there was a surreal irony to the situation, there was a romantic realism attached to the couple that seemed profound if inevitably doomed. Some people wondered whether the relationship mirrored Sid Vicious and Nancy Spungen, or Bob Dylan and Edie Sedgwick, but these were spurious notions.

In early September, following three weeks of unbridled, unsaddled and mutually satisfying time together, hairline cracks in the relationship began to show. Another *Spinal Tap* moment occurred at a Buddy Holly birthday party (thrown by Paul McCartney) that Costello was asked to attend. The invitation was declined due to *Armed Forces* recording commitments, but Buell went in his place. Retreating to Wings guitarist Denny Laine's house with her girlfriend and Generation X's Billy Idol, Buell woke up the next morning on a pool table, draped with a blanket. She phoned Costello, explained what had happened, but 'he didn't believe a word. Can you blame him?'[28] Shortly afterwards Costello re-entered the studio, only to be returned to Bebe later that night. He was tired, emotional, and very, very drunk.

'He hung his head over the side of the bed and threw up all over my shoes. That's when he confessed to me how much he loved me ... Between puking I was getting Shakespearean speeches. I was crying and telling him I loved him more than anybody and that none of these boys meant anything to me. The next day he would barely speak to me. He really thought I had gone off and shagged Billy Idol.'[29]

All told, it was a delicate matter for the rock star and the model, and whichever stance they took they were bound to be sniped at. Buell believed that Costello's 'team' were not helping the situation, seeing her as more of a hindrance than a help in the plans to establish him on the international scene. Costello believed Buell was reverting to pre-New

Wave habits. It was a messy business, for sure, with mutual recriminations and frayed nerves adding to the emotional war of attrition. A major insult added further fuel to the fire, however, when Buell – a woman who had slept with some of the coolest and richest 1970s rock stars – was accused of sleeping with John Cooper Clarke. Righteously indignant, Buell realized enough was enough.

It wasn't enough, though, for the couple to split up, and as the relationship staggered from one emotion to the next, Costello dived into the writing and recording of *Armed Forces*. 'I view it as a progression,' he revealed to *NME*. 'I want to plough in more emotions, not because people have drawn this one-dimensional picture of me but just . . . for my own sanity, really.'[30] Not that he had reason to doubt his emotional turbulence. The recording of *Armed Forces* (originally titled *Emotional Fascism*) was streaking ahead amidst personal and professional upheaval, but his popularity was surging to a point where it threatened to undermine his reasons for doing what he did in the first place.

The year ended in a mixture of high tension, celebration, and no small degree of personal loss. Following another Jake Riviera-orchestrated heavy-handed backstage fracas at a nostalgic warm-up gig in New Brighton, Merseyside (a local journalist suffered a broken wrist and five stitches to his head), Costello and The Attractions headed to the Far East and Australia. Playing five nights at Sydney's Regent Theatre should have been easy. It would have been if, at the end of the first night, Costello had come back on stage for an encore. He didn't (the response from the audience wasn't emotional enough, he claimed) and the crowd began to riot, initially throwing beer cans and rolled-up papers at the empty stage, but quickly progressing to chair covers and balcony seats. On the way out of the theatre, some of the audience smashed glass display cabinets and tore down banners, eventually blocking the street outside the venue while chanting such revolutionary delights as 'Elvis Sucks' and 'Elvis Is A Capitalist'. Meanwhile, the street arrest at the CBS Convention of some time back was replayed in Japan. In

Tokyo, Costello and The Attractions played a few songs on a lorry until they were arrested. Costello was fined 4,000 yen (around £10) for disturbing the peace.

Meanwhile, a new single was released, 'Radio, Radio' – 'Costello is in tune with nothing at all,' barked one reviewer[31] – and dates were announced for his highest-profile London concerts yet at the Dominion Theatre. They would be the first rock band ever to play there. Playing seven consecutive nights at the venue, from 18 to 24 December, with support from Richard Hell and The Voidoids, together with John Cooper Clarke (!), all the concerts sold out. Costello's father, Ross, came to see his son play at the venue, and was impressed by the gig but worried by the atmosphere. 'They just want to see you die,'[32] he told an unperturbed Elvis. Perhaps he didn't appreciate that the aggressive energy emanating from the stage was readily returned by the fuelled-up audience.

The sell-out series of seven concerts at the major London venue (*Star Wars* was ditched in place of the shows) told a rewarding and unquestionable tale: Costello had well and truly arrived. He had it all. The critical acclaim he had always wanted. Public adulation he thought he didn't need. A feisty and fisty manager. A public image that disturbed those who thought about it. A new apartment in Kensington. A model mistress. An imminent album release. And a wife and child in Whitton he was just about to separate from.

Happy days were indeed ahead. Oh, yes . . .

CHAPTER 3

Question: *'Why aren't your songs on karaoke machines?'*
David Ryan, Colchester, Essex.
Answer: *'Too many words. Can't fit them on the scroll.'*
Elvis Costello, Dublin.
Excerpt from Cash For Questions, Q magazine, February
1998

*'By Armed Forces, I thought I was God's gift, y'know? I
didn't think I was that cocky at the time, but we totally
thought we were kings of the castle. Whether or not we
were, while making it I was completely convinced; I had no
doubts . . .'*
Interview with Neil Spencer, NME, October 1982

Question: *'Haven't you occasionally been the obnoxious
jerk you're supposed to be?'*
Answer: *'Not really. Maybe once or twice in a confrontation, I would just be exactly what people would
think . . .So, sometimes, yes. But only in a stand-off. The
French call me Mr Hate. I'm not Mr Hate, I'm Mr Love.'*
Interview with David Wild, Rolling Stone, June 1989

Happy days for Elvis? Well, almost. Out went 1978: acclaim
for his second album, singing in Nashville, and being chased
by lawyers wanting to serve him with divorce papers. In came
1979: his public dirt hanging out on the washing line, and a
new album ready to go. Yet there was pressure of another
sort, the personal vying with the professional. A three-month

tour of America was in the offing, and the US label, CBS/Columbia, wanted to do to Elvis Costello and *Armed Forces* what they had done with Bruce Springsteen and *Born To Run*: make him a megastar.

While *My Aim Is True* quickly became the biggest import album of the decade, *This Year's Model* didn't sell as well. It 'lacked' that all important radio-friendly song that FM stations pick up on to bolster the sales of the album, a reflection more on the stringent conservatism of the radio programmers than on any quality-control problem on behalf of Costello. *Armed Forces*, therefore, was the one chosen to do the business, and everyone involved in the campaign knew it. While Costello and his band were steeling themselves for a three-month tour of US cities coast-to-coast, Jake Riviera was wondering what would happen if the album didn't cut the commercial mustard.

'We either make it all the way with *Armed Forces* or we don't,' he said to *Creem*. 'If this album doesn't break in America, then Columbia will still keep us but we'll be considered pretty much a spent force.'[1] There was little choice but for the campaign managers to go all out to capture the audience and radio play. There was one thing in their favour: the album was Costello's most concerted attempt at fashioning a pop record. It's the best kind of pop record: tuneful, insightful, subversive. Here was Costello playing the game, knowing full well he was going to win it. Perhaps for the first time in his career to date, he had everything sussed. Musically, the Attractions (welcomed into the fold by being mentioned on the sleeve for the first time) were in top order, having coalesced into a superb band who weren't afraid of embracing influences as broad as *Abbey Road*-era Beatles, Bowie, The Byrds, Roy Orbison and Abba.

From start to finish *Armed Forces* is chock full of melodies and tunes (only one of which, 'Busy Bodies', was over three-and-a-half minutes in duration) that gave the lie to the accusation that Costello was a mere Van Morrison and Graham Parker clone. The magisterial sweep of the material also firmly lifted the album out of the New Wave arena (or whatever you wanted to call it) and into the 'Pure Pop For Now People' aesthetic embraced by Stiff. In particular, Steve Nieve's keyboards (Elizabethan in 'Green Shirt', very grand in 'Party Girl', metronomically European in 'Oliver's Army') were outstanding. Bruce and Pete Thomas, meanwhile, surrounded Costello with a tight cloak of rhythm that acted as a dense backdrop.

Lyrically, Costello moved away from the personal (although 'Party Girl' allowed a glimpse into his current extra-marital relationship) to the international. From the album title to the song titles to the lyrics, military metaphors abounded, all of them wrapped up in punning so outlandishly clever they were impossible not to admire. Like Dylan in many respects, Costello's songs on *Armed Forces* were many layers thick, and not a weary one-stop shop to the heart of the matter. His lines were getting smarter and better, it was simple as that. As if driven by a creative marketing strategy of hitting the listener with as many words as possible (in the fervent hope that if one lyric didn't connect, then another certainly would) Costello deliberately trowelled on the wordplay, compacting the songs with imagery so romantically and dangerously powerful that it hurt. Such clever wordplay leaped from the album with lightning clarity. But there was no hint of self-congratulation, and the seriousness of the album soon became apparent.

The album's original title, as previously noted, had been *Emotional Fascism*. This, perhaps, threatened to limit the overall scope of the record. The Americans didn't like the title, anyway, and this may have had a slightly stronger bearing on the name change, particularly as Costello was ready to admit that it was far too harsh for the marketplace. The new name, coined by drummer Pete Thomas, nevertheless continued a singular Costello theme – that of control and domination over both governing and individual bodies. Besides, if *This Year's Model* had retained its original title of *Little Hitler*, the Nazi elements would be seen to have been overplayed and to be stating the obvious, something that Costello avoids.

'Oliver's Army' started the ball rolling: a glorious pop song that focused on the plight of a young soldier and how he had been manipulated by the powers that be. Institutionalized violence is the target of most of the songs, and along with the occasional barbed aside concerning paranoia ('Green Shirt'), sexual authoritarianism ('Big Boys') and the British (wrong) way of life ('Sunday's Best'), he fashioned a political record of extreme importance while simultaneously honing his pop skills. *My Aim Is True* sounded like a bunch of rough demo songs compared to the sophistication of *Armed Forces*. And who else would allow the first line of the first song on the record to ponder precisely how they might begin proceedings?

Armed Forces quickly became Costello's most succesful record to date, showing him on one hand to be someone who barely dwelled any more on the fringes of the New Wave, and on the other to be an artist who just may have composed a collection of such radio-friendly pop songs that America could be his for the taking. Unfortunately, great record though *Armed Forces* undoubtedly was, it didn't work out quite like that.

Elvis was very much aware of the importance of the upcoming US tour, but was burning the candle at both ends. Jake Riviera was as much an obsessive as his charge, figuring out ways to market the man in the horn-rim glasses that didn't appear either dubious or stereotypical. There was more than speculative talk about Costello appearing in his own 'rock' film. Dismissing the likes of Malcolm McLaren's concept for *The Great Rock 'n' Roll Swindle*, Riviera's idea was to concoct something along the lines of the quintessential 1950s rock movie, *The Girl Can't Help It*, an acerbic satire on public relations, rock 'n' roll and advertising. According to Riviera, the completed script for the Costello film was already in place.

This wasn't the first time Riviera had such an idea. When Costello was starting out he made overtures to the BBC documentary department to chart the rise from obscurity of a young singer/songwriter called Declan Patrick MacManus. Nothing ever came of it.

Costello, in the meanwhile, was writing songs as if he had

but a week to live. Already, most of the songs for the next album were completed. Bassist Bruce Thomas, who normally roomed with Costello while on tour (oh, those happy-go-lucky twin-bedded Holiday Inn days) claimed that at this time Costello had enough new material to fill four albums. He also contended that the singer was a workaholic insomniac who paced hotel bedrooms furiously writing songs. Was Costello serious about what was once a hobby, but was now his work? You bet.

He was already smarting from unguarded comments made by a fringe associate who attested to Costello's lack of edge and artistic drive. The thought of that possibility frightened him. 'Sometimes it's just fatigue, other times you really start to doubt yourself,' he confessed to *Creem*. 'Sometimes it can be healthy, because complete conviction about one's right-ness at all times is the worst sort of vanity . . . I've got areas of megalomania which are sometimes the only things that keep me going. Sometimes, even now I can feel absolutely washed up. If two days go by without a idea for a song, I become obsessive about writing. That's what taking it up as a career does as opposed to it merely being a hobby. The thought of me drying up doesn't scare me so much as the thought of me just repeating myself in a series of diminished echoes. Watching someone you admired struggling to be inspired is the most pathetic sight imaginable. Ultimately, I just want control over what I'm doing. Complete control.'[2]

Again, things didn't work out exactly like that. For starters, the track listing to *Armed Forces* was rejigged by Columbia bosses, deleting 'Sunday's Best' (too darned 'British' for US tastes?) and replacing it with Nick Lowe's '(What's So Funny 'Bout) Peace, Love And Understanding?' – the record company executives' pitch for the crucial radio-friendly hit single. It was a good choice, but one that must surely have sent alarm bells ringing in Costello's head as to how much trust Columbia had in him as a writer of pop songs.

The US tour commenced in February. Support acts included Rockpile, The Damned and old friends Clover (as backing band for Carlene Carter). Beginning on the West

Coast, the tour, in keeping with the most obvious interpretation of the album title, was organised like a military-style task force. Jake Riviera outfitted the roadies in army fatigues. The maroon-trimmed Silver Eagle touring bus had the words 'Camp Lejeune NC' on a one-foot-high banner. Full-page press advertisements included one of Costello pictured with a gun in his mouth, the words 'Pay Attention' and 'Be Mercenary. Get Armed Forces' accompanying the disturbing image. While provocation was inevitably part of Riviera's game plan, no one had anticipated the lengths he would go to in adhering to the principles of antagonism. And no one foresaw just how awry matters would go with Riviera's and Costello's unwise strategic manoeuvres.

'By turns petulant and rabid, Elvis and his troops did not seem equal to the grand military metaphors of the promotional campaign that preceded them,' wrote Fred Schruers in *Rolling Stone*. 'They seemed, rather, to be conducting a messy police action bound to make doubters and even enemies out of his strongest American partisans.'[3]

Even from the beginning, the omens were not good. In Seattle, Costello's sound crew organized shrieking feedback to drown the negative audience reaction when a normally hour-long set was cut to forty minutes of barely-contained venom and contempt – something UK audiences, reared on a diet of punk rock, would probably have appreciated. At a gig in Berkeley, California, following a set of similar length, members of the audience threatened to break open the box office and get their money back. Costello, already irate that the Clash, who were playing San Francisco the same night, had promotional posters pronouncing them as 'The Only English Band That Matters', turned in a hot-wired forty-minute performance and stormed off the stage. Incensed, the audience ripped out a portion of the venue's seats, then went outside to vent their spleen on the tour bus, breaking windows in the process. When matters took a turn for the worse, Costello and Bebe Buell were shepherded from backstage to the safety of their hotel.

This preceded the Grammy Awards in early February, a

glittering industry night built round the awards system that Costello despised. Such was the response to *My Aim Is True* and *This Year's Model* that Costello was nominated, along with Cars and Taste Of Honey, for Best New Artist of the Year. Despite the prestige nomination and the US success of *Armed Forces* (the first 'New Wave' record to attain gold status, and this in the post-*Saturday Night Fever* heat), word had it that champagne corks would not be popping at Riviera Heights. The winners of various categories on the night included Barry Manilow, Anne Murray, The Bee Gees and Billy Joel, so it came as no great shock that Taste Of Honey beat Costello to first place.

And still the beat went on, mostly negative, expletive-deleted, crawling the walls. At a 3,000-plus gig at the Kiel Opera House, St Louis, Costello drove the first real nail into his own coffin when he dedicated 'Accidents Will Happen' to KADI radio station, soon after nixing the goodwill of another local radio station (KSHE, and the show's unofficial sponsor) by introducing 'Radio Radio' with a petulant dig. Costello's three albums went from heavy rotation to no play at all on KSHE, a situation rectified several days later when Alan Frey, boss of Costello's US management company (the not so cryptic acrostic ARSE), smoothed out the radio station's ruffled feathers.

Columbia was not impressed, but the feeling was mutual. There was discontent in the Costello camp that the US record company was not using its major league status and financial might in the way it should have been. Disillusionment set in ever more deeply when a New York radio station held a competition for 1,200 Costello tickets for a forthcoming concert in the city. Over 250,000 callers jammed the switchboard, giving Riviera the managerial leverage to request extra finance from the record company to book Costello for Shea Stadium. After due deliberation, Columbia said no. The following day, a number of Columbia executives were surprised to find a present of a shovel awaiting each of them as they arrived for work. As quoted in *Uncut*, Riviera had attached a note to the consignment: 'If you really want to bury my act, I thought you could do with some more help.'[4]

After St Louis, a crooked necklace of one-off gigs awaited Elvis Costello and The Attractions. Physically gruelling, mind-numbing and devoid of any spark of individuality, the cities were just staging posts on the inexorable march of the *Armed Forces* campaign. Rochester, Cleveland, Harrisburg, Syracuse and Dayton blended one into the other. And then came the events at Columbus, Ohio, a pivotal moment in Costello's professional career and personal life that came to overshadow him for at least five years. Reports of what exactly happened vary from account to account, but one thing is certain: Costello's mouth, at times so eloquent and articulate, had a huge and ungainly size-twelve foot in it.

Situated halfway between Cincinnati and Cleveland, Columbus is the capital of Ohio, with a population of over 500,000. Picture the scene: a bar at the not-so-salubrious Holiday Inn, with bassist Bruce Thomas and Elvis at the bar drinking after a mundane gig. They were not drunk yet. Also in the bar, having arrived back at the hotel after his own gig in the city en route to another town, was founder and former member of the once vital Buffalo Springfield, Stephen Stills. A member of one of the most popular US groups of the 1970s, Crosby, Stills, Nash & Young, Stills was now viewed as a songwriter on the wane. His most recent album, *Thoroughfare Gap* (a collection of self-pitying songs inspired by the break-up of his marriage to French singer Veronique Sanson) had been released in 1978, and to many represented a low point in a career that had already been going downhill. Drug problems and a bad 'attitude' had not helped his current status.

Along with Stills and his entourage was back-up vocalist and hard-living woman Bonnie Bramlett, a singer who, under her maiden name Bonnie Lynn, had sung with noted soul and blues figures such as Little Milton, Albert King and Ike and Tina Turner. She had also acted as back-up vocalist for some of the major figures among 1970s US white blues artists – Dickie Betts, Duane Allman, Rita Coolidge and Leon

Russell (whose 'Delta Lady' was said to be inspired by Coolidge). Bramlett had enjoyed some success as part of the husband-and-wife duo Delaney & Bonnie (the first white act to be signed to Stax/Volt) but they had divorced in 1972. Now struggling in her career, she had come through the other side of alcoholism and, now rehabilitated, she had joined Stills as part of his band.

Costello was certainly aware of Stills' history and his part in the Buffalo Springfield legend, but in his twisted logic on matters American, quite likely loathed what Stills had come to represent. Nevertheless, both Elvis and Bruce accepted an invitation to join the Americans for a post-performance port, and soon the two groups which were at different ends of the rock spectrum but were connected by their respective artistry, were chatting noisily, each fielding off amiable jibes from the other. Also in the bar were several Costello fans who had wanted to see their hero up close.

One of the fans asked Costello what was surely a devil's advocate question: what did he think about America and its people? Costello prepared to meet his maker with a reply that characteristically bit the hand that fed him. 'We hate you,' he spat. 'We just come here for the money. We're the original white boys and you're the colonials.'

Provocative humour in the wrong company is no laughing matter, and when words with no sense of irony are spoken specifically to raise hackles, the results can be ugly. Those familiar with the type of ferocious verbal spat emanating from the mouths of Costello and Riviera knew the score: keep a low profile on the way out, and breathe a sigh of relief that the scorn heaped upon some unfortunate individual didn't land anywhere near you. People who weren't used to the oral onslaughts either cowered or confronted. Stills' reaction was not to sense any spark of humour at all in the remark, instantly squaring up for a showdown.

Reports of what happened next vary. One description reports a member of Stills' road crew assaulting Costello. A report in *Rolling Stone*'s Random Notes section claimed that Costello then called Stills' percussionist Joe Lala 'a greaser spic'. Now it was Stills' turn to lunge at Elvis, after which the irate American walked out of the bar with the words 'Fuck off, steel nose'[5] ringing in his ear – a reference to the reconstructive surgery Stills reportedly had on his nose following his cocaine addiction.

This left a drunken, seething Costello and Thomas, and an angry Bramlett. Perhaps in an effort to tone down the rising tension, Bramlett told Costello how much she admired his music. So far, so good. Then she asked him what he thought of James Brown. Big mistake . . .

'A jive-ass nigger,' replied Costello. All right, then, said Bramlett, how about Ray Charles?

'He's nothing but a blind, ignorant nigger,' retorted Costello, and it was now completely beyond a joke. His reply, though, was also beyond being tolerated. Telling him to keep his opinions to himself, Bramlett swung at him. 'Fuck Ray Charles, fuck niggers, and fuck you!' was the response.[6]

What followed was either mayhem, or according to the hotel bartender a small fracas that soon petered out. The Stills crew shuffled out to their waiting tour bus, while Thomas and Costello (the latter gingerly rubbing an injured shoulder) made their way up to their rooms. That would have been that, but for one crucial decision on the part of Bonnie Bramlett.

The following morning, Elvis was hungover and smarting from a sore shoulder, 'I only remembered that the thing had even taken place when I returned to my hotel room and discovered that my arm hurt somewhat,' he told *NME*.[7] Costello and the rest of the crew drove on to Cleveland, where he played a blistering two-encore show at The Agora. He learned that *Armed Forces* had reached No. 10 in the Billboard charts.

The following few days saw no public outburst or recriminations. The events at Columbus were slowly receding into a twilight zone of barely-recalled drunken rudeness, the kind that is begrudgingly forgiven in the cold light of day. The tour would reach New York in less than two weeks, and already a poster blitz was covering the walls of the city publicising

Costello's gigs. Scheduled to play two shows at The Palladium at the end of March, the remainder of the Big Apple itinerary included three gigs on 1 April. On the so-called 'April Fool's Day Marathon', Elvis would play at The Lone Star Cafe at six in the evening, The Bottom Line at nine, and at midnight at The Great Gildersleeves. New York, it was thought, would finally catapult Costello into the big-time arena. Such a gig blitz would surely gain no end of media coverage, would it not? In the end, Costello did garner massive media coverage, but not for the right reasons.

What he wasn't aware of was the seed of loathing that remained in Bonnie Bramlett's consciousness *après* Columbus. Shortly after the insurrection, Bramlett had been on to East Coast news agencies, newspapers and magazines supplying them with unambiguous minutiae of what had happened at the Holiday Inn bar. She had spared little, stig-matising Costello as a bigot and a racist.

By the time the *Armed Forces* tour trundled into New York (by now battle-weary and somewhat unfocused), the story had broken coast-to-coast. The strategy of the April Fool's Day gigs had been swamped by the details of the Columbus incident. As the story emerged from local and national media in a destructive ripple effect, Costello came to be looked upon almost as a threat to the nation. There was a certain irony about this: in the UK, Costello had latched on to the coat-tails of punk, but had caused as much anarchy as an altar boy. In America, he dismisses two of the country's great black artists in a drunken stupor and gets hauled over the coals. By the end of March, the East Coast media 'were whipping themselves up into a frenzy of liberal indignation, demanding explanation, public apologies and retractions of what they had already decided were Costello's racist views.'[8]

'I don't think anyone really believed that Elvis hated niggers, blind or otherwise,' former *Rolling Stone* writer, Kurt Loder told *NME*, 'but because of the attitude he'd had previously towards the press, he really set himself up . . . Stephen Stills and Bonnie Bramlett, these real burned-out guys. You can imagine what they were like . . . But he should've known that people like Stills and Bramlett, they needed publicity, they were bound to build it into a major incident. I mean, he [Costello] is touring America, putting down Americans. Some people, they're gonna think that's bad enough, and they're gonna want to get him for it. Then he picks on Ray Charles. You're talking about stuff that people grew up on. Like, everybody thinks Ray Charles is the greatest. I'm sure Elvis felt the same. So what he said was just dumb . . . Nobody's gonna get away with shit like that. It was the stupidest thing anybody could've said.'[9]

The New York press wanted to know what had taken place between Bramlett and Costello, and they wanted to know immediately. In order to counteract any further negative publicity and adverse public opinion, a press conference was arranged to take place at the Manhattan offices of Columbia Records on 30 March. Assembled there were fifty journalists, quite a number of whom had been waiting for a pot shot at Costello for a long time. The atmosphere, inevitably, was hostile. Quite simply, this was payback time.

Costello arrived in the 14th-floor record company conference suite wearing a polka-dot suit and tie. A green badge affixed to his jacket lapel read 'Desire Me', Costello even at this juncture showing his trademark ironic sense of humour. He began in a faltering manner, picking up speed after a plea to the assembled photographers to stop using flashes until after the press conference ended. Explaining that he was misquoted out of context in various publications, he went on to say that he didn't want to get involved in a minor fight with the likes of Stills and Bramlett. It concerned him, he continued, that people would take what he had said as his opinion, and not as heated, provocative words spoken in the course of an argument.

'I'm sure,' he said as coolly as he could under the most trying of circumstances, 'that everybody's had occasion to go to absolute extremes . . . in order to, you know . . . even to say things that you don't believe, you know. Ask Lenny Bruce.'[10]

And so it went on, the collected journalists' reactions ranging from mild bemusement to near apoplexy. Questions were flying thick and fast, Costello answering them as pointedly and with as much finality as he could. A reporter asked why his comments focused on black performers. Costello replied that the remarks he made about Crosby, Stills, Nash & Young went unreported, as did Bramlett's opinion of Englishmen in general: '. . . all lousy fucks who couldn't get it up any more,' according to earlier Costello biographer Krista Reese.[11] And Bramlett was also quoted as saying, 'I told him anybody that mean and hateful has to have a little bitty dick.'[12] This comment also went generally unrecorded in the battle to nail Costello to the media cross.

The press conference eventually ground to a halt, with most of New York's fourth estate feeling that Costello's defence was a waste of time, albeit delivered in as sincere and penitent a manner as he could muster. The damage had been done and reported, the perception of Costello as anything less than a stupid bigot lost in the hysteria. Curiously, what Costello didn't raise at the conference was his Rock Against Racism connection (he had played alongside reggae bands such as Aswad in an Anti-Nazi rally in Brixton the year before), nor the fact that he had a history of writing anti-fascist songs. No matter, the press had it in for him. As hard as he tried, he lost. Ironically, though, a report in the July 1979 issue of *Creem*, written by Susan Whithall, noted that the majority of journalists present at the press conference who asked questions in an 'offensive self-righteous tone' were themselves major participants in the New York New Wave scene, itself 'lethally racist'. Critic Lester Bangs, wrote Withall, penned a primer on New Wave racism for *Village Voice*, 'describing the insidiousness of it in that scene, because it's on the lips of the hip elite more often than not.'

The New York shows went ahead, despite calls from civil rights groups and anti-racist bodies screaming for a boycott. And then there were the cranks. Within five days of the Columbus incident being reported in New York, Costello had received well over 120 death threats, a number of which

Riviera took seriously enough to engage the services of armed bodyguards for round-the-clock protection. 'There were two guys with guns with him at all times,' Roberta Bayley, a friend of Costello's from the days of *This Year's Model*, told *Spin* magazine. 'A car would backfire and everyone would hit the floor. It really was that bad.'

The shows went ahead, with pickets outside The Bottom Line, Costello perversely singing The Merseybeats' 'I Stand Accused' at The Lone Star, and death threats still trickling through. Security was as high as the spirits of the entourage were low. There were several more US shows, but most people just wanted to hop on the plane back home. The resulting mess affected Costello personally as well as professionally. His break-up with Bebe Buell was quite probably hastened by what took place at Columbus, and the subsequent psychological strain it placed on their relationship. Costello flew back to England with death threats still ringing in his ears, leaving Buell inconsolable and on the brink of a breakdown. 'He started flipping out on me,' she later said to *Oui* magazine. 'I think Elvis derives a lot of inspiration from not being happy.'[13]

The US tour was a strategic disaster. As the tour personnel approached New York they were hopeful of a Top Five *Billboard* chart position. By the end of April, *Armed Forces* was out of the Top Thirty, with Costello never selling as many copies of an album in the States again. It would be close to two years before he would tour America once more, and it would take many more years for the unfortunate results of the incident to subside. It was undoubtedly the most horrific event of his career, and was for years the first thing that many people thought of in relation to his work.

'It was a drunken brawl, and I wanted to say whatever would outrage those people the most, but that's no excuse,' he said of the nightmare scenario to the *New York Times*. 'A lot of people were very angry and rightfully so. Those words I used certainly don't represent my view of the world. I had always just assumed that people would recognize my allegience to R&B, to black music, but it wasn't obvious enough. I suppose if you allow uncontrolled anger to run away with you, and if you make a career of contriving anger, up on stage, whether you're feeling anger or not, sooner or later you'll find yourself saying some things, using words you don't mean. It'll all come back at you. But I don't want to sound like I'm making excuses. There aren't any excuses for saying things like that.'[14]

'If it had been a considered argument,' he reasoned later in Rolling Stone, 'I probably would have either not pursued the argument to such extreme length, or I would have thought of something a little bit more coherent, another form of attack, rather than just outrage. Outrage is fairly easy. Not in terms of dealing with the consequences, but in terms of employing it as a tactic in an argument.'[15] The personal repercussions were such that Costello kept his head down for some time. From a career point of view it was a small death (from an American perspective, anyway), and one that changed him for the better.

'I thought it would make for a more original exit than the usual motorcycle accident,' was the comic aside Costello gave to an NME journalist two months later,[16] referring to the over-the-handlebars experience of Bob Dylan some thirteen years earlier as symbolizing an implicit if pivotal change of public attitude.

In the US aftermath, readers of the Village Voice and Rolling Stone had their say. One letter described Elvis as a 'twerpy punk', claiming that he had visited America to 'make big bucks and hire goons to kick the shit out of his audience and then cut down Ray Charles.' The letter writer advised for stricter immigration laws. Another missive writer was shocked at how Bonnie Bramlett struck a visitor just because she didn't happen to agree with his opinions. Mostly, the letters were as irrational as Costello's now much-regretted remarks. One letter, however, appeared in Rolling Stone a few weeks after the rumpus, and shone like an intelligent beacon amidst all the ranting. It was written by Costello's father, Ross MacManus. It began by thanking the paper for its perceptive review of Armed Forces. It continued:

59

'"Oliver's Army" is an important track for me, and your reviewer, Janet Maslin, so quickly picked up on the 'white nigger' significance. My grandfather was an Ulster Catholic, and, as a child, I lived in an area where bigotry was rife. So we are those white niggers.

'This brings me to the disturbing reports that I have seen branding Elvis Costello as a racist. Nothing could be farther from the truth. My own background has meant that I am passionately opposed to any form of prejudice based on religion or race. And El's mother and I were both branded as hotheads and Marxists or anarchists.

'So you can see that we don't have any chic, white liberal attitudes (and El has publicly despised the latter many times). This is the water that Elvis has been born and bred in, and he swims in it as naturally as a goldfish. His mother comes from the tough, multi-racial area of Liverpool, and I think she would still beat the tar out of him if his orthodoxy were in doubt.'

Another measured form of support came from Ray Charles himself. Asked his opinion of what had taken place at Columbus, and as quoted in *Uncut*, his reaction was succinct and sympathetic: 'Anyone could get drunk once in his life. Drunken talk isn't meant to be printed in the paper, and people should judge Mr Costello by his songs rather than his stupid bar talk.'[17]

In 1989, on a visit to America, Costello summed up not only that specific incident but also the general chaotic lifestyle that he, Jake Riviera, and The Attractions experienced: 'I had never made my living with music. Suddenly I had all these ludicrous sort of things to live up to. And I reacted badly. That made good copy, not just the Columbus thing, but other punch-ups that we had with various photographers who wouldn't take no for an answer. We were all moving very, very fast. And there's a tremendous amount of fun to be had in terrorizing people that are so thick-skinned. So we kept going along like some sort of bizarre episode of *The Monkees*, running around, drinking lots of vodka and turning up in these places where things were so comical that we'd just push 'em right up into the absurd rather than even try to rationalize them.'[18]

In May, 'Accidents Will Happen' was released. Come June, the single reached the Top Thirty, and Elvis was reunited with his wife and child. In the interim period after returning to England, Costello had gone from performing on stage to studio work with the likes of J Geils Band and The Specials (whose debut, *Specials*, released in November 1979, was produced by Costello). He had also appeared in his first film, *Americathon*. Written by Firesign Theatre's Phillip Proctor and Peter Bergman, the movie is a 'comedy' featuring, among others, Meatloaf. Costello appeared briefly (and whimsically) as the imaginary British rock star Earl Manchester. This would be the first of several generally misguided attempts at 'acting'. 'It was awful,' he admitted to *Trouser Press*, 'though I only had a cameo part in it . . . I couldn't see myself acting . . . The camera doesn't like me. I know that from watching myself on *Top of the Pops*. Every time we've appeared on that programme, the record's gone down the following week!'[19]

Facing 1980 head on with his next album (*Get Happy!!*) completed, Costello had record-company difficulties to contend with. Radar had collapsed leaving its founders, Martin Davis and Andrew Lauder, and its acts, Costello, Lowe, Bram Tchaikovsky and The Yachts adrift. It had been financed by WEA Records (the international wing of Warner Communications), who had similar arrangements with several other small labels, notably Real and Beggar's Banquet. WEA originally owned half of Radar, but became a majority shareholder when it bought out Davis and Lauder in November 1979.

Ordinarily, WEA's financing would have given Warner Bros the freedom to have released Radar product in America, but Costello and Lowe – Radar's big boys – were already lined up with Columbia via a licensing deal with Riviera Global Productions. Not that Warner Bros wanted everything that Radar had to offer. Bristol's perversely-named Pop Group were seen perform by a Warners executive whilst on business in England. Appalled by the band's apparent lack of melodic structure (what, no hit singles from a band called the Pop Group . . .), he cancelled any further collaboration between the two companies. While the likes of The Yachts and Bram Tchaikovsky were eventually licensed for North America to Polydor, racking up small but significant success, Radar nevertheless began to run into difficulties. It started when Lauder left the label, following an argument with Davis. 'Warner Bros' UK book-keepers were scrutinizing the lack of profitability of a company that should have been making an enormous profit,' remarked Dan Loggins, then Warners' Executive Director of International A&R, to *Trouser Press*. 'Radar had an exceedingly high overhead – big offices in Covent Garden . . . I guess they wanted to go first-class once they were successful, but there wasn't enough cashflow to keep it going at that level. They were earning money but not making the kind of money the original premise of the label was based on. When option time came, Warner Bros had to take a serious look at it from a business point of view.'[20]

Officially and legally, Radar as a record label still existed, so WEA naturally assumed that Costello and Lowe were contracted to it. Riviera, however, claimed that there was no written contract between the two artists and Radar – each record was released on an album-by-album basis on a hand-shake agreement. Riviera decided that as Radar (with Lauder and Davis at the helm) no longer existed, then any contract was null and void. WEA, less than pleased at buying a label with the two main reasons for its purchase out of the picture (and also so with hot property Costello's new album waiting in the wings) did what any major corporation would do: they went to court to get Costello and Lowe.

In December 1979, meanwhile, Riviera teamed up with Andrew Lauder on a new label. Initially called Off-Beat, it was abbreviated to F-Beat (reportedly toned down from the racier Fuck-Beat). A plan to release a cover of Sam & Dave's 'I Can't Stand Up For Falling Down' on Two-Tone (The Specials' label) was an idea that Costello particularly liked, connecting the label's main act with his production work on their debut album. Despite the fact that 13,000 copies of the single had been pressed by Chrysalis (Two-Tone's distributor) a good idea came to nothing. Although some copies were sent out to UK-based reviewers, the release was scuppered by bad timing, lack of operational clout on behalf of Two-Tone, and hints from the Specials' organization that 'there wasn't enough collaboration on the project.'[21]

F-Beat was also landed with an injunction, which forced Riviera and WEA's Managing Director, John Fruin, to look at new arrangements. The option was for F-Beat to wade through court proceedings while the new single and album sat in limbo, something that no one involved, least of all Costello and F-Beat, wished to happen. Under the new agreement, WEA manufactured and distributed F-Beat. The advertising, promotion, choice of releases, and more, were left to the F-Beat troops. Was everybody happy? Suppose so . . .

'The best situation was had by all,' claimed Dan Loggins. 'We should make money. Elvis should make money, and Andrew's . . . obviously more important as an owner than he was with Radar.'[22] When Jake Riviera was contacted for his comments by Loggins, he replied, 'We've got a lot to do and we want to get on with it, so fuck off.'[23]

Case closed, then?

CHAPTER 4

'This business sucks you in after a while. It's not really based around truth and I've had the disturbing feeling that what I do is a perversion of truth for quite a while.'
Elvis Costello on The South Bank Show, November 1981

'All the time I'm fighting a battle against myself to escape mediocrity and to do better. All creative people are like that. But the difference between myself and the vast majority of songwriters is that I'm not content with a sloppy phrase when a better one will do. How many people can honestly say that?'
Elvis Costello talking to Marc Shapiro, 1977

WEA eventually absorbed Radar in January 1980. In the wait for legal issues to be settled, more problems arose in relation to record releases. A scheduled date of 11 January was slotted in for 'I Can't Stand Up For Falling Down'. The single was reviewed ('guaranteed to spin some heads,' chirruped *NME*'s Max Bell), while acetates of the song received steady airplay on London's Capital Radio. In response to this, Warner Bros filed for an injunction to prevent the BBC from playing the record, which the corporation had been sent. It was a warning shot across the bows of Riviera Global Productions, one of a number of writs being prepared by the company.

Something like this didn't exactly help Costello's career. Apparently, he didn't wish to sign to Warners (not yet, anyway), and the grapevine hinted that he was prepared to

do one of two things: retire from the music business altogether due to the frustration of it all, or limit his career to
continuous touring. Neither of the two scenarios seemed
likely, but at this point what was to happen was anyone's
guess. F-Beat, meanwhile, launched itself with *Get Happy!!*
A change of approach was obvious, and it was much needed.
Throughout the previous year, Costello had experienced
many personal and professional problems, making *Armed
Forces* an unhappy event in general.

The pivotal personal episodes of 1979 – the break-up with
Bebe Buell, the Ohio incident, reuniting with his family – had
been exacerbated by the machinations of the record business.
The process of making *Get Happy!!* (recorded mostly in
Hilversum, Holland) was similarly tiresome and frustrating.
But there seemed to be something of a coherent method
behind it. Having toured America in 1979 as a full-blown
New Wave act, all the time on stage furiously belting out
songs in a manner fitting the perception of what a New Wave
act should sound like, Costello and The Attractions knew that
they could only carry on creatively if they moved away from
skinny-tie white post-punk pop-rock. While crisscrossing the
US, staple diets on the tour bus included Iggy Pop's *The Idiot*
and David Bowie's *Low* and *Heroes*. Mixing these with
Abba's greatest hits only confused matters, and the initial
sessions for *Get Happy!!* came predictably close to the sound
of the keyboard-led, tremolo-guitar-driven *Armed Forces*.

Already, this distinctive sound had acted as the blueprint
for a number of copycat pop acts, notably The Jags, whose
September 1979 hit single, 'Back Of My Hand', could easily
have been a third-class discarded item from Costello. In a
similar vein, songwriters such as Joe Jackson and Any
Trouble's Clive Gregson (although soon to bloom as credible
artists in their own right) were being lumbered with Costello
comparisons. It was time to move on.

'It got to the point where I felt the next record we made
would end up sounding like a parody of ourselves,' noted
Costello in *The Face*. 'On the *Armed Forces* tour of America
we had arrangements of half the songs on *Get Happy!!* in

our old style. We went to start recording and the result *did* sound like clichéd new-wave music. It would have come out sounding like a cross between *Armed Forces* and *This Year's Model*. It would have been less well arranged than *Armed Forces* and slightly more maniacal, more out of control, because we were out of control by that point. I felt it wasn't right . . .'[1]

A story initially deemed apocryphal actually turned out to be true: in October 1979, Costello was seen coming out of the Rock On record store in Camden Town, an oldies record shop that worked miracles in bridging the gap between pub rock and punk, run by Ted Carroll, another member of the extended Murphia clan. Costello left with a bunch of old Tamla Motown, Stax, Hi and Atlantic records – a mere £50 very well spent. These records, constituting as they did the sounds that Costello, as a discriminating mod, listened to in his mid-teens, were the effective homework for *Get Happy!!*. Other records from the participants' own collections completed the research.

The decision to alter the blueprint for Costello's fourth album was taken following a few drinks in a pub near the studio booked for the sessions. Knowing that they definitely wanted to avoid the sheen of 'quirky' new wave groups, the band's idea was to play some of the *Get Happy!!* songs in a slower, more soulful way. Whereas the musical accompaniment on *Armed Forces* was tight, fussy and twitching, skimming on the surface of the groove-oriented songs, here they wanted to delve underneath the skin of the songs, making them more rhythmic and more considered.

With no shame about borrowing from the soul greats, and with frail nervous systems and a considerable amount of drink and drugs, the new sessions for the album began. Taking existing artists and songs as the basis for their own ('Temptation' uses a riff that echoes Booker T and the MGs' 'Time Is Tight'; 'Opportunity' is a mental steal from Al Green; 'Clowntime Is Over' from Curtis Mayfield; 'Love For Tender' and 'High Fidelity' contain references to Supremes' songs; the Four Tops' 'Reach Out (I'll Be There)' influenced

'King Horse' . . .) the sessions were conducted in a haphaz-ard fashion. Names and songs would be invoked as the inspi-ration for a particular number, the experienced musicians easily recalling the original songs to mind. Some of the songs had more direct connotations. 'Black And White World', for instance, was written after watching a Barbara Stanwyck movie, *Ball Of Fire* (an inversion of *Snow White And The Seven Dwarfs*, with Stanwyck playing the improbably-monikered Sugarpuss O'Shea). None of the songs on *Get Happy!!*, according to Costello, were written about what took place in Ohio.

Inevitably, there were tensions behind the sessions, and these would become apparent after the album's release. 'Riot Act' was the song closest to the naked truth, a reaction to all of the personal and business strife that threatened to push Costello over the edge. He had determined that *Get Happy!!* was to be his final record in the current set-up, and was considering the option of a solo career. He had even recorded a cheap demo of 'New Amsterdam' with thoughts of a solo single.

The album title itself, taken from the Harold Arlen and Ted Koehler number of the same name, was a heavily ironic comment on the record's lyrics, which were steeped in discontent. As a necessary reaction to, and exorcism of, the events of 1979, there's a rough quality to the record that is in stark contrast to the production values of *Armed Forces* – a subconscious move away from clinicism to something a tad warmer and more emotional. If *Armed Forces* sounded, well, forced, then the new album was more relaxed, despite its creation amid external friction and inter-band factions.

'It was made under extreme self-inflicted emotional stress,' Costello recalled in *The Face*. 'It was a very extreme record from the point of view of the condition that I and the rest of the band were in . . . the aftermath of what happened in America and just generally very emotional, you know, shat-tered nerves. Too much drinking . . . I was taking enough drugs. Too many. Any is too many . . . That's why it sounds unfinished because it's about all we were capable of doing.'[2]

The album, radical though it was in relation to what had been released before, was well received and critically lauded as being a step in the right direction, both musically and lyrically. The Attractions locked in hard and tough when the occasion required it, while Costello said what he wanted to say with a leaner, more direct sense of autobiographical candour. Concomitantly, there seemed to be a dual sense of purpose about the songs. The Attractions were able to breathe or blow in them, and Costello didn't seem to be stumbling under such an enormous obligation to keep coming up with the puns and canny couplets he had established a reputation for. There was no consistent theme, though of course Costello was asked whether the single-word songs 'Opportunity', 'Temptation' and 'Possession' were regarded as constituent parts of a lust-fuelled trilogy. For the record, there was no link between the three songs, although Costello admitted years later in *Record Collector* it would have been great if there had been. 'Once I'd written the first two, it was inevitable I'd write 'Possession'. We went for a cup of coffee in Hilversum, because the hotel we were staying in was ghastly. We were very bored, and we went in to a cafe there . . . I fell in love with the waitress and wrote the song in ten minutes. It was a total lust song, it had nothing to do with any art concept . . . I then insisted on learning it on the way back to the studio. We were quite drunk, as it happens!'[3]

A UK tour followed the album's release, after which Costello actually left The Attractions to fend for themselves. He decided that he simply didn't see the point of carrying on in his present capacity. Such a decision was destined to be short-lived, and as one month blended into the next, as *Get Happy!!* reached No. 2 in the UK Album charts in March, and No. 11 in the US in April, a compromise developed.

In the UK, Costello's popularity showed no sign of diminishing, but in the US, *Get Happy!!* didn't have the staying power of *Armed Forces*. In part its sales suffered from the time it took to release the album, undoubtedly lessening its chances. Other influencing factors included the Bramlett/

Stills episode and the fact that, stylistically at least, the record was so different from his previous one. It's also quite likely that Costello's less informed American fans didn't appreciate what they perceived to be a musical defence of his Columbus outburst. Whichever way one views it, *Get Happy!!* failed to retrieve the commercial ground lost in the previous ten months. Costello had yet to tour America again in the aftermath, and wouldn't until much later on in the year.

It didn't prevent him from gigging all the way to Canada in August, at Toronto's Mosport Park Heatwave Festival. Promoted as the first New Wave rock festival to be staged in North America ('Punkstock!' screamed the promoters), over 50,000 people witnessed the combined forces of US and UK post-punk acts. On the US side, Teenage Head, Holly and The Italians, Talking Heads and the B-52s delivered the goods. For the Brits, Rockpile, The Rumour, Costello and The Pretenders (with Chrissie Hynde, an American Anglophile as lead singer) did the honours.

As the crowd grooved, journalists and photographers milled around the backstage area only to be informed that no one was allowed to photograph either Rockpile or Elvis on or off stage. Such decisions were standard bully-boy tactics from Jake Riviera, who was reported in *NME* to be cruising backstage 'threatening dire harm to anyone caught taking Costello's picture. Paranoia fills the air, good times soured by manipulation.'[4]

Such managerial action was apparently OK with a defiant Costello, who eventually stepped up to the microphone and announced himself and The Attractions as The Clash (who had been advertised to play but cancelled). The gig was a good one, the basic difference in approach on stage not just competing with what the other bands had done before but distinguishing them from it. 'All the others tried, in one way or another, to entertain and to please. Costello couldn't care less about that, and didn't play to the audience at all. He's here to make his points, to deliver his ultimatums to the world, with no attempt to ingratiate. He just lays it out, take it or leave it.'[5]

In the lead-up to 1981, a US-only compilation of out-takes, demos, and UK singles was released. *Taking Liberties* showcased 'throwaway' songs from all four of his studio albums, many of them shedding new, somewhat poignant light on Costello's public persona, dashing the cynic's view of the man who, in some people's minds, was little more than a caricature of bitterness and retribution. The collection was released in the UK on cassette only and with a different track listing as *Ten Bloody Mary's and Ten How's Your Fathers*.

Pleased so much with the fundamental premise of *Get Happy!!*, Costello could only be disappointed with his next studio album. Released in January 1981, *Trust* (the original title was *Cats and Dogs*) was conceived as *Get Happy!!* without the blatant outside influences, and *Armed Forces* without the Abba chords and squeaky-clean keyboards. Whereas the soul/Stax-influenced record was predominantly rhythmic, its core elements swathed in either short, jerky utterances or mellow tunes, the songs on *Trust* were, stylistically, all over the shop.

Complex and metaphorical, the material ranged from 'Different Finger' (a country adultery song that Costello wrote when he was nineteen, in an attempt to emulate a Tammy Wynette tune) to 'Shot With His Own Gun', a stark and skeletal not-just-another-failed-relationship song that contains some of the writer's most controlled lyrics. *Trust*'s creative strength variety was also its commercial weakness. Up to now, it was quite easy to pin Costello down as a surly, misanthropic singer/songwriter, someone whose nervous impatience bore down even the most understanding and sympathetic of observers.

His career thrived on people misunderstanding him. Was he an articulate punk rocker? Was he a frustrated and sour Randy Newman? To call the album *Trust* was another joke along the lines of his previous album title. How could anyone trust an artist who changed his tune(s) so much? Anyway, an over-adherence to trusting someone leads to complacency and being taken for granted. Costello could never allow that, could he? It was virtually impossible to get a handle on

Costello now, all too easy to be confused by his stylistic stance, and to be alienated by his own deliberate distancing of his fans. He was that rare breed of pop star who (apparently) loved his work but hated the environment in which he laboured.

Of course, for the number of his fans who actually connected with what he had to say (and how he went about saying it), Costello's continuing series of jerky leaps and bounds was a huge recommendation. At last, here was someone who wasn't content to rest on even the freshest and most fragrant of laurels. The motives of 1970s and 1980s music people were usually based on greed. Standing at the self-service counter of life, they took with both hands but gave back very little of substance. By comparison, despite an image that fluctuated from good to bad to worse and back again, Costello was a role model for the integrity-fuelled craftsman.

The variety of material contained in *Trust* highlighted his growing concern at being pigeonholed. Considering the vast array of stylistic changes that had been displayed on his previous four records, this amounted to an obsessive need to be even further recognized as a person who could push out the barriers wider and further apart. Likewise, while the lyrical content of the songs embrace his normal love 'em 'n' lash 'em issues, he imbues them with less cynicism and more culpability than before.

The revenge and guilt cards, so clearly marked, were shuffled to allow a minimum of irony, a direction that hadn't been conspicuous since the majority of songs on *My Aim Is True*. The fact that lyrics of 'Watch Your Step', 'New Lace Sleeves' and 'Different Finger' had been largely written when Costello was a lot younger may have had something to do with their comparative lack of ambiguity. 'It wasn't that I was out of material,' explained Elvis in *Record Collector*. 'I had always hankered after using those verses. Even the tune of 'New Lace Sleeves' was old. I just hid it away for years. It was one of the fluky, more sophisticated songs I wrote when I was messing around with trickier chord sequences than most of the early stuff.'[6]

There was a clarity about the voice and the conscience, and Nick Lowe's production work was an exercise in frosty sonic crispness. The one track Lowe didn't produce was 'Big Sister's Clothes', but Costello, the culprit, manfully takes away all blame from Lowe for this. Despite the inside sleeve depicting Costello and The Attractions playing within the confines of an orchestra (Joe Loss/Ross MacManus, anyone . . .) there was little or no clutter from the band. Pete Thomas' drums in 'Lover's Walk' echoes a Bo Diddley figure, while Steve Nieve's keyboard playing is scattered about the album making sarcastic references to various pop eras. From the grandiose arpeggios of the dramatic 'Shot With His Own Gun' to the honky tonk traces of 'Different Finger', Nieve once again stamped his authority over the general sound.

Lyrically, the album is one of Costello's finest. Although it can never be clearly explained why his often confounding and confusing lyrics work, they obviously do. The details of the songs are probably drawn from his very own real and personal world, but whether they are or not increasingly tends not to matter. Simply, they stand up on their own as classic self-confessional vignettes.

While in strictly rock-music terms he is leagues ahead of most, there is always a hint of the schoolboy taking pleasure in rolling out the puns, giving erstwhile lame lines the once-over, and tired clichés a slap on the cheek. Occasionally, the word-play can be tiresome and exhausting, but when one takes into account that *Armed Forces* was quite likely a concept album not of a story but of a metaphor (sexual trysts as military tactics), one can begin to appreciate that the man is no ordinary wordsmith.

So it is with *Trust*, a verbose record the success of which depends not on how confessional Costello himself is, but how honest the words themselves are. In this sense, he came into his own as a lyric writer with *Trust*, taking the first important step to becoming a songwriter who sings words of which he clearly knows the full implications. It's not too surprising that he stepped from one level of songwriting to another. He admitted to American TV chatshow host Tom Snyder, that he admired the lyrical craftsmanship of people such as Cole Porter and Lorenz Hart. Fusing the influence of diction-proper lyricists with his own pet loves of culture, money, sex and love, Costello steered himself away from conventional pop-song writing. Through linguistic bravura, technical knowhow and a firm emotional base, the results were remarkable.

'I don't even notice it,' he said in *Record Collector* regarding the avalanche of *Trust*'s wordplay. 'I got tired of reading about that in articles about what I do, because I don't see it as a dominant thing at all. Maybe it was more obvious on *Armed Forces*, where there were some really terrible puns. But all good pop lyrics try to work on that basis, unless they're really trying to be Esperanto and not use any words they won't understand in Taiwan . . . I took my cue from Smokey Robinson, and songs like 'I Second That Emotion' . . .'[7]

Trust left the committed Costello fan with a warm glow. Despite the initial lack of a thematic front, which to the casual listener might well have been intimidating, the songs were themselves cohesive. 'I was taking a lot of drugs when I wrote some of those songs,' Costello told *Record Collector*. 'Some of them are pretty affected by that. That's not to say that I don't remember what they're about, but the logic is quite deliberately fractured. It's like short bursts of attention span, gathered together into songs.'[8]

Costello moved from accusing to exploring on *Trust*, believing in his own instincts as a developing and growing songwriter, and embracing those elements within himself that he had previously shied away from. He himself didn't particularly like the record, feeling that it was a disappointment and an under-achievement, a bogus album with a mixture of fine and poor songs produced in a low-key way and played in a conservative manner. In retrospect, however, the results – sharp, genuine, touching and biting – were quite superb. Rather than viewing it as a piecemeal operation, it's actually a stylistic triumph that displayed the full range and variety of Costello's songwriting. In a different light, it can also be looked upon as a comment on the pretentiousness and light-weight nature of the then current pop scene.

Shortly after finishing *Trust*, the record's associate producer Roger Bechirian and Costello co-produced Squeeze's *East Side Story*. The band's Glenn Tilbrook had guested on *Trust*'s 'From A Whisper To A Scream', and the association was continued on a coast-to-coast American tour in February. It had been almost two years since Costello had toured the US. Requests from journalists for interviews were refused, Costello reserving his promotional time for a safe TV chat show, NBC's *Tomorrow*, reasonably secure in the knowledge that probing questions would not be asked. Unsurprisingly, the host, Tom Snyder, asked Costello nothing of the Bramlett/Stills debacle (it's possible Snyder knew nothing of it, but it showed poor research that the subject wasn't even tentatively broached). He concentrated instead on a career overview from Costello, who amused his host with tales of pre-Stiff days. Snyder in typical chat-show host mode veered from fawning to cutting. The younger members of the audience sniggered occasionally at the line of questioning. Two interesting questions were asked: had Costello learned to control his anger (a direct reference to Ohio?), and did he love his father? While he said yes to the latter, he declined to answer the former. As quoted by Krista Reese, Snyder then asked him if he thought he'd matured. Costello demurred, saying it sounded 'like cheese or something.'[9]

The US shows were a revelation to the audiences and to the media, which was probably expecting a return to bad form. Instead they witnessed a man (and a band, especially Nieve) whose edges had been rounded out somewhat, who had been shaped by the experiences of the past four years into an altogether more approachable artist. An *NME* review of a gig in New York perfectly captures the flavour of the 'new' Elvis: 'His aesthetic used to be to exhort an exciting momentum out of audience antagonism. He used to use lots of red and green lighting, unflattering psychologically provocative colours. His stage sets and lighting design had the principles of Leni Riefenstahl's film *Triumph Of The Will*

74

applied to a rock show, while Costello portrayed himself as a most unaccommodating and nasty Little Hitler . . . His character now is less starkly drawn, a lot harder to define. He regards his American audience with a lot less suspicion than he did two years ago . . . The stalking around the stage, the tantrums and mock psychosis, have gone. He sang to, rather than at us. The result is that he's more effective as a pop dramatist. He hasn't 'mellowed' or dampened his fire; instead he has, finally, started to make the passions, heartaches and crises of his songs seem like potentially universal, shared experiences instead of private nightmares.'[10]

The set comprised an abundance of riches culled mostly from *Get Happy!!* and *Trust*. A surprise cover version was 'She's Got You', the Patsy Cline hit. Costello altered the gender of the title, of course, and his vocal and phrasing exhibited both warmth and sensitivity. Country music was hardly the next big thing in 1981. As one of America's indigenous musics, country had never achieved the critical respect and rigorous analysis that many afforded to rock music. Like its native compadre jazz, country has a century-old tradition, with numerous styles evolving over the decades. It's a resilient form of music, taking on all manner of outside influences and feeding on them. In the early 1980s, it had lost its ragged edge. The likes of Willie Nelson, Waylon Jennings and Kris Kristofferson took a hike out of Nashville to formulate the sub-genre 'outlaw' country, leaving the likes of Kenny Rogers and Barbara Mandrell to croon bland country clichés. For many of its earlier fans, it appeared as if the music had lost sight of its roots.

There were interesting, often invigorating sideshows, not least being the emergence of country rock, the spiritual leader of which was Gram Parsons. He revitalized The Byrds and co-founded The Flying Burrito Brothers, as well as shacking up with Emmylou Harris, arguably the real queen of the new country sound. It was these aspects of the music that had initially spurred Costello into action, from as far back as the early 1970s. Alongside country rock, Costello focused on the greats of the 1950s and 1960s: Hank Williams, George Jones, Patsy Cline and Loretta Lynn. Williams, in particular, was a major influence. Costello had sung some of Williams' songs amidst the usual rock'n'roll whilst dragging his heels and acoustic guitar around the folk clubs of Liverpool and London.

His old band Flip City was a loose bluegrass/folk outfit. His song 'Stranger In The House' had been left off *My Aim Is True* because Stiff decided it would confuse even the most accepting of punk-rock fans. *Trust*'s 'Different Finger' was another remnant of those early days. The evidence was there for all to see. You could take Elvis out of country music but you couldn't take country music out of Elvis: that darned C&W influence just wouldn't go away, and something had to be done to accommodate it.

In mid-May, Costello and The Attractions went to Nashville to record *Almost Blue*. The producer was the legendary Billy Sherrill, whom Costello had previously met on his first visit to Nashville to record a duet with George Jones a few years back. The idea behind making *Almost Blue* stemmed as much from the fact that he was getting bored singing his own songs as from the wish to reach people he wouldn't normally have touched with his 'own' records. He also hoped to turn his steady fanbase on to music they might not have voluntarily listened to. Patsy Cline singing 'Sweet Dreams'? No way. Costello covering the same song? Worth a listen, if just to hear what it was like . . .

'Both things appealed to me quite a lot,' he told *The Face* in 1983. 'I was completely obsessed with country music at the time, although I hardly play country records now. I've exhausted that love, though I still have my particular favourites. There are other darker things involved in that. It's a rather fatalistic type of music. I listen to that record (*Almost Blue*) now and think, "God! I was never this depressed, was I?" It is a very depressed sounding record . . . Maybe that was the aftermath of 1979, maybe that was the final exorcism of all the unhappiness.'[11]

Costello toyed with making an album of ballads, a sad

record in homage to Frank Sinatra's *Only The Lonely*. He was even planning to cover a couple of Sinatra songs, but the arrangements (or the actual idea itself) got lost in the rush. 'I went in there in a depressed frame of mind, anyway,' he told *NME*. 'I had this sad feeling. I dunno why, it wasn't anything specific in my life, I'd just wound myself up to it . . . I can't imagine how I was so miserable sounding. It was a genuine feeling, so I never accepted the criticisms that the singing wasn't authentic.'[12]

Costello and company spent about eight days in Nashville, a period of time that flashed by in a whirl. The recording was being filmed for a *South Bank Show* special (to be shown shortly after the record's release at the end of October), a factor that added extra tension to already on-edge proceedings. Although Costello wasn't aware of it at the time, the initially bemused Billy Sherrill eventually became quite indifferent to the recordings. Showing more interest on some days than others, Sherrill's lack of enthusiasm stemmed from the fact that he considered the material Costello chose to record as tired songs resurrected from country music's knacker's yard. 'They weren't worn out to our audience,' Costello said many years later to *Record Collector*, 'and those people that didn't freak out at the mere thought of us doing a country record bought it.'[13]

Despite Sherrill's lacklustre approach to the recording, the sound of the record was spot-on. The famed producer knew Costello wanted the classic George Jones/Tammy Wynette torch'n'twang atmosphere. It was how he got it that made Costello smoulder. 'Sherrill's not interested in 90 per cent of the records he makes. He mixes half of them from his office where he's got an intercom . . . He's an odd character. He doesn't seem to have a lot of love for anything really, least of all music. God knows why he's in it. It seems to be a habit he can't get out of, making million-selling records.'[14]

They recorded the album in the old Columbia Studio A, a disappointment in the sense that Studio B was where 'Stand By Your Man' and *Blonde On Blonde* were recorded. According to Costello, recording was also affected by what he termed extracurricular activity. Prior to *Almost Blue*'s release, its appearance was pre-empted by a secret one-off filmed gig at Aberdeen's Country & Western Club in the town's Hotel Metro at the beginning of August. To tie in with the *South Bank Show* documentary, Costello and The Attractions booked themselves into the club incognito.

Club regulars might have suspected that something was going on when they arrived at the venue in search of shit-kickin' rhythms only to be greeted by TV cameras, no-dancing signs, and the front-row spaces filled with tables and chairs. The venue was far from full, but those that were in attendance wore the regulation uniform of cowboy boots and hats, patterned plaid shirts, and strategically placed slicks of hair gel. Costello and band had also splashed out on fine country-style clothes for the occasion. The gig was in two parts, and Costello appeared to rev it up in the second half, confident that he and the band (which was supplemented by pedal-steel guitarist and old friend, John McPhee) had earned their country chops and pork scratchings.

Almost Blue was released in October 1981 to an unsuspecting public (although jazz fans could clearly see the inspiration the cover owed to Kenny Burrell's *Midnight Blue* sleeve). Unless the average Costello fan happened to glance at the sticker on the album sleeve that screamed 'Warning! This album contains country & western music, and may produce radical reaction in narrow-minded people' they might have been led to believe that it was just another collection of (probably) good songs. Fact is, it was another collection of good, even great songs. Those people blinkered enough to dismiss it as a creative aberration were missing out on one of rock's finest and enriching sidesteps. There was respect for the genre, too, which, taking into consideration Costello's noted affection for it wasn't too surprising. His Liverpudlian/Ulster Irish background was also a factor, for the c&w tradition and culture had been steeped into both regions from the 1950s onwards, a subliminal influence that rose to the surface when he began to sing in public in his early teens.

If respect and affection were at the root of *Almost Blue*, then so also was an enduring tendency to blend the authenticity of Billy Sherrill's production with the traditional rock flavourings of the Attractions (who were assisted once again by John McPhee, his mercurial pedal-steel guitar playing adding lachrymose-colour blue, naturally, to the proceedings).

It's unlikely that many other British rock stars could grasp the nettle of 'genuwhine' country music and get away with it. Costello was brave and foolhardy enough to do just that and succeeded in a way that was neither ironic nor perverse. The man likes his country music straight, and *Almost Blue* has a razor-sharp crease down its centre. The music suits him, generally speaking the lyrics reflect his own concerns, and he's smart enough to figure out the genre's keen sense of humour as well as its integral sense of mourning.

The only aspect of the album that might have grated with the hip young things of Chelsea was old country's core and its reactionary assessment of morals. The songs said it all: 'Got problems? Then drink 'em under the table with a bottle of Jack! The wife ain't got dinner on the table when you walk in after a hard day's truckin'? Then go ahead and walk out on her!' If the PC fan could withstand the contradictions, then *Almost Blue* was an unspent match made in heaven. The tunes are brilliant, and the sentiments are as strong and binding as superglue. The record, needless to say, didn't sell very well. You won't find it in many reference books on country music, either.

Critically, *Almost Blue* split the jury. Some critics thought it complete and utter rubbish (and noting the look of incredulity and indifference on the face of Billy Sherrill throughout the *South Bank* documentary, it's possible he thought the same). Others thought it a brave move but one that lacked business nous. Very few (*NME*'s Paul Du Noyer and *Hot Press*'s Niall Stokes being two exceptions) thought it was more than a good idea. Critics aside, the record was a bigger hit with fans in the UK than *Trust* was, and probably connected with people outside his regimented fanbase. The diehard country audience treated it with the contempt they reckoned it deserved. In America, for instance, the record only made the Top Fifty, indicating a fanbase purchase only.

'Nashville didn't do a single thing to promote it,' Costello said bitterly in *NME*. 'I've heard vague reports that it got played on a couple of obscure country stations, but I guess they thought it was too weird that an English group at all would do that, let alone an English 'new waver'. Country & western stations, they probably think I'm a punk still . . .'[15] Inevitably, disillusionment set in. Gearing up for another coals-to-Newcastle-type tour of the US, to promote a country album in the land that invented the music, Costello was well placed to ponder on the overall subdued reception of *Get Happy!!*, *Trust*, and now *Almost Blue*.

Reckoning that he had paid dearly for the dispute between him, his management and Warners, he also accounted his fall in popularity to changing fashions and trends, and loss of hip status. Although *Almost Blue* had generated a fair amount of media interest and one Top Ten hit ('A Good Year For The Roses'), it wasn't exactly music the 'kids' wanted to listen to. Costello made regular appearances on *Top Of The Pops*, but his was music the kids' older brothers or sisters liked. As for this country stuff well, even mums and dads liked that!

The failure to follow up on the success of *Armed Forces* was apparently a deliberate one. Costello knew he could have made another record just like it, but that would have been formulaic. Hence, there was no major disappointment (he made the records wilfully and of his own volition, m'lud), but rather a feeling of increasing bewilderment at how to up the commercial ante. At its base was Costello's lingering distaste for the workings of the music industry, and his growing fear and loathing for the waste of money on what he saw as fripperies.

'People are always making excuses for the massive waste of money,' he told *NME*. 'The situation where companies have to hype and if you don't, you get pushed right out of the picture has got completely out of hand. You can't call a truce because nobody will agree to it – there's gonna be somebody else doing it. It's got like controlled corruption, the whole thing is sickening. I can't think about it. If I did I couldn't operate at all.'[16] Yet still he couldn't extricate himself from the mess of the album/tour/album syndrome. Flying off to America to tour, he went back to Nashville. He'd been there several times before, obviously, but mostly to record. This time was to play at the hallowed Grand Ol' Opry, where he would bring his brand of country music to those who had heard and seen the greats. He was better received than he had been on an earlier occasion, some time prior to his perceived 'conversion' to C&W.

'We opened with three Hank Williams' songs, and that didn't go down very well,' he admitted to *Record Collector*. 'The kids who came to see us in Nashville didn't want us to be country; they wanted us to be even more punk than we were perceived to be in the rest of America. We were accepted wholesale as the real thing in America because the real thing didn't get to them. The Sex Pistols did one short US tour, The Damned did a tour before that, and the Clash came afterwards, so we were the first group that many people in America saw that was anything like a punk band. So there we were, walking round Nashville, and these kids started giving us a hard time because we had short hair. Which was strange, because a few years earlier we'd have been beaten up for having long hair . . .'[17]

There just ain't no pleasing some people sometimes.

CHAPTER 5

'Do you believe in the supernatural?'
Elvis Costello: *'Er . . . I once saw Al Green. That was pretty close to it.'*
    Interview with Paul Rambali, The Face, *August 1983*

'The thing is, I never was an angry young man, I was always an angry old man. I always felt older, and always looked older, than I was. Things can still get me really angry . . . and I'm afraid my response to that is not a logical one, it's not calm or intelligent, it's fuck this, let's just get into major physical violence right away. The thing is, I am a good bloke, I don't actually hate myself, and I don't think I deserve the vitriol dealt out to me . . . All it shows is either their self-disgust or the fact that they simply don't know me. And they don't.'
    Interview with Barney Hoskyns, NME, *October 1983*

In January 1982, Elvis Costello and the Attractions cocked a snoot at the class of 1977 when they headlined at the Royal Albert Hall with the Royal Philharmonic Orchestra. Costello looked like Tony Bennett after a 3 a.m. bender, his black bow tie and matching glasses a fitting fixture amidst the decorum of the venue and the sobriety of the 'serious' musicians. As *Trust* had shown (and as his forthcoming album, *Imperial Bedroom*, would further demonstrate) he had improved radically as a vocalist.

The crooner ambience was justified, with Costello singing both passionately and in ghostly manner, wringing his hands in silent intensity while the Attractions and the audience drew breath. The first set was himself and the Attractions in full swing. This was followed by the discreet sawing of over eighty members of the RPO, an experiment that began as a interesting proposition, sidled into being a novelty and ended with a fizzle. Was the orchestra there merely to complement the songs, or were the songs going to be reshaped to accommodate the orchestra? No one was really sure. The high point was worth the wait, however: a terrific 'I Can't Stand Up For Falling Down' revisited as an orchestrated classic soul song. Costello lost himself in the achievement, back arched, limbs pointed, hands grabbing at the air. There was no conclusion reached by the critics other than that the concert was one of style over content, an intriguing and often brilliant sidestep that didn't seem to go anywhere. Perhaps that was the point.

One of the songs Costello performed at the RAH was 'Town Crier', a song he had written for his next album. A marked change of approach was adopted for *Imperial Bedroom*. For starters, it would not be produced by Nick Lowe, the man in the studios from 1976's *My Aim Is True* sessions to 1980's *Trust*. Five albums with one man at the helm seemed to be pushing studio stability and familiarity a bit too far, and although *Almost Blue* had Billy Sherrill's intercom-driven hand at the controls, Costello himself guessed that his ideas for the next record might prove somewhat exacting for one-take Nick 'Basher' Lowe.

In relation to his previous albums, Costello preferred to group them into batches of three, each 'set' changing gear as they went along. Refuting the idea that each subsequent set was better or bigger than the first, he nevertheless maintained that they were created by the same person, albeit with different attitudes. Neither did he look upon the first three records as a trilogy, but he realized (particularly following *Armed Forces* and the US tour) that it was time to get serious, to become more diligent and committed.

Besides, his attitude towards record making had altered. From a state of ineffectual ignorance at the time of *My Aim Is True* Costello confesses he didn't have a clue as to what was happening to him between that time and the state of god-like superiority by the time *Armed Forces* came out. He had surged through the spectrum of industry demands, quirks and idiotic tendencies like a man possessed. The defining point was, naturally enough, at the fag end of the *Armed Forces* US tour. He had turned into a caricature of himself by that point, and the music was in danger of folding in on itself also. Hence the disparity of music across *Get Happy!!*, *Trust* and *Almost Blue*. And hence the experiment with orchestra. To the casual observer, Costello looked as if he was a busy-bee dilettante, hopping from one project to the next in search of the ultimate buzz.

He came back from America psychologically (and occasionally physically) bruised and battered by drugs, drink, women, men, touring and an incessant need to drive himself onwards. He realized that he had, somewhere along the line, lost sight of why he had begun to write songs and perform in the first place. Thinking himself unassailable and protected by arrogance, he finally knew it was time to wind down. Simply, his songs became more introspective and vulnerable. The bile and bitterness and rage and torment was still there, but added to these was a sense of self-understanding and self-questioning. It was time to stop the madness.

Another less aesthetic factor reinforced the decision. The sales of *Get Happy!!* and *Trust* obviously hadn't matched those of *Armed Forces*. *Almost Blue* was a superb experiment that went wrong in marketing terms. It captured a new audience, but in America it fell foul of music-biz types and their ideas of niche markets and music categorization. As such, effectively it fell between two stools, putting a heavy dent in Costello's already falling popularity and calling his creative decision-making processes into doubt.

Another less well-publicized factor (at the time) was his involvement once again with Bebe Buell. Despite having gone back to his wife and child towards the end of 1979, Costello had began seeing Buell again in the early 1980s. 'I would meet him in hotels,' Buell told *Mojo*. 'We had pseudo names for each other; I was Jane or Candy, he was Henry.

He'd leave me his key at the front desk. And I would very discreetly come when he was at the show and be waiting for him when he'd return. This went on for months. And it culminated with me getting pregnant.'[1]

Frightened of having another child out of wedlock, and scared of losing the man she loved so deeply, Buell took the decision to have an abortion. 'I was a little bonkers at this point. I don't think that I understood the truth, or anything about it.'[2] Some time after, when Buell finally contacted Costello again, she could guess that he had been wondering what had happened. She informed him that she had had a miscarriage: 'I just lied through my teeth,' she confessed to *Mojo*. 'I wanted to say whatever I could to hurt him. And he put the phone down and never spoke to me again. Ever. To this day I still cry over that termination. I don't think Elvis knew what I was going through; I think he thought I was an unobtainable, non-committal, incapable of fidelity, frivolous sort of It Girl.'[2]

Originally titled *This Is A Revolution Of The Mind* (a direct lift from the James Brown song, 'King Heroin', and a proposed title that would blatantly publicize the health-conscious change of attitude) *Imperial Bedroom* was to add another element to this new attitude. It was the first Costello album to actually *sound* brilliant. It was also the first record of his to be recorded without 'road testing' the songs. Work on arranging and writing continued through rehearsals and into the sessions at AIR Recording Studios (where, just along the corridor from Costello's studio, George Martin was producing Paul McCartney's *Tug Of War*).

A number of the songs that Costello had written around the time of *Almost Blue* didn't make it on to the record. With the batch of songs he nevertheless knew he wanted to record, he and The Attractions travelled to the West Country where they rented a cottage in Devon to rehearse intensively for an uninterrupted week. Ending up with a double-album's worth of finished songs (the idea for another *Get Happy!!* bounty was quickly dismissed), they went back to AIR. Once they settled in, serious doubts began to emerge about the shape of certain songs, and some were restructured accordingly. Other songs were actually rewritten in the studio, something that Costello had never done before. He put this down to being fully in control of the recording environment, again something that had not occurred in the past.

The co-producer of *Imperial Bedroom* was Geoff Emerick, a colleague of George Martin, and engineer on a number of the Beatles' finest recorded moments (*Revolver* and *Sgt Pepper's Lonely Hearts Club Band*, to name but two). Along with some of Costello's best songwriting to date, Emerick's guiding hand transformed the record from what was probably originally a decent eight-track demo album into an aural tour de force. Studio time was (for Costello, anyway) an unprecedented and extravagant twelve weeks, a period long enough for Emerick to try out as many vocal and instrumental experiments and additions as he wished, without having to watch the clock.

In July 1982 the album, Costello's seventh, was released. It took longest of all to make, primarily because of his role as co-producer – he had to charge out of the control room to the studio to hear every take of a song. The fitness regime kicked in to every quarter of the record: everything about it was different. The sleeve painting by Barney Bubbles was inspired by Picasso's Three Musicians (a reference highlighted by the spelling of 'Pablo' in separate letters on the sleeve cover's snaking zippers). Costello's voice had never sounded better. And, most surprising of all, the lyrics were printed on the inside record sleeve. Like a Reuters dispatch with no commas or full stops. Naturally. The man who was recognized as being the most literate British songwriter since the days of Lennon/McCartney had finally decided to allow his fans full inspection of the words to one of his albums. No more would they begin to sing a line of a song only to give up because they couldn't make out precisely what Costello was singing. The fun and frustration of trying to decipher the words had been taken away by the man himself. But he made them difficult to read nonetheless. Drat and double drat.

'I've never been terribly comfortable with the thing of

having these little poems on the sleeve,' he told *Record Collector* apropos the decision. 'I think it makes too great a claim for the words. Later on, I got less worried, but at one point I was very uneasy, and I didn't think the words stood up to being read in that way. I intended them to be heard. So I thought I'd make them like a telegram where somebody forgot the punctuation. It makes for quite interesting reading. You can make up your own lines, starting in the middle of one song and into the next one.'[3]

The degree of confidence and power that was made apparent from the studio to the album sleeve could be heard all over *Imperial Bedroom*. He explained the processes behind some of the songs on a promotional double album called *A Conversation With Elvis Costello*: 'On "Beyond Belief", the first track, I noticed that the backing track had this great conviction whilst my initial melody was weak and needed drastically rearranging. The original lyric was garbled because it was at more than twice the speed. So I halved the lyrics and halved the speed of my vocal delivery which makes for a nicely disconcerting effect of calm vocals over this rattling back-up, instead of yet another frantic track which we've done too often before.

'Similarly, "Tears Before Bedtime" . . . It needed a more buoyant feel because the subject definitely isn't lightweight but tended to sound a bit too angst-ridden to begin with. People have had enough pain and misery anyway. Particularly on our records! . . . "Pidgin English" is a political song. I think it's pretty disgusting the way the English language is being taken to pieces particularly by certain newspapers. The way the *Star* and the *Sun* are trying to turn everyone into morons, people actually won't be able to talk in fifty years' time . . . There's nothing wrong with slang as shorthand . . . but when it becomes this degeneration of intelligence then it's dangerous because you end up being manipulated by people who've taken away your ability to say anything different. The whole reason for me writing a pop song about that issue is that it's become a popular disease.'[4]

Reviews of the album treated it with due respect. After the sincere sob stories of *Almost Blue*, it was good to get critical teeth into something meaty again. Once more, Costello was critics' favourite (the majority couldn't understand how someone as good as Costello wasn't hugely popular, anyway) and no longer the public's whipping boy. The majority couldn't understand why Costello had had to go all 'funny' on them. Country music? 'Shot With His Own Gun'? What were they all about then? Despite the key decision to contain his misery to himself ('people had enough of me whinging on', he told *NME*[5]) *Imperial Bedroom* remains a defining confessional album of the '80s. Through rehearsals, rewrites, rearrangements, Geoff Emerick's production and engineering expertise, and Costello's prodigiously accomplished abilities both as lyricist and melodicist, the record is sophisticated and sensual. Each arrangement adorning the songs dovetails seamlessly with the words. What are the songs about? Are they private or public? Can we believe what he sings?

The only way someone as private as Costello can say what he thinks through a song is to sift through what is real and what is not and layer the chosen lines with enough ambiguities and verbal resonances to confuse even the most erudite listener. The large amount of quotable lyrics on *Imperial Bedroom* may or may not amount to a man breaking down and confessing (or addressing) various issues close to his heart. The core achievement of the record is that, for once, the music also works on varying levels. Between the two of them, Emerick and Costello created a synthesis of words and music that had little to do with contemporary pop fashion.

While *Get Happy!!* and *Almost Blue* blatantly flirted with soul and country, respectively, *Imperial Bedroom* was the creative offspring of *Trust* – a diverse multi-layered collection of songs whose seductive sound oscillated from track to track. Ultimately, there was nothing strange about them, rather they were recognizably classic pop songs that made some people rave about them, and most others tune out. Costello reckoned he knew the reason why. 'Most people, I think, are confused regarding their identities, or how they feel, particularly about love. They're confused because they're not given a voice, they don't have many songs written for or about them. On the one hand, there's "I love you, the sky is blue", or total desolation, and in between there's this lack of anything. And it's never that clear cut. There's a dishonesty in so much pop written, possibly, with an honest intent . . . all that starry-eyed stuff. I believe I fulfil the role of writing songs that aren't starry-eyed all the time.'[6]

Emerick had full responsibility for the rococo'n'roll sound of the record, which chimed with Costello's marked reservations in relation to modern recording techniques. Ideally, what they wanted was to revert back to the sound on 1960s albums from the likes of The Walker Brothers and Dusty Springfield, where the musical backing is compressed and where vocals play a much more important part in the overall sound. With Emerick's background, he was able to create a larger and more expansive framework for his charges to work in. 'He was used to being thrown an incomprehensible garble of sounds and musical directions, and making some sense of it,' noted Costello in *Record Collector*. 'After working with The Beatles at the height of their psychedelic era, he was used to innovation, and to the direction being a bit berserk.'[7]

Despite a rash of great reviews, the album still didn't take Costello out of the commercial doldrums, failing to sell appreciably more than his other records. The troubles he had with his record company (the album was an F-Beat release, but a licensing deal with WEA enabled the major to call a lot of the shots; in America, his record label was Columbia, with whom he experienced similar difficulties) became more apparent with each record release. An incredulous Costello maintains that the record company could not single out any potential hit songs to market. He naturally considered the record had a number of possible hit singles.

'They just released the wrong tracks. The trouble all along has been that we make records and they sell them. And if you're making them, you're always looking for something new that excites you. But when I did what I thought was a really original record in *Imperial Bedroom*, the record company still thought of us in terms of *Armed Forces*. They hankered after that. So instead of releasing a bold piece of music like "Beyond Belief" as a single that would have marked this album out as a departure, or maybe "Almost Blue", a ballad that was very heartfelt, they released "You Little Fool" which is a good pop construction but was the track most reminiscent of what we'd done before. It was idiotic. It was so cowardly on their part. Then, when the excitement for the album had been defused by that mistake, they released 'Man Out Of Time', which again would have been a bold first single. Then when it flopped they said, "Well, we told you it wasn't a good record."'8

While he had more control over releases in Europe, it was still a problem. The pressure applied to videos as well. By this time, promotional videos were an established part of music-business currency. Although stylistically still in its infancy, the music video was becoming a convenient source of promotion, enabling bands who might be holed up somewhere, anywhere, to be seen on television worldwide.

While no one could claim that Costello and The Attractions were the visual equivalent of Duran Duran, Adam Ant or Human League (three early-'80s UK pop acts whose popularity was undoubtedly founded on their stylish videos) they nevertheless took to the video age with a combination of gritty determination and a sense of humour. The videos for 'Oliver's Army', 'I Can't Stand Up For Falling Down' and 'Hi Fidelity', for example, now look very amateurish, but at least it seems as if most of the people involved were having some sort of Chaplinesque fun.

It was becoming plain that Costello, in the age of Duran Duran, was swimming against the commercial tide. The facts had to be faced: having released over seven albums (not one of which was found wanting in song quality) in five years (not one of which was without headline-grabbing incident), Costello's star was waning. In strictly marketing terms, he didn't make fluffy pop records. Despite a certain, er, rugged charm, he certainly wasn't a pin-up. More often than not he looked like a miserable sod, straight out of a Tony Hancock half-hour – when he laughed there was often melancholy behind the mirth.

The paradox was that he wasn't prepared to give up making music just because a record company had failed to realize his potential and market his talents. He knew he wanted to continue writing, playing and performing for years to come, but realised that the then current trend for New Romantics, and synth-pop groups such as Depeche Mode, Human League, Soft Cell and OMD, wasn't exactly conducive to his own highly individualistic techniques. Those bands and indeed, most of the pop music of the day, had a high turnover and little quality control. Superficial noise and glamour was the new order of the day, and while Costello was aware that he was part of this scene to a small degree, he also knew that he couldn't successfully compete with fashionable trends he had little or no truck with. So who exactly were the faceless ones that bought his records?

'There are millions of people out there,' he told *The Face*. 'Even if your record gets to number one, even if you are Kajagoogoo, there's still something like 70 per cent of the population who have never heard of you . . . There is always an audience out there, even if it's quite small. I mean, we toured last year having watched at that point four, maybe five singles fail to make the Top Forty. And yet at a time when bands that had had hits were having to cancel, we were still doing 75 per cent-to-capacity audiences all over the country. If you sell 100,000 records, maybe they're the only 100,000 people in the country that like you, but that's still a lot of people. 20,000 is still a lot of people. It's a damn sight more than you reach playing your songs in your bedroom. You can get very spoilt by success, not least in that you think you have a God-given right to an audience. If I really felt that there was someone doing what I do better than me, then I'd be worried.'[9]

Such an attitude can only stem from a remarkable degree of self-confidence or arrogance, but there was something peculiarly unassuming about the way in which Costello said these things. Truth is, he was right and people knew it. In comparison to the current crop of feather-boa'd and made-up pop stars (Adam and the Ants? Puhlease! Duran Duran? Beg pardon!), Costello was your above-average avuncular Oxford professor.

He was supremely singular in his stance towards his own music, a throwback, perhaps, to his solitary four-track demo days in Whitton. He might not have had a God-given right to an audience of 200 or 2,000 or 20,000, but he knew damn well that he liked what he did. 'If everybody else hated it, I'd have to reassess it, but if I did genuinely believe in it then I'd have to go ahead with it. I have held out on things . . . ideas about the direction of a track, particularly on *Imperial Bedroom* where I was making all the production decisions. It's very hard when you're judging your own work. Some of the things that I held out for when everyone said I was wrong – six months later I found I *was* wrong! There's that song 'Kid About It', which I insisted on singing in an entirely unsuitable octave. I was trying to get away from having one vocal feel throughout, the sort of one-man-tortured-by-his-art thing, so I went completely the other way and used overlapping and conflicting styles to suggest there was more than one attitude going on inside the songs. Some of it worked perfectly well, a rather more theatrical way of singing, if you like, because I wanted to get away from that sort of soul singing and do something cooler, in the old-fashioned sense.'[10]

To promote the album in America, Costello and the Attractions began a two-month coast-to-coast tour, also darting into the Midwest and South, playing numbers from the new record as well as some unreleased songs, old favourites and a couple of *Almost Blue*'s country standards. Overtures from *Rolling Stone* for an interview were enthusiastic enough for him to talk to the magazine's leading rock writer, Greil Marcus. When the cover-story interview was published, pictured on the magazine's front was a sober-looking Costello: dark jacket, bright shirt, dickie bow peering over the banner-size words 'ELVIS COSTELLO REPENTS'.

The interview was specially arranged as part promotion for

Imperial Bedroom and the US tour and part explanatory apologia for the Ohio occurrence on the *Armed Forces* tour. Costello knew full well that certain matters relating to the nasty event had to be cleared up once and for all. Marcus, perhaps America's leading socio-musicologist writer, was intelligent and sympathetic enough to realize that Costello wanted to get things off his chest. America still hadn't come to grips with Costello's racist slur, anyway. His record company knew that, too, becoming increasingly wary of each subsequent 'product' that they had to service and market.

In the UK, Irish and European territories, such an attitude didn't exist. The man might be a prickly bear occasionally but he wasn't a fascist. Although Americans had seen Costello touring with subsequent albums, a nicer chap altogether despite the downsizing of his career – or, probably, because of it – they still couldn't take to him the way they took to, say, Journey or Boston. He just wasn't *obvious* enough for them. Probably the majority of record consumers in the US had never heard of him, anyway, or if they had, his name registered low on the recognition scale. Which was, presumably, another reason to go for *Rolling Stone* instead of any other US publication. While the interview went some way to explaining away the damage, it also highlighted the fact that he had well and truly tired of his self-defining 'revenge and guilt' remarks made over four years previously.

'It's only fun for so long,' he confessed to *NME*. 'Also you become a bit pathetic after a while if you're still ranting on. You can only hit people with rage when they're not expecting it, otherwise they just switch off. You've no divine right to their attention. To hold their attention, you've got to be a bit more cunning. You've even got to get them to like you. Maybe later you decide to rub 'em up the wrong way again. I'm not saying that would never happen. If I wanted to make a very aggressive record I wouldn't feel inhibited about it as long as I felt it. It was then that the attitude started to dictate to the music and not the other way round; that's when I got disturbed. When I found what I was saying was making better copy than what I was singing I thought, "Well, hang on, I gotta be a bit more . . . not deceitful, but careful and cunning about it." '[11]

Costello's game plan at this point was to put across to people that their negative image of him demanded a change in their own attitudes. It clearly couldn't happen overnight, however. In the US, he reckoned, he would have to wait about five years for people to catch up on his career movements. In the UK, he was up against a different wall. A visit to Manchester's Hacienda club – the Northern Mecca of modern dance – brought him face to face with people who looked like they were unused extras from David Bowie's video for 'Ashes To Ashes'. Not his audience, then – but who was? According to Costello, he had an estimated 50,000 diehard fans in the UK. A small number by harsh commercial standards, maybe, but as he had alrady observed, more than he could play to in his bedroom.

As for his game plan, he was seriously thinking of using a different name for future record releases. He realized the inherent dangers of such a move, but the other options of losing command of himself and of his original aspirations, and the way in which the public persona could easily cross over into his private life, were unthinkable. A song on *Imperial Bedroom*, ' . . . And In Every Home', pointed to the way in which he felt powerless and redundant to stop the downward slide into commercial cultdom.

He explained to *NME*: 'The fact that we make the records and people buy them and appreciate them, and the work that's gone into them, but at the same time, the loss of greater interest in them . . . It's something I'd like to arrest . . . I've thought of hanging up the name or doing something drastic like recording under a pseudonym, 'cos I'm actually beginning to think that the name is a jinx. I'm actually starting to get superstitious about it because I think, "Well, what more is there that I can do?" I don't want to put any more in because I don't want to be one of those people like Pete Hamill who's tearing his own head off in private.'[12]

Part of the perceived problem was lack of radio play. Costello looked beyond that towards the offices of WEA, judging the predicament to be politically-based, and one that was launched between the end of Radar and the beginning of F-Beat. Inevitably, as always, he found it an onerous task to equate business with the supposedly simple need to make records. At one end of the scale, here was an artist who clearly made serious records that made serious statements about love, human and social relationships, politics and the whole damn lot. At the other end was a bunch of bands with silly haircuts and silly clothes. Some made great pop music, and others didn't, but the fact remained that the two opposing factions were in competition with each other. It got to the point where, once more, Costello didn't even know if he wanted to slug it out with them.

NME again: 'At the moment I'm weighing up what the next record should be, or whether there should be a pause of some kind . . . On the one hand, I'm just a songwriter who sings and does my best and puts my heart into it. On the other hand I understand the business better than a lot of people, I know where I stand in it. That side of me says hang on, what is the point of bashing your head against a brick wall, to throw it away, because you're not gonna put all this work in and people are not going to accept it because of who you are? They've decided they don't like you so you might as well not bother to make records and be off like John the Baptist. It's a question of presenting it, the production, the kind of song even.'[13]

Irrespective of who or what was directing the political strategy, the loser was still Costello. For someone who breezily admitted that he could write dumb lyrics as good as the next dumb lyric writer, there was no real evidence to support that. He might have written intelligent words and phrased them in an obtuse way, but he surely realized that was a different thing altogether.

Although it took some time for the wonderful people at national and international radio programming level to realize that subversive pop music is never subversive if you're informed that it is, radio in general hasn't been good or kind or agreeable to Costello. For a while on its release in 1978, the radio bods loved 'Radio Radio'. They played it to death on BBC Radio One until they listened to the words in the verses. Then it dropped from playlists and the single hit shitsville. Not that the pragmatic Costello minded. He didn't hold any grudge against the programmers for their cowardice and underachievements. Not in the UK, anyway. American radio by comparison, stated Costello, was virtually sinister in the play-listing of his records, something that he reckoned was not only a bitter leftover from colonialism but also from a harsh form of cultural superiority.

'America's fairly intimidated by England culturally. The one thing England's got and they haven't is history and a lot of old culture, and I think that gives clout to what comes afterwards. I think they try to be very dismissive about it, but every so often they give in to one particular thing, whether it's The Beatles or more recently, Human League. It doesn't have to be a huge revolution for them, it just proves that their chauvinism isn't watertight. I think they get bored with what they've got over there. What's sad is that they pay so little attention to the good stuff under their noses. They've got great singers and writers in every field . . . Then they have the nerve to champion these awful groups, that's where I start to get annoyed. The British take it to extremes and champion the most obscure people who aren't worth championing, but the Americans are so disrespectful about the great things they've got.'[14]

By early 1983, Costello and the Attractions had reached a decision – they had to start having hit singles again. From the Spring of 1980 to the Summer of 1983, they had released a dozen singles. Of these, only two had broken through to the Top Ten (1980's 'I Can't Stand Up For Falling Down', No. 4, and 1981's 'A Good Year For The Roses', No. 6). Significantly, both songs were cover versions.

With his next album now in progress Costello wanted to revert back to the sound he had successfully avoided on *Imperial Bedroom*. To a degree, he had already started this process with 'Shipbuilding', a song written by Costello and Clive Langer. The latter was late of Clive Langer and the

Boxes, producer of some of the best early-1980s pop music, and the soon-to-be co-producer, with partner Alan Winstanley, of Costello's next pop opus, *Punch the Clock*. Initially sung by Robert Wyatt, 'Shipbuilding' surely contains the most plaintive and angelic British voice ever to be captured on magnetic tape in the 1980s. Costello wrote the song – in essence, an extremely effective, admonishing war ballad in response to the Falklands 'conflict', and about how a father's eventual re-employment in the UK shipyards of Swan Hunter, Cammell Laird and Harland & Wolff led in turn to the death of his young son who had signed up to fight against the Argentinians. The original idea was akin to a Brill building song concept, except somewhat more sombre and not as fulsomely poppy. Clive Langer had written the tune with Wyatt specifically in mind. The producer had contacted Rough Trade but deliberately not mentioned Costello's part in its creation for fear of the project not going ahead.

Another possible reason for Costello wanting to utilize Langer and Winstanley was that they were currently the hottest production team in the UK. Costello was only too aware that his songwriting cachet (although still looked upon with huge favour by many music critics and his thousands of fans worldwide) was waning in terms of hit singles. While six of his seven albums had been Top Ten hits, Costello knew that recurrent hit singles, the regularity of which allowed prolonged contact with a mainstream audience, provided the basis for popular longevity. If that contact was cut off, the freedom to have a broad artistic licence was consequently taken away. He decided to see what would happen using a current name producer.

'In the past, we'd never conformed to any great production design,' he explained in *Record Collector*. 'Nick Lowe's idea had always been to capture what we did, Billy Sherrill's was to put up with what we did, and Geoff Emerick's was to let us go along until we exhausted the possibilities and permutations, and then try and make sense of it. This was the first time we'd taken a formal approach, and to some extent it really worked.'[15] In some ways it did, but not before Costello did what he had been threatening to do for some time. The change of name beckoned, and it was, er, The Imposter. Like a languorous sexual build-up that leads to a miserable anticlimax, and with a name taken from a song of the same name on *Get Happy!!* the connotations are a tad too obvious. Costello rush-released a new single called 'Pills And Soap' on his own label, Imp, through Demon, then a one-off release subsidiary of F-Beat.

It was launched in a limited edition of 15,000 copies at the end of May. Costello wanted the record out fast to circumvent record-company lawyers who might prevent its release. FBeat's licensing deal with WEA Records had expired, and negotiations were underway for a marketing and distribution deal with RCA. While the legalities were being thrashed out, the single – a potent posie of politics and bile, with a metronomic melody inspired by Grandmaster Flash's 'The Message' to boot – became his biggest hit single in two years, reaching No. 15. Of course, this may have been helped by a marketing scam directed by Costello towards not only the retailers but also BBC Radio One – he threatened to delete the single within a week, and this undoubtedly assisted its passage up the charts. It showed Costello was shrewd enough to play the suits at their own game and win. The single *was* actually deleted on the eve of the general election.

There was one snag, however, something that Costello would probably never have foreseen. 'Pills And Soap', despite being a great protest song, and in spirit a broadside across the bows of 1983's political conservatism, was Elvis Costello's last UK Top Twenty singles entry.

Shortly after, *Punch the Clock* was released, a snappy piece of work that lacked the sultry, sleazy sophistication of *Imperial Bedroom* but brimmed with as much bright and bouncy pop music as *Armed Forces*. A step forward for Costello's great plan of survival in pop music, it nevertheless contained his own version of 'Shipbuilding', and 'Pills And Soap', two songs that could not by any stretch of the imagination constitute typical chart fodder. That said, he succeeded yet again to display his knowledge, use and conceits of the English language, as well as an envious show of pop history from the obvious (The Beatles) to the arcane (Lewis Furey). Ultimately, it was another stylistic triumph from a pop star who wasn't all that popular. There was a breezy horn section that deliberately echoed Dexy's Midnight Runners, vocal responses and backing from the two-woman team of Carol Wheeler and Claudia Fontaine (Afrodiziak), and a plethora of pop hooks and snags.

There was a puzzle to ponder, however. Of the songs on the record that entered the charts, 'Shipbuilding' by Robert Wyatt, 'Pills And Soap', 'Everyday I Write The Book' and 'Let Them All Talk' – it was the improbably-named Imposter's song of 'Pills And Soap' that charted the highest. The previously established critical notion that people steered clear of Costello because of his pensive and convoluted song compositions was beginning to look decidedly out of date. For the moment, he was back where he belonged. Where would he go to from here?

Perhaps Tony Bennett knew. One of America's greatest living crooners had, after all, invited England's greatest living pop solo songwriter to New York. The venue was Le Parrot night club, and the occasion was the filming of a US nostalgia show called *Swing It Again*. With backing by the Count Basie Big Band, Costello and Bennett sang 'It Don't Mean A Thing If It Ain't Got That Swing' before an invited black-tie audience of 1,000 Big Apple hipsters. Working with Tony Bennett was a dream come true. Childhood memories of the first time he saw him came flooding back. It was going to be a night to remember.

Alas, the dream of singing with one of his mother's crooner heroes turned into a nightmare of the kind where you're walking down the street gaily greeting people only to discover you have no clothes on. Costello lost his voice the night before, but couldn't pull out. The results are on tape somewhere in NBC's television vault and they're very embarrassing. 'Who is that cat?' enquired Basie's trombone player

of the bespectacled English singer. The name is Costello.
Elvis Costello . . .

'Never heard of him! Can't sing neither.'[16]

Costello fully expected never to hear from Bennett again,
but did when he was contacted by Bennett's manager son for
a guest spot on his father's MTV *Unplugged* album: 'I think
he knew my heart was in the right place,' said Costello on
RTE Radio. 'So I got a second go at it. I was nervous, and
Bennett leaned over and said, I learned from Frank Sinatra
that being nervous makes the performance better. I was okay
after that.'[17]

CHAPTER 6

*'Most people in groups are dullards . . . The best thing they
can do is make records. There are not that many hidden
meanings in my songs that I have to sit down and do an
interview to explain them, 'cos I'd feel the songs have
failed if they don't speak for themselves. There may be
oblique things in there that I put in and I still wouldn't
choose to explain them; they're set in there to work on the
imagination of the listener, or work on my imagination
when I sing 'em again.'*
Interview with Neil Spencer, NME, October 1982

*'I was tired of the way people saw Elvis Costello: they saw
this funny pair of glasses and a load of mannerisms, and
they had all these preconceived ideas of what I was and
who I was. I started to think of it as a bit of a curse. I
started to wonder if there were people who were not listening to my records simply because they associated me with
1978 or 1979. Elvis Costello was becoming a brand name,
kind of like Durex.'*
Interview with David Fricke, Rolling Stone, April 1986

In October 1983, Costello began a British tour with his most
ambitious on-the-road entourage yet: The Attractions, the
TKO Horns and Afrodiziak. The great entertainer was taking
a show with colour, musical-trappings, rock'n'roll and back-
up singers around the standing-only venues of England,
including three in London (the Hammersmith Palais, the
Tottenham Mayfair Ballroom and, quirkily, Streatham's Cat

101

Whiskers). The tour had been planned to go ahead in June, but had to be put back due to contractual problems.

Costello, therefore, was raring to go. He was relatively content with the poppy *Punch the Clock* as an album that utilized solid-state technology and sounded up to date, as opposed to *Imperial Bedroom*, which languished in the warm afterglow of valve power. He had put down the new record's success to the discipline of the production team, people who took ideas and placed them in logical order. Now realising, in retrospect, that *Imperial Bedroom* was overdeveloped (his ideas clearly ran riot, and Geoff Emerick was not the man to rein in his excesses), he felt that *Punch the Clock* was no less ambitious. He felt it was less diverse, a pop record with successful hints of soul, but without the frayed nerve endings of *Get Happy!!* He had wanted to make a record that was brighter and more forceful than the previous one, and achieved this. He was vindicated in his use of Langer and Winstanley, who had the patience to apply down-the-line pop principles to the record, something which previous producers lacked. 'Nick Lowe is like Stax,' was Costello's explanation in *NME*, 'whereas they [Clive and Alan] are more like Motown or Van McCoy.'[1]

Once more, though, he soon found fault with the record. He reckoned that some songs on *Punch the Clock* were weak, singling out 'King Of Thieves' as being one whose heart was in the wrong place, and 'Love Went Mad' as one that he performed well, but which didn't particularly mean anything. It was an old problem rearing its head again, a disenchantment with content and style, with fashion bibles and stock-in-trade clichés. 'If something lacks substance, lacks anything to move you, then it's only of any use to the people who like that flavour of candy-floss, but I don't have a hatred of it. I've been somewhat amused that I'm a good guy now, which seems to be the current popular opinion. Last year I was supposed to be in search of an audience, which again was a blanket opinion subscribed to by both people who don't think and people who think too much.'[2]

Punch the Clock was outward looking, a deliberate

connection between the songwriter and his audience. The audience responded in kind, and informed Costello that an interest was indeed there, but he was concerned about the lack of direct communication between himself and his fans. He was by no means a man of the people, but he had no wish to place himself on a pedestal from which his words of wisdom would be bestowed on his followers. To a degree, however, he was treated with suspicion by people who seemed to want exactly that.

Conversely, the popular socio-political causes espoused by the likes of The Jam, UB40 and The Specials were being greeted with enthusiasm. What soured the relationship was the audience wanting more of the same. Artists such as Paul Weller, Ali Campbell and Jerry Dammers, who had beliefs beyond the political arena, were therefore drained of audience empathy. Like a scene out of *Monty Python's Life Of Brian*, pop fans *en masse* declared themselves to be individuals. And if a pop star had a bit of sound advice for them, then all the better. Does any pop star *really* want to be a spokesperson for their generation?

'What I find a little sad,' noted Costello in *NME*, 'is if somebody is going to take that position, it's important that they do it with some intelligence than just in a rather empty way . . . What you really want is not songs that tell you what to think but songs that teach you to think for yourself. It's not a mantle I would want to pick up, and clearly no one else wants to either.'[3]

Despite not wanting to place himself in such an unenviable position, by virtue of the fact that he was writing such politically-charged material as 'Shipbuilding' and 'Pills And Soap' and getting hits out of them into the bargain, he was inevitably if unwittingly painting himself into a corner. Just as he was gaining ground in the commercial mainstream, he was writing political songs that couldn't have been further away from the Conservative manifesto. On record, he was scabrous about current political processes, while on stage he would appropriate The Beat's 'Stand Down Margaret' and then knowingly lead straight into 'Beyond Belief'. With heavy irony, he would dedicate 'The World And His Wife' to the adulterer Cecil Parkinson.

Costello had things to say, and while he refused to serve up his lyrics as pointers towards a better and more realistic world, he was clever enough to know that if he alienated himself from the mainstream audience, fewer and fewer people would get the chance to listen to his songs. 'Everyday I Write The Book' and 'Pills And Soap' on the same record, sung at the same gigs? Now *that*'s subversive.

By this time, Costello was gearing up for two events that would take place in 1984: the release of his ninth album, *Goodbye Cruel World*, and the start of divorce proceedings with his wife, Mary. There were other problems, too. How does one concentrate on crafting a batch of songs when your personal life is screwing up before your eyes, and how do you maintain humour and sanity when threatened with bankruptcy? Clive Langer and Alan Winstanley were once more asked to produce the record, though what Costello probably needed was a therapist, not a record commitment. Besides, his recurrent crisis regarding his attitude to pop music had arisen again. While 'Pills And Soap' had sneaked into the Top Twenty, Costello's final single of 1983, 'Let Them All Talk', had barely managed to scrape into the Top Fifty. Pressure was being brought to bear on him by some people in the record industry to conform to the style dictates of his chart peers, an idea that he considered absurd.

'They're people who want to see everybody in those terms,' he told *NME*, 'because they run scared whenever this happens in pop music. And it does happen periodically, that you get a load of people pretending to be homosexuals in shorts. There's nothing worse than that fake effete pop. Some of these groups write good songs, but when the record company people start trying to get me to do that . . .'[4]

A commercial follow-up to *Punch the Clock* seemed unlikely, although with the magic fingers of Langer/Winstanley at the controls nothing could be discounted. If Costello had been on form, it's possible that brighter, more appealing songs could have been salvaged from the wreckage, but it was not to be. He recorded the album over a two-week period, and it was a tense affair. A single, 'Peace In Our Time' a companion piece to 'Pills And Soap' and also credited to 'The Imposter', (on The Imposter label) was slotted in for release in April. Disappointinly it only reached a poor No. 48, despite the jaunty melody and protesting lyrics. This did not augur well for the imminent release of the album.

Matters were now getting somewhat confused. Most people might not have known who exactly The Imposter was until they heard the voice, which was quite identifiable anyway, yet the single came from an Elvis Costello and The Attractions' record. It was a marketing exercise that appeared both fruitless and directionless. It's a moot point, but it's quite likely Costello seriously didn't know what to do anymore. He'd played most, if not all of his cards and none had come up trumps. He was too recognizable to alter the public's perception of him. The subterfuge was, to all intents and purposes, quite pointless. Costello wasn't David Bowie, a person who had his finger on someone else's pulse and who was quick enough to transfer exactly what they doing into his own body rhythms. Bowie was great at adapting his music and mood to suit the fashion of the day. Costello found it extremely difficult to do so. His heart just didn't seem to be in it. Besides, wasn't 'Elvis Costello' itself a pseudonym?

'The name changing and all that stuff . . . such psychological meanings have been read into it,' he commented in *Record Collector*. 'On the one hand, it's obviously a blessing to have such a powerful image from your first few records, but in another way it's limiting, as people only see you in those terms. And when your own record company defines you in those terms then it becomes difficult, because they're not even helping to promote the new image. The country record was one attempt to escape, *Imperial Bedroom* was another and not just attempts either, I was actually doing it. It just goes to show how powerful the original image was. Until you come up with a suitably contrasting one, you won't really get it over to people.'5

Not that it mattered. When *Goodbye Cruel World* (another perfect title) was released in June, it was drubbed and dragged over the coals. Within eight years, Costello had released eight albums and a cartload of singles with B-sides that contained some of his best writing. He had written and showcased in the public arena more than 100 songs, many of which tested the formal structure of modern pop music. He had reshaped the three-minute pop song and had shown up most of his chart contemporaries as time wasters. The bubble had to burst sometime, and with *Goodbye Cruel World* it popped very loudly. The weakest album of his career was coloured by external and internal factors, primarily the finality of a relationship in songs such as 'Home Truth' and 'Sour Milk Cow Blues'. There isn't a song that isn't undermined by a sense of unhappiness, and whereas on other records there was always a burst of instrumental encouragement or lyrical deftness to lower the pain threshold, too many of the songs go over old ground in *every* respect. Most of the songs were written on an enforced 9–5 basis, and it shows.

The truth is, he was experiencing abject misery during the writing and recording of it. He knew he'd screwed up most of the record, but there was little he could do to rectify the situation. He couldn't even shelve it. 'We were locked into releasing it or else I would have gone bankrupt at the exact moment when I couldn't have gone bankrupt because I was getting divorced. I couldn't scrap the record, so I let it come out, warts and all. When I hear it now, there are some passionate performances in there, but they're muted by the arrangements. It was no fault of Clive and Alan. I feel apologetic to anyone whose favourite record it is, but I can't lie and say it's a good record – particularly the pop songs that were put on there with an even more calculating ear for the nuances of the charts.'[6]

'That was a really fucked up record,' he succinctly told journalist Nick Kent. 'That's the worst one, really, because I had all the arrangements arse-backwards, picked the wrong producers, then asked them to do an impossible job . . . My marriage was breaking up. It all sounds like a fuckin' sob story now but it probably was the worst period of my life.'[7] A few years later one of the songs on the record, 'The Comedians', was rewritten especially for Roy Orbison's 1989 *Mystery Girl* album. By the time the rewrite came about Costello had forgotten what the lyrics actually meant. This occasionally happened to him, something that Costello put down to being a songwriter who had extra-marital flings.

'To be blunt about it, the trouble with being an adulterer and a songwriter is that you always write songs in code . . . When I started I swore to myself that I'd always try to avoid writing songs about hotel rooms. But then inevitably many of my most lurid experiences in the past have taken place in hotel rooms, so that's just part of the job . . . I'm not glorying in that. And I'm still not at all happy about all the pain it caused my ex-wife . . . But it's a fact and I'm not going to try and hide from it. It's just life. You get over it. That's why most of my early songs are more obscure . . .'[8]

In order to get away from the mayhem that followed the recording of *Goodbye Cruel World* and the interim period of fretting about how it was going to be received by the public, Costello effectively jumped ship and went over to America to commence a solo tour. It was the first time he had performed without The Attractions since the sessions for *My Aim Is True*, and the first time he had performed solo since he packed in the day job. Costello had the time of his life, enjoying the artistic freedom to pick and choose any song to sing on any night without fear of upsetting anyone. He sang lots of covers he'd never attempted before, selecting the best and dropping songs he had no wish to sing again.

The support act was American singer/songwriter T-Bone Burnette, a kindred spirit whom Costello admired as a person and a writer. Together they formed a loosely-formatted duo called The Coward Brothers (Howard and Henry). By combining off-the-cuff glibness with no-nonsense country classics and dishevelled cover versions, The Coward Brothers prevented the worst possible scenario for solo singer/songwriters on tour – a pathetic descent into maudlin bedsit sensitivity. It was also an excuse to make light of the various harrowing situations waiting back home, the confronting of which Costello couldn't postpone forever.

'We did the whole act as if we were on a reunion tour,' revealed Costello in *Rolling Stone*, 'and we talked as if we were doing all our old hits. But people didn't know what to make of it, particularly if I said anything funny. They'd be nervous of laughing in case I would come down and strangle them. People get this weird notion of what I'm about. They stop seeing me as a human being. I think they were almost a little upset that we were being so flippant. I sensed a couple of people in the audience that didn't like me making jokes, as if I'm supposed to be bitter. Isn't that ridiculous?'[9]

In the meantime, come August the third single from *Goodbye Cruel World* was released. 'The Only Flame In Town' represented the nadir of Costello's chart career, stalling at No. 71 in the UK. Back from his round of college-circuit clubs in the US and Europe, he dived back into touring with The Attractions, offering a mixture of musical ferociousness and stand-alone solo material. The gigs were received in a half-hearted way, but the general consensus was that if they had been performed by anyone else, they would be regarded as a triumph. The only problem with a Costello concert is that he sets such high standards, and anything below these may be looked upon as a failure. A new song performed at most of the gigs (later to find its way on to *Blood & Chocolate* via the *King Of America* sessions) was 'I Hope You're Happy Now'. Not everyone got the message.

Towards the end of the year, Costello also began producing *Rum, Sodomy and the Lash*, the second album by The Pogues. The band were then a major force, their combination of punk-flavoured Irish trad and the songs of Shane MacGowan displaying a brutal eloquence that did not find favour with traditional-music purists. Costello's attitude was that the band were a caustic antidote to the fossilization of folk by these purists. The irony about him producing The Pogues was his long-time distaste for traditional music, an attitude he had harboured since his days of suffering from the blinkered stares of woolly-headed folk 'fans' in Liverpool and London folk clubs.

'Any idiot can get up at the end of the night and sing "The Wild Rover", and go down a storm,' he asserted in *NME*. I used to hate the fucking "Wild Rover". I got my own back on it, I got a version on the Pogues B-side; talk about a demolition job! And Ewan McColl fell asleep in the front row the first time I ever played in public. I imagine he's not the kind of guy who would be appreciative of The Pogues' rendition of "Dirty Old Town", from the way he carries himself. But I'm sure he'd like the money . . .'[10]

Along with the ribald revelry of it all, Costello also realized a connection at the heart of what The Pogues were trying to do with his own work. The Irish 'thing' was there, too, but in an understated way. And while producing the record, Costello began a relationship with Pogues' bass player, Cait O'Riordan. Costello also toured solo, playing dates around the UK and Ireland with T-Bone Burnette as guest. Another first: unless someone had seen him play in the small folk clubs of Liverpool and London, this would have been the first time his British fans would have witnessed him in a real solo capacity. Once more people were looking for clues: was this a nostalgic journey back to his folk-club roots, a reclamation of the same, or a pointer to future career plans? At the end of it, no one was really quite sure. There were no real answers. A few surprises popped out amidst his acoustic trawl through his back catalogue, notably a wonderfully bleak rendition of 'A Smiling Shore' from June Tabor's *Abyssinians* album, and a few songs from *Goodbye Cruel World* that showed up the LP versions for the poor renditions they were. Apart from that, it was another night of Elvis Costello songs, far and away the best in British pop but miles from the glory days of feral sweat, spittle-flecked words and a barely-hidden contemptuous glance. Time to take a holiday.

From early 1985, it was clear that Costello wasn't going to fling himself headlong into recording another album. The solo dates with T-Bone Burnette in America, Europe, and then Japan and Australia had serviced his internal engine. So he bummed around, finishing production work on The Pogues' album, courting Cait, playing live with the band (at one point on a particularly ramshackle tour of Scandinavia he even played drums for them) and supporting them at various gigs, including a St Patrick's Night soiree at London's Clarendon Hotel. Dressed in a shamrock-adorned green rugby shirt, he sang a brief set comprising a George Jones number, 'A Man Can Be A Drunk (But A Drunk Can't Be A Man)', and a new song called 'The Big Light'.

As well as the production work with The Pogues, he had also begun to dabble in the business side of the music industry with his own label, Imp. Already, several singles had been issued through the label: Irish punk rocker turned Brecht/Weill fan Philip Chevron's version of Brendan Behan's 'The Captains And The Kings', and The Men They Couldn't Hang's 'Green Fields Of France'. Imp served as a release valve for music that would probably never have been touched by the majors. In Costello's case, the issuing of 'Pills And Soap' and 'Peace In Our Time' indicated his dissatisfaction with F-Beat's then present label-in-arms, RCA.

'I didn't think the record ['Peace In Our Time'] was really commercial,' he claimed in *NME*. 'It was a personal thing to release it, and it would stand or fall on whether people felt any sympathy with it. I didn't want them [RCA] hyping it or doing peace-sign picture discs . . . It just devalues the song. The song is sincere, whether people like it not.'[11] The fundamental basis behind Imp was just putting a record out if it was felt (by Costello and by his unofficial A&R man Chevron) that it was good enough. Sales didn't matter. Imp had no staff or premises and no regular overheads. It had nothing except a tough quality-assurance test for prospective candidates to pass.

'Quality control is the closest we get to a policy,' stated Philip Chevron in *NME*. 'We put out records that other people wouldn't touch with a barge pole and in so doing we're tapping a need in a certain constituency of the record-buying public that other people wouldn't understand in a million years.'[12] Unusually, Imp was not a rock star's hobby, but something of practical, utilitarian service to be used whenever it was needed. The first album to be released on the label was Agnes Bernelle's *Father's Lying Dead on the Ironing Board*. A Dublin-based Berliner singing adapted German absurdist songs on a album produced by a London-based Dubliner and ex-punk rocker on a label owned by a Liverpudlian Ulsterman who once wrote a song called 'Night Rally'? Go figure. If you consider that Costello's voice and lyrics can blend jocular detachment, eye-brimming intimacy and lacerating satire, then you'll appreciate the pre-war Berlin connection even further.

Of course, there was a method behind Costello's extracurricular activities. His prolific diversifications in the areas of production, thoughtful songwriting and even relaxing were something he had wanted to do properly but rarely had the time. He'd been busy for over seven years without any longer than four weeks' holiday. The past two years he had had less than a week's break. A good time to stop, then, and take stock. 'I was getting bored. Not even bored, really. Getting a sort of maniacal nervous energy. I was working on complete nervous energy for the last couple of months in 1984. I was still enjoying it but I don't know how much the rest of the band were. I was playing longer and longer shows, it was a sort of hysterical energy you get when you're tired. I like being hysterical sometimes.'[13]

In early July, the only new Costello record release of the year, discounting the single 'Green Shirt' put out on the back of a TV-advertised *Best Of* collection, was released under the umbrella title of The Coward Brothers. 'The People's Limousine', a brisk skiffabilly song as if performed by Buddy Holly accompanying The Louvin Brothers, didn't bother the compilers of the *Guinness Book of British Hit Singles*, but was instead a carefree trundle along an Americana path. Based on their tour of Italy, the song surreally outlined their travels there in a limousine provided by a concert promoter who professed to be a Communist. The record cemented a mutually-realized partnership that would bear even more fruit on the album Costello was currently writing and working on, with T-Bone Burnette taking over co-production duties alongside him.

Shortly after the single's release, Costello played a brief solo spot at Live Aid. Introducing it as a folk song from up North, he sang The Beatles' 'All You Need Is Love'. For many he crystallized the event in the space of a few minutes – no guff about rocking'n'rolling the world, no communing with the audience, no flash showing off, but a simple, common link between performer and crowd. It was the perfect song to sing in such circumstances, something that Costello, with his Liverpool connections and pop-history expertise, had to be aware of. Sung live, it hurtled around the world's TV satellite stations for the second time. The first was on *Our World*, a pioneering live TV broadcast on 25 June 1967, when The Beatles unveiled the song over a 24-country satellite link.

At that time, the words of the idealistic song title were no more and no less than a hippy plea for peace. On 13 July 1985 Costello's rendition thoughtfully banged out on an acoustic guitar in front of millions of people worldwide sharply brought into focus the wayward materialism of the 1980s. Strange to say, it was the high point of a career that was bereft of such transcendental moments.

And then, as quickly as he appeared, he was gone. In a puff of smoke from his own gun, Costello was unmentioned in dispatches until early 1986. He might have disappeared from view, but he was still active: recording his forthcoming album in Los Angeles throughout the summer, falling in love with Cait O'Riordan, and writing songs not only for his own record but also for inclusion on the soundtrack of Julian Temple's *Absolute Beginners,* none of which were used because of budget restrictions. The media, in the meantime, commented upon the sorry decline of one of Britain's greatest living songwriters, speculating that his 'disappearance' was due to marital breakdown, alcoholism or a prolonged bout of writer's block.

By February of that year, the new album that he had been working on throughout 1985 was released. 'I have no position in pop now, I resigned my post. I'm not in competition with anyone. The best people are in a class of one, and I'm the best example of what I am,' was his defiant message to *Record Collector*.[14] With these words Costello returned. Or should that be Declan Patrick Aloysius MacManus returned? Almost ten years after he had relinquished his real name in search of a place in the pantheon of pop, the erstwhile Declan MacManus became the erstwhile Elvis Costello. The new album, *King Of America*, was credited to The Costello Show. The original songs on the record were credited mostly to Declan MacManus (though 'Indoor Fireworks' was still credited to someone called Elvis Costello). The co-production credit was shared between T-Bone Burnette and Declan Patrick Aloysius MacManus, the 'Aloysius' a fanciful and heretofore hidden adoption of Tony Hancock's middle name.

But there was more to the name change than just mere whimsy. Although his then passport still read 'Elvis Costello', he had by this time legally reverted to his real name. This was not just a chameleon-like transformation, but a forced re-evaluation and metamorphosis of his public image, private life and creativity. He might have had no self-imposed position in pop music anymore, but he knew precisely where he stood in relation to his work and life. With the exception of *My Aim Is True*, his new album was the first he had completed without assistance from The Attractions. Appearing on one track only, the band, who expected to work on half the record, were subsequently banished from the studio sessions.

'Originally, it was supposed to be half with them and half without,' he explained in *NME*, 'but it just didn't work out. Every session before they came seemed to be more productive than I had anticipated, and the record was at least three-quarters done by the time they arrived. Because of the tension of suddenly shifting from working with them to working with other people, I think it put them on edge and made them defensive and hostile, which made me hostile . . . The sessions were a disaster. We just managed one track ['Suit Of Lights'] and then they left . . . I finished the record with various combinations of people . . . The experience of doing *King Of America* without The Attractions showed me one of the problems on the records we'd done with Clive Langer and Alan Winstanley: the band was simply falling apart. We'd seen too much of one another, familiarity breeding contempt and all those clichés. Time had gone by so quickly . . .'[15]

The various people that Costello was working with were superlative US session men, chosen specifically for their natural low-key virtuosity rather than for showy effect. The alternating cast, which was connected via rotating studio bands, included New Orleans drummer Earl Palmer, LA drummer Jim Keltner, bassist Ray Brown, Mitchell Froom and T-Bone Wolk. Other musicians who played a part included members of Elvis Presley's TCB (Taking Care of Business) band, guitarist James Burton, drummer Ron Tutt and bassist Jerry Scheff. The irony of backing another singer called Elvis was not lost on anybody . . .

The band of wandering musicians were great, but they weren't The Attractions, which was precisely the point. With the exception of friend and co-producer T-Bone Burnette, Costello hadn't met any of these people before, so he knew he couldn't assume a deep-rooted emotional rapport with them. 'It was like a football team, really,' he told *Rolling Stone*. 'They stood around while I went through the songs, explaining everything, even my colloquialisms, to ensure that the meanings were clear. I was as honest with them as I could be . . .They came along with very few prejudices, very open-minded and hearted. They didn't say "who's this weirdo, then?" '[16]

Co-producer Burnette acted throughout the sessions as editorial assistant to Costello, who dissected each song's component parts, deleting any lyrics that appeared too glib and cutting back any gristle from the vocals. 'We had to remind ourselves how good the good songs were. That means taking up only as much space as you can handle. If you know what you're singing about and really, really mean it, you can appear as large as life.'[17]

King Of America was released to cheers of praise from

the critics and muted applause from the public. The reduc-
tionist sound and structure of it was the antithesis of *Imperial
Bedroom*, completely different to *Punch the Clock* and a
huge improvement on *Goodbye Cruel World*. It was grossly
unfashionable, too: mostly acoustic instrumentation and
pared down rock 'n' roll. Like *Almost Blue* it was a very
American record, this time unsentimental. Still as sincere, but
devoid of schmaltz, this wasn't a record desperately documenting more than a year on personal skid row (as a number
of gossip-mongers had expected it to be). Instead, the songs,
ranging through TexMex, country, folk and cajun, were
measured, calm explorations of love, hope and disillusionment, neatly parcelled in words freed from the usual meticu-
lously-crafted metaphors and perfect puns. The lexicon of
love was trimmed down, edited and given a good seeing to.
Costello's wordplay was in danger of short-circuiting itself, so
using fewer words to better effect made good sense.
Directness and clarity was the name of the game here.

T-Bone Burnette believed that the songwriter's best work
was done when he wasn't parading his talents for all to see.
Burnette's main criticism was that a portion of songs Costello
had written were too superficial and lacking in forethought,
banged out just for the sake of sticking to a formula. What
Costello learned from friendly critical advice such as this was
to leave songs well enough alone. Of course, not everyone
was happy with *King Of America*. Where was the acrimony,
the vitriol, the bitterness and spite? What happened to the
unhappy man we all knew and loved? Where, not to put too
fine a point on it, was the poison? The bile of previous
records had been replaced by an overall atmosphere of
compassion and by a spirit of generosity. From the chess-
board acrostic of 'King Elvis' on the front cover of *My Aim
Is True* to the title of the new record under his real name – it
was all beginning to make perfect sense.

For *King Of America*, Costello wanted a fair hearing and
specifically asked for one. Tired of being misinterpreted and
misunderstood, Costello campaigned hard on the album's
behalf. Was this weariness the reason why, in an apparent fit

115

of Van Morrisonesque pique, he included a particularly virulent version of The Animals' 'Don't Let Me Be Misunderstood'? If so, it was too obvious a plea for appreciation, and it was also the only song on the album that seemed, stylistically at least, out of place.

In America, he called off his war of attrition with the media and embraced print interviews and radio and television promotion with all the enthusiasm of a man who knows he's got something really good to talk about. The change of spirit took the press by surprise, but Costello had his particular reasons. He desperately wanted to get his points regarding *King Of America* across to as many people as possible. The non-music press coverage he received when he first arrived in America (from the likes of *Newsweek* and *Time*) was, he felt, detrimental to his cause. The major UK punk band, The Sex Pistols, had imploded before they could be got at, and so Costello was the next best thing.

'I was the tame punk that could actually speak and didn't spit,' was how he put it in *Record Collector*. 'But I was actually more obnoxious because of the very condescending way they treated me. As a result, it was defeating for both sides. They didn't get a good article, and I didn't get anything across that I wanted to say.'[18] A truce was declared, then, but clanging like a wake-up call amid the peace and quiet were accusations that *King Of America* was unorthodox to the point of being, well, plain peculiar. In terms of what was taking place musically in 1986, the people who said this were probably right, but they missed the point. Inevitably, and justifiably, Costello was amazed by the finger pointing.

'It seems crazy to me that a record with such solid sounds on it could be regarded as unconventional,' he griped. 'It's all voice and all songs. No fancy arrangements, no all-star guest performances. It's not the soundtrack of a movie, I'm not on heroin, and I don't have AIDS. So, I have no chance of having a hit . . . [*King Of America*] is a punk record made by old people. But it's all confrontation, isn't it? It's just that this is less obnoxious than the tactics we had before. We weren't always in the right, but we weren't always in the wrong, either

. . . If this record isn't a hit, then I'll make another one that is even more wilful. I won't make the same record again.'[19]

Nor the same mistakes. In an item in the *Irish Independent*, Costello's forthcoming marriage to Cait O'Riordan was announced. O'Riordan was reported to have said, 'I want to have seven kids and I'd like the majority of them to be girls.' The news article was dated 1 April. However, following the finalization of divorce proceedings from his wife, Mary (and after O'Riordan left The Pogues), Costello did get married in Dublin on 17 May, the day he played a brief acoustic set at Ireland's biggest charity concert, Self Aid. Mary Costello has since kept a low profile regarding her former marriage. She has refused to speak about it to the media, who long ago gave up on the tabloid newsworthiness of Elvis. She remains in London, and has presented a roots music show on local radio.

As *King Of America* was about to be released, sessions for the next record began. For some curious reason, The Attractions were back in the fold, a surprise bearing in mind their short sojourn in Hollywood. Another pleasant surprise was the return of Nick Lowe to the producer's chair, the first time since 1980. Was there something niggling Costello about the divisiveness created in Los Angeles? Or did he really need to make another musical change in order to adhere to his principles of never wanting to make the same record twice?

In the studio for the recording of *Blood & Chocolate* (a title to be found in the lyric of the album's first track, 'Uncomplicated') a far greater degree of compactness and directness was achieved than on their previous liaison. 'I thought that if I could do it in Hollywood with guys I'd never met before, surely I could do it with these people I've worked with for all this time,' he reasoned in *Record Collector*. 'We set up and played as loud as we did on stage. It didn't really sound like *This Year's Model*, but the component parts were just the four of us, and we did very few overdubs. We played as much a combo sound as possible.'[20] The friction, however, continued. As Nick Lowe remakred to David Wild in *Rolling*

117

Stone magazine: 'It wasn't a cosy album to do, but by that time I was used to the odd bass guitar curving in a graceful arc from one end of the studio to the other, towards the drummer's head.'[21]

Still playing with names (the in-joke was getting tiresome, and also led to suspicions of megalomania: King Elvis, Imperial Bedroom, King Of America) Costello was now Napoleon Dynamite. The name was apparently taken from the painting on the front cover by one 'Eamonn Singer', another pseudonym. The album was released in September, six months after *King Of America*. It wasn't so much a change of direction as a backward step to his more raw and intense albums. Those who were expecting a continuation of *King Of America*'s humane concerns weren't necessarily disappointed, but they were mystified. Preconceptions were duly shattered – always a part of Costello's plan – but there was something in the sound that seemed to be straining at the leash. If it was a return to the nitty-gritty belligerence that marked his early records as classics of their kind, and a resurgence of a mean streak that *King Of America* deliberately and successfully submerged, then it was also a record that was unlikely to win him any new converts. *Blood & Chocolate* didn't get any further than No. 16 in the UK and a risible No. 84 in America. The pre-album single, the six-minutes-plus 'Toyko Storm Warning', reached a feeble No. 73, his worst chart showing yet.

The album was issued on Costello's own Imp label, marking the end of his relationship with RCA in the UK. In America his relationship with Columbia was also on the decline. 'They kept saying, "If you could just give us *This Year's Model* or *Armed Forces* again, everything would be sorted out,"' he told *Record Collector*. 'So we gave them stuff that, without actually sitting down and working it out as a formula, was as close to that as we could get. With *Blood & Chocolate* we said, "This is us truthfully, we're thirty-two, a couple of us have got divorced, we're pissed off, and we've taken all the drugs and we've done all that stuff and we're still alive, and this is what we sound like. And you know what?

We're much better at it now." They didn't like it. They hated that record at Columbia. So then I went to them and said, "Listen, I don't want to fuck about like this anymore. You tell me what record you want, and I'll make it for you. You name the producer, I'll go in with him. I'll fight with anybody, I don't care, with Mutt Lange or any of these guys that were making the big hit records of the mid-'80s. I'll pit my musical personality, voice and strength of will against his, if that's what it takes." But they didn't want to do that.'[22]

In between writing, recording, singing, changing names at will and marrying, Costello took time out to appear in various TV and film projects, despite his frank opinion that the camera didn't like him. His dreadful appearance in *Americathon* notwithstanding, there seems to have been more than just a wilful perversity (and diversity) at play in the number of roles he was intent on playing. In 1984, he played an A&R man in the comedy series *The Bullshitters*. In 1985, he appeared in Alan Bleasdale's ITV drama *Scully*, for which he had written the theme song, 'Turning The Town Red'. Also making his acting debut in the series was Liverpool footballer Kenny Dalglish, as well as other members of the Liverpool squad. Costello played the uncle of the 16-year-old Scully, to no great effect.

The following year, Costello appeared in another Bleasdale-scripted vehicle, the excellent *No Surrender*. An acerbic allegory on the state of modern Britain, it tied together religion and politics as two parties of OAPs, one Protestant, the other Roman Catholic, mistakenly gather together in a seedy Liverpool club for New Year's Eve. Costello played the part of a bungling magician, had no funny lines (there were plenty to go around), and was embarrassing to watch.

The same year, he was roped in (did he need much cajoling . . .) to appearing in Alex Cox's *Straight To Hell*, a knotted spaghetti western that *Time Out* generously described as a 'yawning indulgence'. A poor substitute to what was originally planned as a filmed concert (by Cox) of Joe Strummer, the Pogues and Costello in Nicaragua, the film utilized the

119

free time the musicians had already pencilled in for the gig. With Nicaragua nixed, Almeria, Spain, took its place. Shane MacGowan and various members of the Pogues, Courtney Love, Joe Strummer and Elvis, along with Cait, lolled around in the heat waiting for their turn in front of the cameras. Costello was cast in the role of Hives the butler. Other actors (real ones) who had bit parts in the film included John Cusack, Dennis Hopper, Grace Jones, Sy Richardson and Ed Harris.

Costello followed up what, in all fairness, were extracurricular bits of fun with his most unusual tour yet: a traipse around the intimate theatres of America and Europe with an all-purpose revue show that mixed music hall, game shows and pop. Comprising musical bits and pieces from the lives of The Attractions, The Costello Show, The Confederates and The Coward Brothers, the concerts featured mystery guests (one night Tom Waits, another Tom Petty, the occasional Bangle or two), audience requests, solo interludes and the Spectacular Spinning Songbook, a veritable wheel of musical fortune that contained up to forty numbered song titles which audience members were invited to spin, choosing a song at random that would be played by Costello.

It was a cool way to end a most cathartic year. Costello changed name God knows how many times, divorced, remarried, and released two albums of distinct and disparate natures. In *King Of America* he showed that, like Bob Dylan, he could express sentiment and bitterness side by side. In *Blood & Chocolate* he dethroned himself, and said goodbye to his American record company.

It's all over now, baby blue? He wouldn't release another album for almost two-and-a-half years. But no, it wasn't over. Not by a long shot.

'Few would have guessed that Elvis Costello was to be spawned in the miasma of punk rock.' (Above)

'The only one to match him in terms of lyrical deftness and conscious iconoclasm has been Bob Dylan.'

The thrift shop era: how Declan Patrick MacManus turned into Elvis Costello.

'Enter The Attractions, a seasoned trio of musicians, culled from the ranks of dear departed pub rock and the more refined environs of the Royal College of Music.'

'You don't necessarily go and get a new set of clothes because you're listening to a particular set of music, but something about your frame of mind filters through to your dress.'
Costello in the *Telegraph Magazine*, 1994.

Anti clock-wise:
at The Stone Pony, 1977; 1982; Glastonbury, 1989; 1991; 1995.

With Jake Riviera (above) and Nick Lowe (below).

Costello with
The Attractions,
in Chicago, 1979
(right) and
(below) in 1994.

'Being in love doesn't necessarily mean that you start singing about moonbeams and puppy dogs. I think I'm playing better now than I've ever done, and I wouldn't be able to get through doing all of this now if Cait wasn't with me.'
Costello in *Rolling Stone*, 1989.

CHAPTER 7

'I once tried to explain to a lawyer why I run my career like I do. He was completely perplexed, because it runs against all logic with the lawyers and accountants and all the record company people when you tell them that you deliberately try to lose money. I do things to keep interest in my career, bold things like a gig with the Royal Philharmonic, an eight-six-piece orchestra. It was a disaster, but it was interesting. Like doing the last tour with the Spinning Wheel and two different bands while playing 1,000-seat theatres. Do you know how much money I lost on that? But it was worthwhile because people damn well talked about it.'

Interview with David Wild, Rolling Stone, *June 1989*

'I find the actual impetus to write these songs pretty mind-boggling. I'm thinking these horrible thoughts about, say, Thatcher, and I have to face the fact that loads of people think she's wonderful . . . There is no rational explanation for the way she is dismantling everything. Yet people seem complicit . . . It's extremely disturbing. There is no liberal or logical way forward anymore. I firmly believe that. There is no future for the reasonable voice.'

Interview with Sean O'Hagan, NME, *February 1989*

'We're both left-of-centre anarchists and we talk about politics a lot. We see the injustice that usually comes from the right. Music is our everyday air that we breathe, then we get going on politics and say, 'What about that swine . . .' and we'll get the wax dolls and needles out.'

Ross MacManus talking to Markie Robson-Scott,
Sunday Times Magazine, *1994*

121

With the Spectacular Spinning Songbook revue having been enjoyed by all those who took part, Costello's next foray into live shows was with The Confederates. Befitting the name, this band were singularly American, culled from the musicians that played on *King of America*: James Burton, T-Bone Wolk, Benmont Tench, Jerry Scheff. From a 'live' perspective, this was Costello in defiantly non-Britpop mode, 1980s' style. Investigating the core of Americana with US musicians, he played mostly his own material. His previous involvement with intrinsically American music was on *Almost Blue*'s Nashville dalliance. Costello and The Attractions donned the musical threads of country cowboys and played songs written by other people. The Confederates were the real US thing, and played Costello songs that didn't elicit any Attractions' comparisons or touch on their recorded material.

The running order of the shows was largely made up of *King Of America* and a miscellany of prime cuts from the R&B and country catalogues. At a concert in London's Royal Albert Hall in early 1987, Costello showed that his past as a Brit with a sneer (on stage, anyway) was well and truly behind him. He dedicated a transcendent version of Buddy Holly's *True Love Ways* to his wife Cait, joked about not doing 'Peace In Our Time' and previewed a new song with a spot of family history woven into it, 'Any King's Shilling'. Costello the brat had packed up his bags and headed off to America, returning a wiser and happier man. He looked all the better for it, too.

When he wasn't touring, he and Jake Riviera were taking care of business. Relations with Columbia in America were not going well. The company was unhappy with the type of records he was offering them, and apparently unwilling to promote them with a suitable budget. The severance of his contract was looking quite likely, and it seemed that there would be no love lost on either side. He'd been with Columbia for ten years. For the first two and a half, both parties worked well together. Then, according to Costello, and for a number of unspecified reasons, business matters became untenable. By the end of his contract, the company was releasing his records, but not doing much else.

'I had no quarrel with Columbia,' Costello affirmed in *Rolling Stone*. 'They, after all, signed me. I appreciate that. So Columbia didn't sign me and immediately ruin my life. They sort of worked up to it. We could just never reach agreement about promoting my individuality as opposed to promoting my similarity to everything else . . . For a while Columbia kept me around, hoping they'd get back all the money I owed them. But they realized they were taking more and more of a gamble, because I was just never conforming to their expectation of what my records should sound like. Of course, they would never tell me what they wanted, either. But it's no big disaster. Columbia is not going to go out of business just because I owe them a fair chunk of money [$1million]. They've got my back catalogue. One hit record and they get it all back.'[1]

An implicit factor in why relationships deteriorated so rapidly, with mutual, barely-contained animosity, was that Columbia felt severely distanced from both Costello and his manager, Jake Riviera. Indeed, we can safely assume that in the case of Riviera, not many of the then-Columbia marketing and promotions department included him on their Christmas cards list. 'Jake has an unfortunate tendency to attack people personally when he's angry with them about business,' mused Costello. 'Unfortunately, this collides with the fact that American record executives have this tremendous inability to withstand personal insults . . . But some of them are such nancies, you know? I thought these were the guys who were supposed to be bribing people with money and cocaine. If they hated us so much, why didn't they just take out a contract on us? It would've been quicker.'[2]

To make matters worse, Costello never wanted to socialize with the executives, and would never have his picture taken in their company, in case, as he said to Nick Kent, 'it turned up as evidence in some FBI mafia investigation . . . There's always the possibility with those kind of people.'[3]

It was head-below-the-parapet time. Developments in

songwriting were taking place, with new material for future projects slowly shaping up. While discussions were afoot to extricate himself from Columbia, while still finding some way of riveting his future career and recordings to a major record company, Costello began the rare process of co-writing songs, this time with Paul McCartney. He had done this before with the likes of Squeeze's Glenn Tilbrook, producer Clive Langer, friend T-Bone Burnette and spouse Cait, to generally good effect, but it wasn't something he sat down to do in a room, one-on-one, with a furrowed brow. It always seemed as if his need for control was under threat, the constant loner overtaken by a need to share his responsibilities. The examples of co-songwriting were normally without fault, but they weren't necessarily a primary challenge. He had, after all, written 'The People's Limousine', for example, with T-Bone Burnette in the back of a chauffeured car driving through Italy. No formality there, then.

Costello had met Paul McCartney for the first time at the series of benefit concerts for the people of Kampuchea in late December 1979. They would subsequently run into each other when they were recording their respective albums in the early-to-mid 1980s. An amiable person with no apparent hidden agenda, McCartney would have a cup of coffee with Costello and they would play the occasional game of Space Invaders. As years and albums went by they had come to know each other relatively well. However, while they clearly had a mutual respect, they could not term themselves the best of mates.

While making *Imperial Bedroom* at AIR Studios with erstwhile Beatles' engineer Geoff Emerick, Costello once again bumped into McCartney, who was billeted down the studio corridor with his own producer, George Martin. Emerick, coincidentally, was also the main engineer on the album McCartney and Martin were working on (*Tug Of War*). Again, nothing much was said, but another useful connection had been made. They had met, too, at Live Aid, where Costello's use of 'All You Need Is Love' struck an empathetic note with its co-creator. Also, Costello's obvious love of The

Beatles and the band's recurring influences on his work would not have been ignored. And anyway, McCartney was a fan, from the glory days of the New Wave.

'I quite like a lot of the new sounds,' he told *NME* in 1978. 'I quite like Elvis Costello. I like Nick Lowe because I've known him for a very long time. I really do like what they're doing . . . being a bit more adventurous . . . That's why I particularly like Elvis Costello. He writes and performs good material.'[4] McCartney's conspicuous songwriting history does not need documenting here, but if the collaboration was unusual for Elvis, it was doubly so for the ex-Beatle, who had hardly ever worked in tandem with another songwriter since the early 1970s. The initial phone call from McCartney to Costello was plain and simple: would he come down to the studio for a brief chat about writing some songs?

Costello did not know precisely how familiar McCartney was with his material. The important thing to him was that they were attempting to write new songs, and his attitude was as encouraging as McCartney's first communication. He knew that he didn't have the history or the amount of hit records the ex-Beatle had but he realized that his experience as a songwriter made McCartney's contact perfectly reasonable. The press and pundits had their own theories: that McCartney's approach to Costello was an attempt to sponge up some critical kudos, to make him and his music appear hipper, and to add a stroke of vinegar to his own rather 'sweet' songs. As for Costello, there was absolutely no motivation other than one good songwriter wanting to work with another one.

'It's a stupid exercise to talk about things that way,' he told *Rolling Stone* dismissively. 'I hate the way this industry turns people into kind of bubblegum cards or cartoons, distillations of their personality and what they represent, particularly in the last year or two with John Lennon. I find it very disturbing when somebody who meant a lot to me is suddenly remoulded for the benefit of somebody's script . . . I ain't gonna be involved in any of that crap. It's sentimental nonsense.'[5]

Much was made in the media at the time when it was known that McCartney had another songwriting partner and one from Liverpool at that. For the optimistic tabloids and music press baying for a Beatles reunion, it was big news, but not for the participants. For Costello, who wouldn't have wanted to be 'another' Lennon anyway, it was simply a thrill and honour to work with someone who had clearly been such a huge influence on his career. 'It's funny,' he said to Nick Kent, 'you take an opinion poll on Paul McCartney and you'll find that almost all music critics dislike him and almost all music fans think he's great. I mean, compared to *who* is Paul McCartney not any good? Compared to the Inspiral fuckin' Carpets? I don't go in for all this 'knocking' him. He's who he wants to be. Paul McCartney survived being one of the most famous people *ever* in the world and this was back when being famous actually meant something.'[6]

One of the first songs that came to fruition under their association was 'Back On My Feet', which became the B-side of a future McCartney single, 'Once Upon A Long Ago'. McCartney had already started the track, so Costello brought his lyrics to it. Costello then brought in 'Veronica' – he had a verse and the chorus. McCartney assisted on that. So it went on for several songs, each writer lending his craft to their development. In that way they gained an insight into how the other worked. This was the beginning of the collaborative work that would eventually appear on Costello's next two albums, and also on McCartney's.

The two personalities and craftsmen clicked, but in a pragmatic sense. They didn't grow up together and they weren't the same age, but their common purpose was to write good songs that didn't deny each other's histories. Something else also happened, a process that can take place when creative people, normally solitary, are joined together – they switched their assumed roles. McCartney would ferret around for an underdeveloped melody, while Costello would be searching for musical snippets that were not only tuneful but which suited McCartney's voice.

Costello observed in *Q*: 'Inevitably, there's a bit of,

"Fuckin' hell it's Paul McCartney, he's written loads of famous songs." And you're a little bit, not on your guard, but you need to know what he thinks about songs, not necessarily what he thinks about anything else . . . He's very practical about songwriting, very formal, funnily enough. People sometimes say he dashes them off, but that's not really true. If you don't like what he's singing about, if you think the sentiments are not tough enough or something, then that's a personal thing. I wouldn't say this holds true for every song he's ever written but when we sat down together he wouldn't have any sloppy bits in there. That was interesting.'[7]

Meanwhile, occasional live appearances dotted throughout the summer of 1987 gave the public their only confirmation of Costello's continued existence. A show at Glastonbury caught him in top form, duetting with Los Lobos' David Hidalgo (who had helped out Costello with vocals on *King Of America*'s 'Loveable' and 'American Without Tears'. Costello also ripped through cover versions including Abba's 'Knowing Me Knowing You' and Prince's 'Sign O' The Times'. Industry rumours that Costello was about to sign a worldwide deal with a major record label had been circulating for some months, and by the time autumn arrived they had been confirmed: it was WEA Records. The official announcement was issued at the record company's annual conference in Bournemouth in September. A report stating that Costello's first offering for the company would be out by the spring of 1988 proved to be a tad overambitious, however.

He had, however, completed work on the soundtrack to an Irish film, the Joe Lee/Frank Deasy-directed *The Courier*. This urban gangster story was set in Dublin and starred Gabriel Byrne, with Costello's wife Cait O'Riordan as the 'love interest', Colette. They moved to a Dublin hotel for three months, and Costello wrote over half the material that would appear on the forthcoming album. The stay, incidentally, led to an interest in a somewhat purer form of Irish traditional music than that purveyed by The Pogues.

On 30 September, Costello appeared on *The Black &*

White Night at the Coconut Grove Ballroom in Los Angeles, a televised tribute celebrating the genius of Roy Orbison that would be broadcast the following year. Produced by T-Bone Burnette, Costello starred alongside the Big O with kd lang, Jackson Browne, JD Souther, Tom Waits, Bonnie Raitt, Bruce Springsteen and others. By now free of Columbia's indifference, he was in good shape at the show. During a break in recording, Springsteen walked over to Costello for a chinwag. Trailing in his wake was Al Teller, former President of Columbia Records. Really, he should have known better . . .

As Costello recalled in *Rolling Stone*: 'He said to me, "You know, we don't need to not speak just because you're not on the label." It really matters not a damn to me whether he draws another breath, quite honestly. He's irrelevant in my life. He might be a very charming person, but in terms of my career he was nothing but trouble . . . And he said, "So, have you a record coming out?" And I said, "I think there's plenty in the racks, don't you, Al?" He didn't see the joke.'[8]

The remainder of 1987 was taken up with a series of solo shows in Japan and Australia, along with a two-week tour of America's southern states with The Confederates. This was a good experience spoiled only by the inevitable parting of the 'team', who had worked so well with Costello in embracing a peculiarly American sound. Before the end of the year, an album of rare material was released by Demon Records (of which Costello was, and is, a director). Based on the out-takes style of *Ten Bloody Marys and Ten How's Your Fathers*, this compilation was called *Out Of Our Idiot*, a sixteen-track collection of rarities recorded under various pseudonyms. Since there was the distinct possibility of no further original releases for some time, the album acted as a balm to vinyl-pining fans. Their worst fears were confirmed by a statement from Jake Riviera, reported in *NME*: 'There are no plans to release anything at present. Elvis will just put things together as he goes and when the time comes when he thinks he's got something worth putting out, he'll do it. That's the way he works.'[9] The pressures and memories of just a few years previously, when Costello had to release *Goodbye Cruel World* to stave off bankruptcy, had clearly been eased by the financial buffer provided by his new record company.

As for 1988, it was a heady but relaxing mixture of plea-sure and work, including a couple of holidays – Italy at Easter, Greenland in the summer. He found the latter to be spiritu-ally 'meaningful' and wrote new material there. The previous year's Orbison association led to Costello contributing a revised version of *Goodbye Cruel World*'s 'The Comedians' to the American's forthcoming record, 1989's posthumously-released *Mystery Girl*. Costello also penned a couple of songs for the first English-speaking album by Rubén Blades, *Nothing But The Truth*. A New York-based Panamanian musician and actor, Blades regarded his work as a chronicle of urban realities, an attitude that related to Costello's keen sense of social and political exploration. He also wrote the lyrics to 'The Other End Of The Telescope' for 'Til Tuesday's *Everything's Different Now* album. Hey, he was enjoying himself . . .

'I thought, I don't have to be promoting an album, you can just play for the hell of it,' he explained to *Q*. 'You get the offers and they're interesting things to do. I don't do anything with tremendous commercial ambition, sometimes it's just a challenge or really fun to do. Also, to be mercenary about it, I was biding my time for my Columbia deal to run out so that I could get a better deal out for the world . . . So I've done a lot of things, but they haven't all been big career moves. But I've never seen it like that. Since I came off the road as a routine thing – album/tour, album/tour – it frees you to do a lot of things, which you want to do because they're interest-ing . . . I'm not a workaholic, driven by this crazy urge to do anything that comes my way. I'm fairly selective. I turn down a lot of things, high-profile shows, big tours that I didn't think were right, and 'cause' things where I'm not sure about people's motives . . . It wasn't a long layoff by most people's standards. Actually it's a fairly conventional layoff. But I'd done ten years. My parole came up.'[10]

Costello finished recording his next album (which was due for release in early 1989) in August of 1988. Reports of its genrebusting diversity were compounded by sightings of him in recording studios geographically as far apart as Dublin and Hollywood, London and New Orleans. He was working with musicians from varying disciplines, including Roger McGuinn, Chrissie Hynde, Paul McCartney, The Chieftains' Derek Bell, Allen Toussaint, Donal Lunny, Jim Keltner, The Dirty Dozen Brass Band, Benmont Tench and Christy Moore. Appetites were whetted already. Come 1989, and with tour details surfacing, it seemed like he was back in the fray. Business as usual, then.

He was tempted to call the new album *More Important Work,* as a tribute not only to his previously sarcastically-titled records, but also to puncture the very idea of it. He finally settled on the monosyllabic *Spike* (although the subtitle *The Beloved Entertainer* was, perhaps, just as relevant). As usual, it could have meant anything and everything – the bulldog in Tom & Jerry cartoons or a pointed instrument, just like the big nail used as the 'i' on the cover sleeve. The title was in fact a nod to Lindley Armstrong 'Spike' Jones, an American bandleader of the 1940s who took the mickey out of well-known popular songs of the day. This led to his being referred to as the King of Corn, after an album title of the same name; when he butchered a song he would acknowledge the crowd's applause poker-faced, saying 'Thank you, music lovers.'[11]

Spike was wide ranging in terms of musical style and lyrical reach – it was Costello's most diverse album yet. When he left Columbia, he had it in mind to make any number of 'themed' albums. One was an orchestrated record using tuned percussion, akin to the type Burt Bacharach used to create. Another was an album steeped in the hip musical *argot* of New Orleans gumbo. He had upwards of five other motifs that he wanted to pursue, but was unsure if people would have considered it indulgent if he'd made a record on each themed blueprint. He also didn't know if he really wanted to sustain any or all of the themes over an album's worth of material.

A balance was reached on *Spike* where he combined the ideas. The album's brief ranged from the twin Rickenbacker attack of Roger McGuinn and Paul McCartney, the satirical mockery of 'God's Comic', the Noirleans swing of the Dirty Dozen Brass Band, the lyrical deftness and humour of 'Chewing Gum', and the traditional Irish balladry (with the not so traditional invective) of 'Tramp The Dirt Down' and 'Any King's Shilling'. Of all the musical departures, it was the traditional Irish element that was most surprising. He was not consciously working within the genre, but instead making use of musical sounds that derive from it, and he did not regard it as having any greater significance than any other type of music.

'That's read into it from me having an Irish background,' he once told me. 'Some people, particularly in America because of U2 and Sinead O'Connor, have got this notion that everybody in Ireland is a mystic and we're craving for our roots. It's all a lot of nonsense, it's just music. Undoubtedly these traditional instruments embody a certain spiritual quality, the pipes in particular . . . But it's not something I'm putting on like an Aran sweater I've brought home from holidays . . . The difficulty you have when working with traditional musicians is that because it is a tradition, it's like something into which you have to be admitted. Having said that, that isn't the case with the musicians I've worked with.'[12]

It was, by any standards (and certainly by Costello's), a diverse work that managed to mix the lyrical directness of his first two records with a breadth of musical vision he had until now been unable to apply. There were less 'first-person' songs, and more stories about given situations. 'Veronica' and 'Any King's Shilling' were, respectively, about Costello's grandmother and grandfather. Thatcher was given a verbal booting in 'Tramp The Dirt Down' to an Irish lilt snagged on the threads of Stevie Wonder's 'Isn't She Lovely'. 'Let Him Dangle' was a political song which addressed the capital punishment debate, utilizing the real-life 1950s case of Christopher Craig and Derek Bentley. Ultimately, it was a simple record to comprehend, with Costello steering away from what had earlier appeared to be a compulsive need to impress.

'I've been doing that for a long time but nobody seemed to notice!' he told *Q*. 'You see new artists come up, and people are very interested in them, and if you've been around for a while . . . I don't do that anymore. I did it at first, it was just the way I wrote, and then I got a little bit cute with it and then I stopped doing it. Nobody seemed to notice! Fuck 'em. So I'd say that was true of the last couple of records, but more so of this one.'[13]

The sound of the record was far removed from *Blood & Chocolate*. With the exception of a brief appearance by Pete Thomas, there wasn't an Attraction to be heard. Originally, Costello wanted The Attractions as a whole or in part to be involved in up to five songs on *Spike*. This idea was nixed by Steve Nieve, who saw The Attractions as a defined quartet and not something that could or should be split up into musically constituent parts. They argued the toss. Costello won out, leaving the practical future of the band in limbo. From his point of view, if there was a good reason for The Attractions and himself to get back together again, then fine. He refused to entertain the idea that the unit would be regrouped for a nostalgia binge.

'There were a couple of moments that hinted at the old sound,' he admitted in *Record Collector*. 'The bad guitar player's friend, the tremolo guitar, features throughout my career, so there's some of that on *Spike*. But the arrangements were very different to what I'd done before, partly because it was very rare for more than three instruments to be played simultaneously during the sessions. As a result the arrangements were very painterly, with little bits added here and there, and then you rub that bit out and add another bit – it was a very creative use of the studio. But it frightened the hell out of people who were used to safer, combo-sounding arrangements. But then, out of the blue, we had this massive hit with 'Veronica' . . . after years of Columbia saying "if only he'd do what we told him". Suddenly I was a pop singer again!'[14]

Spike was released to rave reviews. The success of the single 'Veronica' only added to the push given to the record by Warners, who were obviously pleased with their new investment. And things were going to get even better. A solo tour of Europe lined up for May was pre-selling a treat, the demand so great that he was in the process of piecing a band together to go out on a summer tour. Things were going extremely well for him. A happy man? Reckon so . . .

'Elvis is not quite as livid as he used to be,' said friend, producer and colleague Nick Lowe in *Rolling Stone*. 'The thing you need to understand about Elvis is that he's never suffered fools gladly. Unfortunately, he happens to work in an industry made up exclusively of fools. I know he's been particularly unpleasant to some people, but generally deservedly so, I've found. He thinks things should be done a certain way, and he doesn't give a toss what anyone else says . . . Plus, the guy's completely in love, and that never hurts.'[15]

Certainly, America was seeing a different man. Shortly after the release of *Spike*, an appearance on *Saturday Night Live* witnessed a man who delivered two songs ('Let Him Dangle' and 'Veronica') without any inherent tension. This was his second appearance on the show in twelve years; the first was in 1977 when he and The Attractions stopped 'Less Than Zero' halfway through and broke into a vitriolic reading of 'Radio Radio'. The passion was there, but not the abuse. Was this a more genteel version of the same man, whose present personal life smoothed by the guiding hand of Cait O'Riordan attested to the power of his recent work?

'Yes, without a doubt,' he told *Rolling Stone*. 'Unashamedly and unapologetically so. But it just goes to prove that happiness needn't inhibit you. Being in love does-n't necessarily mean that you start singing about moonbeams and puppy dogs. I think I'm playing better than I've ever done, and I wouldn't be able to get through doing all of this now if Cait wasn't with me.'[16]

One song on *Spike* confirmed Costello's theory of love not necessarily equalling a simpering, doe-eyed acceptance of things. 'Tramp The Dirt Down' tallied with his philosophy of subversive pop music: a calm Irish folk tune wrapped around lyrics of blistering effect. A protest song that ranks among the best of the past thirty years, it's also a distant cousin of 'Shipbuilding' and 'Pills And Soap', in that it relates and reacts to a particularly harsh strain of Conservative intolerance exemplified by Margaret Thatcher. With the exception of Billy Bragg and to a less eloquent degree, Paul Weller, no one had the gumption to write songs such as these anymore. In love the man might be, but still Costello had no time for what he perceived to be the impotence of the average person facing the bureaucratic might of government departments and leaders.

'It's not some artificial neurosis – oh, I'd better have an angry side,' he explained to Q. 'It's the way I feel about it. That day I woke up and wrote the song pretty quickly, all in one day. And obviously some days it doesn't weigh down as heavily on you; on others, it's all you can do not to kick the television in, just seeing Nigel Lawson, he doesn't even have to speak. You might feel powerless, because it does seem to be irreversible, because there is no opposition. But this is just a song, it's not going to change anything, it's just getting it out. And some people will find sympathy with it, it might comfort some people, who knows how people will hear a song like that? It'll piss some people off, and that's great. If it ruins anyone's day then I'll be a happy man.'[17] The downside to such a bitter polemic was that a baying audience appeared to be commending themselves for their hatred of the same people, a cathartic enough experience, but one for which Costello refused to take any responsibility.

Spike was Costello's most successful album on both sides of the Atlantic since *Punch the Clock*, which, for an artist whose sales rarely if ever matched his creative achievements, was particularly instructive. *Spike* was also his eighth Billboard Top Forty album of the 1980s, no mean achievement considering the paucity of promotion Columbia had given him. The days of Stiff's 'Help Us Hype Elvis' campaign seemed a long way off. Now that he had a major record company pushing his records he didn't need to be pushed an inch. Preconceived notions of his unfashionability were the only thing preventing him from achieving world domination. Well, that was the theory, anyway.

He knew he wasn't competing with other people for chart supremacy. Indeed, he consciously made records that didn't sound like other pop acts. He claimed it wasn't that he didn't know how to make chart-driven pop music, but that he had no interest in doing so (except when his back was to the wall, or, in the case of *Blood & Chocolate*, if he had a point he wanted to make.)

Besides, he was fully aware, like most other people, that the vast majority of pop music was contrived by people with an eye more on their bank balance than on 'art'. A handful of exceptional rock 'n' roll recordings are inspiring and spontaneous performances, surely. Presley's 'Hound Dog'? According to Costello, a mere contrivance. The Sex Pistols' *Never Mind The Bollocks*? Locked in an expensive studio courtesy of EMI, and with Chris Thomas producing, it could hardly be called revolutionary. "Veronica' is a contrived pop record,' Costello pointed out in *Time Out*. 'But although it has the structural reference points of pop music, it also has a heart, life, it says something that I care about: that there's a point where the mind goes beyond the dilapidations of the body . . . I could have written it like, "Oh, the old people and their funny minds", the sensitive version, and given it to Tanita Tikaram and she'd have had a big hit with it. But instead I did it my way.'[18]

Despite his depth of feeling for his work, Costello was astute enough to know only too well that what he did was probably important only to him, some critics, and his fans. He didn't care at this point about his stature in the Rock 'n' Roll Hall of Fame, nor exactly where he fitted in rock history. He had little time for awards ceremonies such as the Grammies, either, which he regarded as corporate exercises in selling nostalgia, or what would be nostalgia in ten years time. Intuitively, he saw this need to make rock 'n' roll a crucial aspect of life as a singularly American thing, prompted by its lack of history and culture. Elsewhere it was just pop music. In the States, it was 'Phew! Rock 'n' Roll . . .', an overwhelming, life-affirming, awe-inspiring experience with a Big Mac in one hand and a large Coke in the other.

But Costello also realized that America fully embraced the commercial breadth of the music it created. It was, therefore, absolutely everywhere, from films to clothes, from food to drink, from work to play, from day to night and all points in between. In America, Costello reckoned, dignitaries and government leaders would go home, slip into their favourite blue jeans and slot Lynyrd Skynyrd or ZZ Top albums into their CD players. Rightly or wrongly, he thought it impossible that a similar all-pervasive pop cultural experience would take place in Britain or Ireland. No, the only aspect of what he did that was important to him was the songs, and even then he was, if not dismissive of them, then casual in his approach about what they meant to people. 'It's just a bunch of songs, you can buy them if you want and it's up to people to sort out what they mean to them.'[19]

His image by this time had changed radically from that in the late 1970s. The people who went to his shows from the very beginning and stuck with him would have seen the same person going through a natural evolvement. Costello could neither understand nor appreciate the all-too-readily presented image of him in the press, which was incredibly narrow-minded and blinkered, and notably unwilling to regard him as anything more than a cipher for guilt, revenge, hate, sarcasm and all the other usual wordy suspects. He naturally wanted to be comprehended on more than just a one-dimensional level. 'Most journalists are just not good enough writers a lot of the time to represent people . . . If you want to be able to move around and do different things, you don't want to be limited by a preconceived idea that you're over here standing with a bloody hatchet in your hand . . .'[20]

To a degree he succeeded by virtue of the diversity of his records from *Trust* onwards, but old habits die hard, as Warners would find out. Diversifying too much came with an

inbuilt debilitating factor – a slow whittling away of the
fanbase that would effectively undermine any long-term
investment. It seemed as if Costello didn't care one way or the
other. He just wanted to continue to do interesting things, to
service the requirements of himself and the people that came
to see him each time he rolled, solo or with a band, into their
town. 'Playing 11,000-seat open-air theatres in Chicago with
corporate sponsorship is not interesting,' he noted in *Rolling
Stone*. 'It's not interesting for people sitting out in the back
. . . And it's not interesting for the band. No wonder people
drink beer and eat popcorn all the way through concerts; how
do you expect them to be involved from half a mile away? So
if [particular pop stars] outsell me on a given day, it doesn't
matter. We're not in the same game, are we? The truth is, I
would rather do it my way and lose money.'[21]

He didn't lose money when he was touring in a solo capacity, though, in America throughout April. There, he bypassed
major markets in favour of college towns, similarly focusing
on promoting *Spike* through college radio. It was a medium
he preferred for a number of reasons; firstly because a newer
and younger audience were less inclined to judge or compare
him on past endeavours, and secondly because it was less
formatted than the more rigidly-controlled larger stations.
Costello had no problem going out to the now-wider range
of radio stations. The irony wasn't lost on him: the man who,
ten years ago, wanted to bite the fingers that fed him on
'Radio Radio' now willingly wanted to shake hands. The
difference this time was that he, and the radio people, were
not the same.

'The misconception is that I was a two-headed monster
. . . I only turn into a two-headed monster when people give
me justification. All impressions to the contrary, I'm a very
nice guy. I trust everybody until they give me a reason not to.
I think they must know I'm daring them to say, "We're not
those guys." And I think people put too much store in that
one song . . . But those radio people know who I am. And I
know who I am; I don't need their confirmation. I don't cease
to exist if they don't play my fucking records.'[22]

Most of the remainder of 1989 was spent touring *Spike*. The solo tour spiralled into a full-blown band gig (including Jerry Scheff, Marc Ribot, Steven Soles, Pete Thomas and Larry Knechtel) for a major US tour in July. The West Coast leg of the tour provided Costello with the opportunity to jam with a musical legend from his teenage years – the Grateful Dead's Jerry Garcia – although it's unlikely that he viewed it with any degree of sentiment. In September, the video for Costello's 'Veronica' won Best Male Video award at the sixth annual MTV Video Awards, while in October, the Demon compilation, *Girls, Girls, Girls,* was released to poor commercial effect. Another gong that Costello clinched in 1990 was, perhaps, more to his liking: *Rolling Stone* named him Best Songwriter in its 1989 Critics Awards.

It was a good beginning to the year, and although he more than likely had a somewhat cynical attitude towards it (he really didn't need a bunch of music critics to tell him that his songs were good) it nevertheless consolidated the feeling amongst the public that here was a songwriter of whom they should, if they hadn't already done so, take note. Of course, there's always a downside, isn't there? Just when things were going swimmingly well – awards, great gigs, love, marriage, the whole enchilada – out of the blue came a book written by The Attractions' bass player Bruce Thomas. He was not a happy camper.

Published in August, *The Big Wheel* was Thomas coming clean and spiteful about life on the road as an Attraction with Costello. Very well written, it conveyed the occasionally hellish existence of being in a band with a bunch of people (and one person in particular) you wouldn't choose as lifelong friends. As The Attractions were, essentially, a band specially put together by Costello for the sole purpose of touring with *My Aim Is True*, logic dictates that there would be a reasonable amount of intra-band conflict that might not have been there had they formed the band at school or college.

So it was that they went through those years from the first album to *Goodbye Cruel World* in various states of mental duress: shock at such sudden huge success (they were the

Herman's Hermits of punk rock, for Crissake), which none
of them had experienced before, despite Bruce and Pete
Thomas' stints in earlier bands. Certainly, the dynamic was
such that it worked in their favour on stage, but one wonders
how sympathetic they were to some of Costello's more
demanding musical experiments. They weren't allowed to cut
loose on *Almost Blue*, that's for sure.

The difference, of course, from choosing two experienced
session men from the pub-rock days and a student from the
Royal College of Music, as opposed to picking up a bunch of
fresh-faced punks from the Kings Road, was musical pedigree
and attitude. From the beginning, it was made clear that
Costello ruled the roost: the songwriter was also the bread-
winner, and there was nothing The Attractions could do about
it. There was also the matter of choice of poison. The ex-pub
rockers and the management system around them knew how
to drink, while those younger musicians who were gaining
notoriety and kudos were too well versed in the lessons of
alternative chemistry classes. 'The drinking might have slowed
a few gigs down,' Costello recalled in *Rolling Stone*, 'but
there was always ways of speeding 'em up again. Whatever
we did didn't do any harm, and it didn't do any good.'[23]

Thomas, through a mixture of rueful retrospection and
well-aimed sniping, enigmatically refers to the other
members of The Attractions throughout as 'the Drummer'
and 'the Keyboard Player'. Unsurprisingly, Costello is
referred to as more than just 'the Singer'. Other sobriquets
include 'Curt Reply', 'the Pod' – 'owing to an increasing
tendency to resemble the shape of those creatures from
Invasion Of The Bodysnatchers'[24] – and 'Manitas de
Concrete', due to Costello's propensity for leaving a trail of
snapped guitar strings across the venues of Europe, America,
Australia and the Far East.

Clearly, time with Costello affected Bruce more than the
others. A couple of years older than the rest of The
Attractions and Costello, it's possible that some of the more
juvenile on-the-road pranks seemed less fun to him. It's also
quite likely that, having been in a successful band prior to the

Attractions, he had already experienced them. Another bout of boys' own humour just didn't fit the bill. 'Bruce just doesn't love music,' Costello said of the strife between the two, talking to the *Big Issue*. 'It makes me sad because he used to be a really good player and still can be on occasions when he concentrates. It just really made being on the road hellish, that's why I couldn't do it anymore.'[25]

While the book certainly didn't help relationships between the two, there wasn't a total split, not for the time being, anyway. Whatever Thomas felt about the situation outside the boundaries of the book, ultimately Costello feels blue that the bilious bass player hadn't enjoyed himself more. 'That's truthfully the answer,' he claimed in *Record Collector*. 'I could nitpick and say, hang on, that punch line wasn't yours to tell because that was somebody else's joke. But we were sufficiently estranged so that I didn't really give a shit at the time. I knew that only about twelve people in the world would read it, and would give a damn. The real inside nuts-and-bolts stuff that was really there to wound the individuals concerned, rather than entertain the general public, passed me by, because the overwhelming feeling was one of sadness and bitterness, that he hadn't had more fun and found the adventure more satisfying . . . It was just an expression of his frustration at the time, just as much as anything I might have said or done.'[26]

And with that, it was bang into 1991. A new album, his second for Warners, was already written up and waiting in the wings. The Attractions were dead. Long live 'The Singer'?

CHAPTER 8

'Hello out there, I'm a guy your mother used to know.'
Elvis Costello greeting an audience of students at
C.W. Post College. From Rolling Stone, *June 1989*

'Some people still have their head up their arse, but there's
nothing I can do about that. Some people want you to
think like them, but I can't. That's their problem.'
Interview with the author, for In Dublin, *June 1991*

'Yes, I do feel I've been too wilfully obscure for my audi-
ence at times. But then it depends on what you're trying
to achieve. If I'm trying to sincerely follow my own feelings
about music, then I'm right to do records like Almost Blue.
If I'm thinking about being ever so famous for a long, long
time, then obviously I was completely wrong. I always find
myself starting to lose interest in the limited areas of
music I operate in. But everything I've done on record,
good or bad, I've done with all my heart. And I stand by
every record I've done, even records that I don't think
nowadays have any virtue. I've made bad records but I've
never made a dishonest record, let's put it that way.'
From The Dark Stuff, *by Nick Kent, Penguin, 1994*

From 1989, Costello had moved house and home back to
the land of his grandparents (and a country whose tax system
was extremely beneficial to those with 'artist' status), settling
in southern Ireland, on the southside of Dublin. He had also
learned to drive within the past year, something that startled

more than several pedestrians on their way to work ('Isn't that? No, it couldn't be . . . Yes, it is!') and in Dublin's city centre. But there was something more than just a vague recognition factor flashing before their eyes. The face was familiar, but it was covered with a facial growth. The head was the same shape, but with far more hair than heretofore. Welcome to Costello's Beard Years. Jamming with Jerry Garcia had obviously had more of an effect on him than he had at first thought . . .

If there was a reason for this dramatic change in appearance, Costello wasn't letting on. Yes, the cold weather in Ireland might have had something to do with it, but the slatternly Satanic look seemed to be a more permanent fixture than an affectation for a mere season or two in an inclement clime.

'It was mainly a private decision to move, really,' he told the *Evening Herald*. 'I wanted to have that little bit of freedom to make noise or not make noise and just be outside of the city in that sense . . . I like all cities where there is one culture laid on top of another, and Dublin to an extent has that when I need it . . . I go there [Dublin] to get away from everything. I don't really get involved very much with the things that are going on there . . . Everything else seems like a temporary place now that I'm there. That's home.'[1]

Cast the mind back to the spring of 1990. Since *King of America*, Costello had toured on a semi-regular basis with The Confederates (Jerry Scheff, Jim Keltner, James Burton and Mitchell Froom). Some members of that band made up the core of musicians who played on *Spike* along with Marc Ribot and Michael Blair, two more members of Costello's now select travelling society. He'd been working with them since 1986 in the studio and from a year later in a live context. Within five years they had become firm friends, and Costello, wishing to capture once more the organic sound they had effortlessly, intuitively forged over the years, moved to a studio in Barbados (well, someone had to . . .) to record an album called *Kojak Variety*. It was a fond farewell to the band, including pianist Larry Knechtel, who was the only travelling Confederate whom he hadn't recorded with up to that point.

The theory was that he wouldn't be seeing them after *Kojak Variety*, that they would go their separate ways for some years at least, and that Costello would get back with The Attractions to see what lay ahead. With that in mind, Costello and company recorded a rake of cover versions for an album that wouldn't be released for another five years. There seemed to be little logic behind this other than record-label shenanigans, but whatever the reasoning behind such a decision, some good came out of it.

Not immediately, however. Costello's original plan to record his new album with all three of The Attractions fell by the wayside. For one reason or another – legal matters, specific member recalcitrance, previous commitments – Costello went to Ocean Bay Studios, Hollywood, to meet up with The Confederates for the new record. Bringing along some floating musicians, including the Attraction who could make it, drummer Pete Thomas (sharing the drum stool fairly evenly with Jim Keltner), The Dirty Dozen Brass Band, Nick Lowe and his own father, Costello began the sessions for *Mighty Like A Rose*.

The album was released in May 1991. Co-produced by Costello/MacManus, Kevin Killen and Mitchell Froom (the latter's reputation as a producer as much as a musician has bloomed since), the album is as sound-sculptured and wilful a miscellany of songs as *Spike*. The title of the record came from a song on an obscure cassette collection of Count John McCormack's that Costello discovered in a roadside petrol station somewhere between Athlone and Dingle. A short time later, a friend found him a cover version of the same song by The Carols, a New York doo-wop group, and Van Morrison's Them also had a version in demo form.

Costello was constantly opening himself up to different musical styles and formats. Nothing was out of the question. From 1989, he and Cait had begun to listen to classical music quite seriously, partly for his own enjoyment and instruction, but also to prepare him for the orchestral arrang-

143

ing and composing for Alan Bleasdale's TV series *GBH*. A portion of that orchestral theorizing transferred across to *Mighty Like A Rose*, most notably on 'All Grown Up' and 'Harpies Bizarre', where Costello utilized minute passages from classical composers and then shaped them into orchestrated riffs.

The opening track, 'The Other Side Of Summer', with its obvious musical references to The Beach Boys, is a tune lampooning Brian Wilson's 1960s' celebration of the joys of the Californian surf, an effective musical joke. 'Hurry Down Doomsday (The Bugs Are Taking Over)' is an impulsive plea for retribution, 'How To Be Dumb' is a thinly-veiled, withering retort to Bruce Thomas' literary whinge, Cait O'Riordan's 'Broken' is a beautiful, romantic Celticized *memento mori*, while 'So Like Candy' as with 'Playboy To A Man', co-written with Paul McCartney, couldn't help but remind some people of Costello's now almost forgotten relationship with Bebe Buell.

The album received extremely mixed reviews. Some attempted comprehension and understanding, but others were downright hostile. The main bone of contention was a lack of musical focus. It was criticized as being self-indulgent and lazy, and while some reviewers were wide of the mark, others were correct in identifying the overall sound as having the imprint of too many hands pressed into it. In the UK it sold almost as well as *Spike*. In the US, it didn't break into the Top Forty. Clearly, irrespective of how brilliant the album had been in theory, in practice it failed to reach the same heights as previous work. Costello reckoned that the bad reviews, especially in the UK, stemmed from critics being somehow unimpressed by his change of image. It's a notion based on a decidedly poor opinion of rock critics. Then again, perhaps he had a point.

He had convincingly altered his physical appearance to look like Catweazle as raised by The Glimmer Twins. Through it, he dug a grave, threw in his skinny runt persona, and buried it forever. Surely no one could object if he grew a beard, even if it was a particularly long one? 'It's my life and

144

my body, and if I want to fuck myself up and have a beard
and wear my hair long, that's my business,' he stressed to
Record Collector. 'That just goes to show that people only
like liberty as long as it's the kind of liberty they like. I have
my own reasons for that change of image, some of them
personal, some of them just damn wilful. I can't say that
when I look back that I think, yeah, what a great style it is.
Some of the pictures with the beard I kinda like; others I see
and think, God, you look terrible.'[2]

By now, Costello had had it with the press. With poor
reviews came an equally critical and suitably intense response
from him. Truth is, he was even more bewildered than usual
about the lack of respect afforded to his music and, by extension, to him. The problem lay in his mixture of arrogance and
contempt. Like a large number of people in his line of business and on his level, he had little respect for the opinions of
music journalists who, he felt, had no right to comment upon
something they did not understand. Their remarks, grounded
in ignorance and spite (with some honourable exceptions –
something he tended to gloss over), devalued his work in
public.

It's a moot point as to whether he was right or not, but it
culminated in his decision to give up doing promotional interviews. In mid-May, he informed *The Chicago Tribune* thus:
'I'm thirty-seven and I feel like I haven't even begun . . . I'm
finally headed towards what I do best, which is to write songs
and perform . . . I want to get away from all that other stuff,
which is why I say this could be my very last interview.'
Coming from a rock figure who is quite probably the most
aggressively articulate and eloquent of his generation, this
was quite a shock. No more interviews sparkling (and spark-
ing) with wicked bonhomie, crushing put-downs and all-round
intellectual rigour? Oh dear . . .

Within a week he was in Kitty O'Shea's pub in Dublin
talking to the Irish media about *Mighty Like A Rose*. The
about-face was not as facetious as one might think.
Costello's clear need to explain most things to as many
people as possible lay at the root of it. Besides, he was right

about aspects of the regurgitated on-file biography-cum-capsule reviews that were published each time he released a record. 'I'm not at school anymore,' he told the *Irish Press*. 'I know what I'm doing, which is more than I can say for a lot of people in this business and the music press. I ask myself, is this really part of the job description? Because it doesn't seem that way to me.'[3]

Like the series of name changes of some years back, it's possible that the radical alteration of his physical appearance was in some ways connected to his desired eradication of image, but he was caught between a rock and a hard place. His own and Riviera's physically-orchestrated PR job at puffing up his angry young man persona had been too bloody good. This previous portrayal was not allowed to be forgotten by the media, and even in his mid- to late thirties he was viewed as a man with bitter attitudes and memories. Not true, reckoned Costello. He had changed, but that didn't necessarily mean he was going to deny his past. 'Or for that matter, that you're not capable of moments of concentrated musical or literal violence and by that I don't mean physical violence,' he told me. 'If you listen to those early records now, they're fairly light-sounding. It was more to do with the attitude. Maybe those were the days when my breadth of expression was limited by circumstances and expectations.'[4]

The recurring themes of rose-with-a-thorn love, red-faced anger, and white-knuckle hate relationships, however, still refused to go away – a major reason why lazy writers still continued to play the cliché card. Some newspapers and magazines were particularly harsh about wife Cait's contribution, not only to *Mighty Like A Rose* but to Costello's life in general, wondering if the transition from 'Mr Horribly Marred to Mr Happily Married', as tagged by *NME*, had affected his quality control.

'There are so many things to sing about, y'know?' he told me for *In Dublin*. 'People say, oh no, not love again, as if . . . Well, it never stopped Shakespeare! There are a large bunch of critics who seem to imagine that the world wants to revolve around contemporary paraphernalia. Therefore, to them, the only real exponents of modern song writing are the Pet Shop Boys, who have their virtues. But to some journalists that's all it can be, it's an absolute. It's Cole Porter or Neil Tennant, and that's it. That's kinda silly. I think you should leave yourself open to everything . . .

'It's like the anger thing. It's only as useful to you as you can employ it. You can't always be in a rage about everything, a curmudgeon. I mean, why would anyone be like that? You'd just make yourself miserable. I guess there are people like that but I'm not one of them. Maybe what you learn over a period of time is how to use it, like a beam on a particular thing you're moved to write about . . . As for hate, on the evidence of *Mighty Like A Rose*, I'd have to say yes, I don't consciously invite it, it's just the way it is.'[6]

Disparate feelings or not, and distinctly diverse as it was, *Mighty Like A Rose* didn't create a huge commercial landslide. In a marketing decision that made no sense whatsoever, there was a six-month gap from the single release of 'The Other Side Of Summer' (naturally issued some weeks prior to the release of the album) to 'So Like Candy'. The smart thing to do would have been to release a single shortly after the album's release, with the hope for a slumbering summer hit. Instead, in a move equal to the commercial stupidity of releasing *Blood & Chocolate*'s 'I Want You' as a single at *any* time, the record company waited until October. Result? 'So Like Candy' didn't even chart.

'I have to admit,' said Costello, 'that none of my songs have the same sort of facile – and I mean facile in terms of easy, not inane – appeal of an MC Hammer or Vanilla Ice. I might be better looking than both of those guys, but you've got to face facts, they're writing skipping songs. I'm asking people to take a bit of time and investigate some emotion in something. What I find harder to accept is not the distance between my sales and theirs, but the notion that we have to be told [that] not only are these people very successful because they write easily digestible pieces of music, if that's what you call it, but that they're some kind of genius for doing that . . . I can't really complain. I'm not saying that

147

ELVIS COSTELLO

what I do is difficult, none of my music is difficult. Musically it's not complex. Not compared to Stravinsky it's not.'[7]

Concerts in America playing with The Replacements and Sam Phillips (spouse of T-Bone Burnette, and on whose *Cruel Inventions* album Costello guested) gave way to a UK tour and an appearance on BBC2's six-part series *Bringing It All Back Home*. The programme charted the geographical and historical development of Irish music into English and American cultures, and how, strengthened and improved by its multi-stranded journeys, it found its way back to the source. Costello's residency status in Ireland clearly had more benefits than just an artist's tax exemption. Further enthused by embracing yet another cultural source (he had already connected with traditional Irish music to a degree on *Spike*) he was now part of the growing number of 'rock' artists who began not to categorize, but to welcome different influences as part of the same common goal.

'Some of the so-called influences are quite obscure, anyway. There might be something lurking in the back of my mind that might not be apparent to anybody else – some motivating connection you're making between the song you're writing and some song you've got in your record collection. I don't see this as a big jamboree bag of influences you can dip into. It's just music. There are no barriers.'[8] This had been Costello's philosophy for some time now, the tacit approval of his record companies allowing him his many experiments. Since coming to Ireland he was only too eager, when he had the time, to assist on projects that reflected his own tastes. *Bringing It All Back Home* was such a one. In what marked the start of his recorded interest in blending a tune of some kind with classical music, he wrote a song specifically for the series. 'Mischievous Ghost' sounded like an elemental mixture of chamber music and traditional Irish melody. The orchestral arrangement is enhanced by the uileann-pipe playing of Davy Spillane and a suitably spooky refrain sung by Mary Coughlan. Typically for Costello he did not wish it to be looked upon as a strictly Irish come-all-ye song.

148

'I wanted to do something different,' he told Nuala O'Connor. 'I didn't think I had the authority to take a traditional piece and sing it my own way, so I thought I'd write something that maybe made some sort of comment on one element of the story.'[9] Described by Costello as 'a life-after-death song'[10], 'Mischievous Ghost' ran in parallel with his prickly individual take on music. The theories behind the television series and the book made sense to him. 'I started with rock 'n' roll and you don't really think of it in a scholarly way, then you start to take it apart like a child with a toy and you see that there's blues and there's country . . . Then you go back from country into American music, and you go back from American folk music and you end up in Scotland or Ireland eventually.'[11]

While working on *Mighty Like A Rose*, Costello's parallel work on the soundtrack to *GBH* continued apace. In collaboration with Richard Harvey, his knowledge of classical and orchestral music slowly grew. He didn't have a command of musical notation at this time, so Harvey would take his themes and occasionally re-orchestrate them radically, moving away from the manner that the singer originally intended. In association with Costello, Harvey must have done a good job: they were rewarded with a BAFTA Award for their troubles.

As their tastes in classical music became more and more developed, Costello and wife Cait regularly attended performances at the Wigmore Hall (András Schiff's cycle of Schubert sonatas and Bach recitals by Tatyana Nikolaeva) and the Royal Festival Hall (whenever the London Philharmonic was in session). A performance of Schoenberg's mighty *Gurrelieder* at the Festival Hall was a pivotal moment in Costello's appreciation. He thought it an overpowering, almost brutal piece, and one that he willingly caved in to. More crucial to his actual recording career, though, were the Brodsky Quartet's recitals of the Shostakovich Cycle at London's Queen Elizabeth Hall, which he had first attended in 1989.

The Quartet took its name from their Russian violinist

tutor, Adolf Brodsky, whilst its four members (brother and sister Michael and Jacqueline Thomas, Ian Belton and Paul Cassidy, who is married to Jacqueline) met while studying in Manchester in 1977. The members of the group had seen Costello in concert several times from the late 1970s (noting that The Attractions also had a couple of members with the Thomas surname), but the experience wasn't immediately reciprocated, with Costello being somewhat busy carving out a reputation for himself.

Over the years, the Quartet expanded their repertoire through noted compositions from Beethoven to George Crumb via Mozart, Schubert and Delius. Known in classical circles as a group who have effectively rewritten the guide book of chamber-music etiquette, they decline to wear white tie and tails in favour of designer clothes by Issey Miyake (at whose Paris fashion shows they have provided the music). For encores, they occasionally play old Dave Brubeck numbers. And they've worked with Iceland's sister strange, Björk, and Costello co-writer Paul McCartney.

The intersection of the Quartet and Costello occurred when a friend of the group ventured backstage after a concert in the early 1990s to inform them that he had been sitting beside Elvis Costello throughout the entire performance. Startled by such news, it became more and more obvious to the Quartet that the singer was attending their concerts on a regular basis. By this time, they had broken the ice somewhat by exchanging CDs. This contact was strengthened by a mutual friend at Warners (the Brodskys were also on the label) who arranged a convenient meeting after a lunchtime recital at the South Bank in November 1991. Repairing to a nearby wine bar, Costello and the Quartet sowed the seeds for future collaboration. After agreeing to work together on a musical project, they arranged to meet informally over a brief period of time, doing nothing but chatting about their respective musical tastes and interests, and playing each other pieces of music they respected and loved. Generally speaking, they were just sounding each other out.

At first, the Brodsky Quartet held Costello slightly in awe.

Underlying that initial feeling was the fact that they knew he had respect for what they did. As the meetings went on, they realized that there was no sense whatsoever in which they were in diametrically opposite factions, and there was no thought of the project being misunderstood by anyone as being a selection of Elvis Costello songs backed by classical musicians. From the very beginning, it was understood that they would work together as a quintet, and that the songs would be written be for the string quartet.

Used to working with musicians with whom he had a natural empathy and dynamic, he was careful not to dent the extremely taut unit of the Brodskys. 'It was a bit like being Mick Taylor joining The Rolling Stones,' he observed in *Q*. 'And finding that Bill and Keith are married. And Charlie and Mick are really brother and sister . . . Inevitably, there are things between the Quartet that I can't gatecrash . . . but it's not like, oh, the singer's arrived. I think we get on great.'[12]

Before he attended the Quartet's Shostakovich concerts, Costello knew nothing about them. He didn't fully comprehend the music (let alone any other type of classical music) but he could see in their exceptional playing a couple of aspects that he could relate to: a singular dedication to the music, and a different-but-the-same presence on stage that was comparable to the magnetism of great rock 'n' roll performers. 'Two things really hit me with equal force,' Costello said in the *Irish Times* of the first time he witnessed The Brodsky Quartet. 'One was the obvious intensity of their performance. And I think that people who find classical music a closed book to them simply miss the "personality" aspect which is sometimes all there is in pop music. Shostakovich's later string quartets, on the other hand, vividly reflect the fact that he had endured a form of living death during the Stalin era. And it made me realize that any perceived repression that has ever been visited on rock 'n' roll is tiny compared to the conditions under which his music was composed.

'Likewise, Shostakovich's string quartets also reveal any perceived rebellion in rock 'n' roll to be the foot-stomping nonsense much of it is . . . Shostakovich was trying to create art in conditions of such emotional and political repression that it is little wonder his works are still so powerful and potent. I'm not necessarily saying that they are superior to forms of self-expression in folk or blues, but they are not the same thing. And on some intrinsic, personal level I responded to those quartets with the same excitement I'd feel on hearing a great Billie Holiday or Hank Williams song, that also seemed to embody some sort of unspoken spirit. It really was a revelation to me.'[13]

When he first met the Quartet, Costello couldn't read or write music. By the beginning of 1992, he could. Undoubtedly, their collaboration was facilitated by his decision to learn how. Partly brought on through his partnership with Richard Harvey on the soundtrack to *GBH* – 'I got slightly frustrated by not being able to be more help to Richard by saying, look, this is exactly how it goes and it should be these instruments . . .'[14] – and by a considerable appetite for the challenge of actually doing it, thereby edging further into another phase of his own musical development, Costello liaised with an Irish composer in Dublin and took a intense course in learning the process. He mastered musical notation quickly, starting in November 1991, when he knew not what a coloratura was, to the end of January 1992, when he could write a foolscap four-part. Soon after he was sending the Quartet his ideas on paper. According to the group, he completed in a couple of months what some people take years to achieve.

'I found out, well, this isn't a bad system,' Costello told *Rolling Stone*. 'No wonder we've been using it for 700 years. The disciplined aspect of writing down allows you to have more abandon inside that structure. The Brodsky String Quartet is never going to be as loud as a rock 'n' roll band, but it wields an attack in its own way.'[15] Of course, advance word on the project was met with raised eyebrows in both the rock and classical worlds. Memories of failed and intriguing experiments between the two disciplines had filled record-shop bargain bins from as far back as the mid-'60s. But it went further back than that. Classical melodies were ravaged by Tin Pan Alley songsmiths from the earliest days of recorded sound. Written in 1888, Borodin's *Polovetsian Dances* was adapted into 'Stranger In Paradise' (a hit in 1955 for Bing Crosby, and a UK No. 1 smash for Tony Bennett).

Towards the end of his life Buddy Holly had recorded with *pizzicato* strings. However, in 1959, Jerry Leiber and Mike Stoller created what was probably the very first successful true cross-pollination of rock 'n' roll and classical music when The Drifters' 'There Goes My Baby' reached No. 2 in the US charts. The song weaved textures and harmonies from classical music into a rock context, creating the blueprint for later experiments that became the byword for pop sophistication. Some of these were just as, if not more successful. The Beatles (icons of the pop/classical crossover) through classically-trained producer George Martin, added a string quartet to 'Yesterday'. Shortly after, Martin, inspired by Bernard Herrmann's score for François Truffaut's film *Fahrenheit 451*, utilized a more daring arrangement for 'Eleanor Rigby' (with Paul McCartney's suggestion of using an idea or two from Vivaldi overridden by Martin).

Other rock bands and pop acts followed suit: The Rolling Stones used strings, Phil Spector's Wall of Sound created 'symphonic' vignettes, Deep Purple raided the concerto form, The Who recorded a rock 'opera' and ELO drew on Copeland, Sibelius, Mussorgski and Ginastera. The concept reached its nadir in the progressive rock era when pretentiousness and drug use weakened what could have been decent ideas. Interestingly, though, Gryphon – four Royal College of Music students – was commissioned by the National Theatre's Sir Peter Hall to compose a piece based on the band's perplexing mix of progressive rock and mediaeval music. The band were fronted by one Richard Harvey . . .

Following the Electric Light Orchestra, no classical composer was safe from the pillaging of rock 'n' pop types, who generally debased both forms of music by haphazardly

153

slapping some strings behind cack-handed rock 'n' roll or ersatz pop. It worked both ways, however. Most examples of classical or operatic names colliding with pop tunes could hardly be described as musical delights, as listening to Kiri Te Kanawa's 'Blue Skies', with the Nelson Riddle Orchestra, or Placido Domingo's 'The Broadway I Love' confirms. In current rock and pop terms, the use of classical music in a contemporary format is not at all unusual, while the regular use of strings in country music has for decades sugared the otherwise bitter domestic subject matter of the genre. Many rock bands have used a string quartet or mini orchestra on stage. Of course, some do it just to have women in slinky black numbers with cellos between their legs. Others (notably The Divine Comedy, The Verve and Tindersticks) apply the basic principles of pop/classical notation in a somewhat more exhilarating way. At the time of Costello's creative marriage with the Brodsky Quartet, there was very little in pop and rock's frame of reference with such ambition. The reason for this is simple: no one had either the will or the knowledge of the reference points.

'I'm not fed up with rock groups,' Costello explained in the *Guardian* of his supposed two-finger salute to the rock establishment, 'only fed up with the concerts. I kept going to concerts and it would be the same ritual happening. Even with artists I liked, there would be moments of inspiration but nobody seemed to take many chances. Therefore it almost becomes like a holy rite, but without the quality to really justify that.'[16]

Of course, the other aspect the participants had to contend with was the breaking down of the already weakened barriers between the two forms of music. Critically, sniffy noses were put out of joint whenever rock musicians such as Frank Zappa and Paul McCartney (whose own *Liverpool Oratorio*, commented *The Times*, made 'Brahms's Requiem* seem like a hotbed of syncopation') seriously attempted to create a piece of music outside the constraints of their own perceived rock or pop domain. Clearly, the complaining masses were missing the point: that rock music was no longer the preserve of the under-thirties any more than classical music was the sanctuary of the over-sixties. The outcome of the project, both sides felt, was that it would help to open up paths of discovery for everyone. And so it turned out to be.

At first, it wasn't certain what form the collaborative work would take, but after Cait O'Riordan showed her husband a newspaper clipping about a curious academic in Verona who had taken it upon himself to act as respondent to letters addressed to 'Juliet Capulet', bells in the bright-ideas department of Costello's brain started clanging. Why not, he proposed, co-write a sequence of songs based on an unconnected stream of letters? Slowly the idea was put into in practice. The first test was for the five people involved, aided by Michael Thomas' wife, Marina, to go home and return the next day with a suicide note. The words and music were eventually worked out over a prolonged period of time. Other types of communication and correspondence – love letters, graffiti, postcards, a scrawled child's note, a begging letter, even a seance session – were considered. By relying on each of the members' voices to provide a particularly rounded and equal collaboration, with Costello acting as onsite editor, slowly but surely the lyrics were fashioned. The music was also written in a democratic manner, with Costello not missing a trick of the trade, cutely grafting motifs from the soundtrack of *GBH* on to some of the tracks.

Prior to the album being released, Costello and the Brodsky Quartet presented the music live at two concerts, one in the UK and one in Ireland. 'The first time we went out 'live' with Elvis,' recalled Paul Cassidy in *Q* 'and this was after months of working on *The Juliet Letters*, we came off at the interval and he turned round to us and said, "Shit, what are you doing out there? It's so loud . . ." As soon as we got on a stage, with the adrenalin and so on, the volume went up about ten times, and he just couldn't believe it – he who'd been standing in the middle of The Attractions for fifteen years!'[17]

Playing at a summer school at Dartington Hall in Devon,

where the Brodskys were quartet in residence, they were pleased to find people embracing what they heard, rather than dismissing it as a gimmick on either the rock or classical side. Classical music snobs would have been well advised to leave their prejudices at the door. 'Those people can't create anything,' said Costello, talking to the *Irish Times*. 'All they do is go to cocktail parties and bitch about things. And if they can't accept something that's done wholeheartedly they should go see a doctor. And any rock fan who thinks *The Juliet Letters* is 'po faced', having truthfully entered into the spirit of the thing, really has a problem with their own conceptions about music and art in general.'[18]

In Dublin's Gate Theatre where the performance was being recorded for future broadcasting by award-winning Irish film-maker Philip King, fur coats rubbed shoulders with biker jackets. The resulting album, *The Juliet Letters*, was released in January 1993. Subtitled 'a song sequence for string quartet and voice', the album passed by many rock reviewers, who failed to see it as an extension of Costello's inbuilt risk factor and an apparently limitless search for change. The grumpiest of them, however, irrespective of whether or not they liked the music, couldn't help but fail to agree on one thing: that the record employed Costello's most coherent and themed set of songs since *King Of America*. Naturally, pulsating with equal measures of indignation, defensiveness and ire, he didn't give a damn what the critics thought.

'I can't be bothered to think about people who have some vision of me as a pop singer or a rock 'n' roll singer and that this should prohibit me from entering into collaboration with so-called serious musicians,' he said in *Q*. 'I'm a serious musician . . . I don't see this as a classical or pop record. It's a record of some songs we've written, and it's there for anyone who'll listen. They'll be disappointed if they expect to find *Death And The Maiden* by Schubert, or equally if they want to find some cherished record of mine, if such a thing exists. They may be disappointed if they come expecting a certain sound they have fixed in their heads as "what I do". But of course I haven't exactly stayed with the one sound over the years anyway.

'Anyone who's really followed what I do would be ready to expect something different. I'm just looking for something inspiring. I defy anyone to find a calculated angle to it. There is no Achilles heel of ambition over content here which you see so much of in collaborative things.'[19]

The idea of art having to be intricate and abstruse was rendered null and void on *The Juliet Letters*. That's not to say the unashamedly individualistic songs weren't challenging to the ear. On a superficial level, the actual sound of the record was smooth, although a few of the songs (notably 'Swine', 'Damnation Alley' and 'This Offer Is Unrepeatable') veered dangerously close to string-heavy Stravinsky and forced comic operetta. Occasionally, although he didn't need to battle against the low-frequency instruments, thus making the performances more intimate than he was used to, Costello's voice lost confidence. For anyone who cared to scratch under the surface, however, the majority of *The Juliet Letters* was expressive, extremely moving and poignant in its lyrics, music and voice. It was also blessed with wit, in a style Costello had never before shown, and some of the best tunes he had been associated with for many years.

While some felt that his previous two records for Warners had been lathered with praise beyond their actual worth, the irony with *The Juliet Letters* is that no matter how good some reviewers felt it was, or knew it to be, it wouldn't garner the same degree of acclaim, simply because it wasn't a rock album. For those who considered it bad, and Costello's involvement in it a betrayal of his punk roots, they were simply missing the point by a mile. Sniping at Costello was one thing – he could, after all, take care of himself in the small-minded world of rock criticism. Those who criticized the Brodsky Quartet were, however, about to sink in quicksand of their own making. Costello wrote the guilty parties a stinging letter. 'There's a certain responsibility on my part to stand up for my collaborators because they're drawn into a petty-minded media position which is informed entirely by my back history, not theirs,' he told *NME*. 'Perhaps it was ill-advised to write, you should probably always be above it. But . . . I got furious because I felt it was unfair to those guys. They didn't ask for any of that shit, or some tired old hack . . . taking us to task, trying to pretend to be dangerous . . .'[20]

In truth, *The Juliet Letters*' boldness and originality set it aside from the norm, where the only connection to the rock world was the amount of media promotion involved. 'It has a life of its own,' he said to *Record Collector*, 'whether or not somebody who writes for the *Melody Maker* likes it. What does that matter? They should be writing about seventeen year olds, not me. I would much prefer it if none of them ever mentioned my name again. Because, frankly, they don't understand what I'm doing. They pretend they know the answer to everything, and when they get to where I am, they'll know they don't know, just as I had to learn that I didn't know everything. Why not celebrate the stuff they do like, and stop wasting their pencils on something they don't understand?'[21]

Warners are not on record as to what they thought of their investment veering so radically away from his usual, eclectic base (nor for that matter are the thoughts of his manager, Jake Riviera, in the public domain), but one might presume, going on his track record, that they weren't exactly over-joyed. At the outset, Costello described the idea to Warner Brothers President, Lenny Waronker, who answered, 'well, that sounds interesting,'[22] a reply that, depending on the tone of voice used, could have meant just about anything.

Ultimately, be it diplomatic or not, Costello credited Warners with having the maturity and the imagination to put out a record that had no obviously defined marketing nor commercial thrust. It has since sold over 300,000 copies, and is still in music industry terms a catalogue item; it sells more than *Spike*, the record perceived to be his most commercially successful. The album also received a full-scale adaptation by the Gothenburg Opera in Sweden in the autumn of 1995. Not bad for an 'interesting' idea. Maintaining that the company liked what they heard, his anxiety lay not with whatever expectations of record sales there would be, but with the type of feeling the audience received when sitting down and listening to the music. It was the only thing that mattered to him. His strong personal belief that music should not be analysed, but should be allowed to take effect with little or no intellectual analysis, was at the base of *The Juliet Letters*. Aside from this, he cared not a bit about any other aspect of the project, least of all where the money was coming from.

'Compared to the money they're throwing out on people like Madonna, it's nothing, it's pocket money,' he told *Musician*.[23] Which is exactly what the US public didn't spend on *The Juliet Letters*, the first album of Costello's career not to chart there. Time to switch back to the kind of strings they're more used to, then.

CHAPTER 9

*'Riding the crest of a wave is a dangerous feeling to take
seriously. The minute you think you're indestructible you
will be destroyed. That's a lesson I had to learn . . .'*
                    Wendy James, interviewed by the author for
                    The Sunday Tribune, *March 1993*

Q: *'Do you listen to techno?'*
A: *'What for? Isn't it something that you have to experience in a certain situation? I don't go to those places,
why should I bother to buy the records? It's not really
designed to be listened to, it's designed to be experienced
at high volume in an environment that I wouldn't choose
to visit. It can't teach me anything about music and it's not
emotional. That's the whole point of it.'*
                    Elvis Costello, interviewed by Adrian Deevoy,
                    Q, *April 1994*

*'We've got a culture now where everybody wants to turn all
the great stuff down into the pygmy world. I would rather
say, listen, just accept it: It's a better world that there is a
Beethoven, that there is Little Richard, that there is
Picasso and James Joyce; and it's a better world that
Apache Indian recorded 'Boom Shak A Lak' because I dig
it. It might not be the record I want played at my funeral.
Then again, maybe it is.'*
                    Interview with Alan Corr, RTE Guide, *March 1994*

In August 1991, Elvis Costello and The Attractions played on
a Gaelic football pitch in Semple Stadium, Thurles, Co

Tipperary. The event was the then-annual, self-styled Trip To Tipp, a three-day music festival that initially featured a large contingent of Irish rock groups. However, in order to ensure its continued success, the festival began to pull in players from the international arena, contracting medium-size and bigger performers to play up in the bill as well as to headline over the three nights. Starting in 1990, the Trip To Tipp (or Feile, as it's known) became the first extended rock festival in Ireland since the early 1980s, and was generally recognized as the only opportunity for the 'kids' to let their hair down and throw up all over their shoes while listening to relatively decent rock music.

On the bill alongside Costello that year was Transvision Vamp, a band who were reviled by the rock press for being a cheap and diluted imitation of various more credible pop and punk-rock bands. Such hatred appeared to be a violent reaction against a group who knew their pop history and who wanted be part of it. Put simply, the band desired to combine the visionary ideals of Velvet Underground, The Stooges and the trash aesthetic of pop art with the pop principles of Marc Bolan and the punk-rock energy of The Clash. The result was a mishmash of plundered styles that threw up some fairly enjoyable hit singles, but little else. In a nutshell, there was little substance amid lots of vacuous panting and pouting.

The p&p element of the band belonged to lead singer Wendy James, a female pop star who talked herself up to be something a lot bigger than she was. In the heady chart-bound years (1988–91) of Transvision Vamp, Wendy was the cover girl, her pronounced sex-kitten imagery and 'what me?' naiveté gaining more acres of print than was subsequently good for her. For some reason, Wendy, not by any means an unintelligent woman, wanted to be on the cover of everything, including *Variety* – when she held the Oscar that she misguidedly said in an interview she would one day receive. She stopped short of trying for *Angling Monthly* and *Gardening Weekly*, but, if push came to shove, and push she had, she could have got them.

161

'At the end of that phase, press reviews hardly even mentioned the music,' she moaned. 'I felt like a schizophrenic, because there appeared to be some other person alive in the eyes of the media. It was *The Face* cover that hit the final nail in the coffin. That killed off Wendy James in my mind.'[1] The cover in question featured Wendy wearing a string of strategically-placed pearls. She draped her body with the pearls because she says she wanted to be tremendously arty. In the long run, it was a decision she was to regret. A similar risqué appearance under the lens of David Bailey for *Tatler* was another.

While Elvis Costello and The Attractions were on stage at Semple Stadium, James stood in the wings listening to music that she clearly far preferred to her own. The fact is, despite a public reputation to the contrary, things weren't going too well for Transvision Vamp in 1991. They'd already had two very successful albums, *Pop Art* in 1988 and *Velveteen* a year later both reached the UK Top Five. Halfway through 1991, however, there had already been a couple of singles that were noticeably less popular than previous outings. With an album (the not exactly succinctly-titled *The Little Magnets Versus The Bubble Of Babble*) in the can but held back by the band's record company, it looked as if their time was up. Besides, when James witnessed Costello and The Attractions in action, she realized she wanted to be involved in something both more organically exciting and honest.

'It got harder to sing the songs with any conviction,' she told Giles Smith for *Q*. 'Bubblegum is fine when you're a teenager, but as I got older it wasn't ringing true. With no disrespect to songs like 'Baby, I Don't Care', I couldn't sing that song anymore, because I wanted to say, I do care, and these are all the things I care about . . . I had no solution to this at that point. I would just start calling things shit and getting negative about everything.'[2]

Following the band's Irish gig, they set about plugging the singles and the forthcoming album in a series of concerts, some of which were in America. In late 1991, at about the same time as Costello was grooving on a different riff with the Brodsky Quartet, Wendy was in Los Angeles conducting pre-publicity media interviews on her own. Also in the same city, by sheer coincidence, was Attractions' drummer Pete Thomas. The two bumped into each other in the course of work and Wendy, who had never actually met or previously talked to Costello, asked Pete if the singer would be able to help her out on a possible solo career. Even at this time, the seeds of a different musical path were taking root in James' head, and she needed sound advice if she were to make a credible impression. James didn't know if Costello had ever heard Transvision Vamp, let alone liked them. Even allowing for his eclectic tastes it's unlikely that he would have gotten off on 'Psychosonic Cindy' or 'Vid Kid Vamp'. Then again, with Costello one never knew.

To his credit (and as someone who knew His Master's Voice better than most), Pete Thomas didn't dismiss the query as the final request of a dying pop star. Instead, he thought it would do no harm to write Costello a letter. In Washington DC soon afterwards, where the Transvision Vamp US tour was starting, Wendy did just that. 'I'm not a big letter writer, but I think I can script a fairly good one if I have to. It was a bit like a letter to an agony aunt. I wrote down all the reasons why I wasn't really a happy person, not with my emotional life, but with my musical life. It would have served me as a diary if I hadn't posted it. But I sent it off and fatalistically tore up my copy the next morning, thinking, well, you're living in cloud cuckoo land. Not that I asked him for any specific help. I simply said, "I need to get better, and you're what I consider is better. So can something be done?" '3

Nothing was heard by James for over a fortnight, but when news came through via Pete Thomas and Costello's publisher that he had written a complete album for her, you could say it shook her world just a little bit. Costello isn't on record as to the exact reasons why he did this for James (although he rigidly denies the notion that he did it as a bet), and James isn't fully sure, either. 'I'm sure Elvis saw all manner of reasons to reply,' was Wendy's measured comment when I

163

interviewed her. 'As much as the idea in the first place to contact Elvis was off the cuff, I'm sure his response to write an album for me was totally off the top of his head. If the idea had been written down on paper and gone through with lawyers and business managers, it wouldn't have happened.'[4]

The possibility that Costello himself was working on a sequence of songs based on different forms of letters might just have added weight to his involvement. It certainly would have appealed to his sense of irony, responding to a genuine, pleasantly-written, begging letter. Another likely and more simplistic reason is that he just wanted to help her, albeit perhaps in a brash pop-Svengali fashion. The plan was marked out thus: he and Pete Thomas would initially do the songs up as a one run-through demo album over a couple of days while Transvision Vamp were on tour in the States. With a bad head cold, Costello double-tracked his voice and played bass, guitar and piano on the slower material while Thomas played drums. It would be waiting for her when she returned to Britain at the tour's end, and if she liked it then it was hers for the taking.

'I didn't want to give her one song to put amongst all this cartoon punk,' said Costello in *Record Collector*. 'I was up for writing a whole album of cartoon punk songs for her . . . It would give her a whole story. I always thought she was much more of an actress than a singer, anyway, so it was an acting role for her.'[5] Due to the time constraints regarding Costello's work with the Brodsky Quartet, the writing of Wendy's album had to be completed very quickly. Costello and his wife went to a nearby park from their London base, where, over a weekend, they completed the words and music. The songs were loosely based on certain aspects of Wendy's life, based on her correspondence with him and whatever information he had of her from sifting through music magazines and TV chat shows.

By the end of 1991, Transvision Vamp had finished its tour of America, but the death knell was sounding and the band split up in the process (guitarist Dave Parsons eventually went on to find far greater success in the US and Britain with Bush). James came home to her London flat, where, weary from jetlag and depressed at how 1992 might look, she found the neatly-packaged demo tape waiting for her. 'I was dying for the first chord to come,' she told *Q*. 'When it did there was this really great riff, played by Elvis with the guitar cranked up full volume. It was a very rough demo . . . The third track (on the demo) was a ballad, and I thought I'd landed in heaven. It was a one-woman fan club in my living room right there.'[6]

James listened to the tape up to six times, astonished at the accuracy at which Costello and O'Riordan (who was able to give a perspective of what it was like to be a woman in the music business) had pinpointed various facets of her life. The trappings of cool, the hypocrisy of self, and the need to remove oneself from the lig 'n' gig circuit were exposed in the lyrics. Despite the swift weekend execution of the songs they were neither throwaway nor old. Inevitably, there wasn't a single song in which Wendy James was let off the hook regarding her past. Well, she did ask . . .

Contacting Costello's publisher to say she wanted the songs for herself, James recorded the album, *Now Ain't The Time For Your Tears* (a Dylan rip-off title), with Chris Kimsey. Kimsey, who engineered a number of Rolling Stones records, kept it rough, raw, and very much in line with the truthful thrust of the lyrics. In fact, Costello would later criticize the production for having Wendy's voice too far in front of the music. He felt it would have worked better if her vocals had been mixed down within an even rougher sound. The album was released in March 1993 to a universally critical thumbs-down. Commercially, it didn't fare much better. Two singles from it, 'The Nameless One' and 'London's Brilliant' were moderate hits. The album itself reached No. 43 in the UK album charts on 20 March. By the end of that month it had dropped out. 'I knew she had a bit of a challenge on her hands, but that was the whole point,' Costello noted realistically, in *Record Collector*. 'If you go round telling the world that you're going to win an Oscar and dominate the world and all the things she foolishly said – though you've got to give her credit for the front she always had – then when that doesn't come off, you've got to develop a sense of humour. I think the songs were probably my attempt to provide her with the platform for that. I can't say she really got the joke all the time, but she did as creditable a job . . . you know, nobody ever said she was Maria Callas. There was no pretending . . . It was a fumbled opportunity. But not my opportunity.'[7]

According to Aimée Mann, with whom Costello co-wrote 'The Other End Of The Telescope' for her erstwhile band 'Til Tuesday, Costello was surprised that Wendy James agreed to record the songs 'because the story told isn't exactly flattering. I think those are some of his best lyrics but she didn't really do a great job on them. Her voice could be so perfectly charming if she didn't try so hard to . . . emote,' she told *Hot Press*.[8] So did Costello ever get to meet Wendy James, having written a set of custom-made songs as an exercise in Tin Pan Alley techniques? Only once. Backstage in the VIP tent at a U2 concert in London, where the connection between all the well-known faces present was U2, but not any particular familiarity or overt friendliness, James spotted Costello sitting in a corner. Still quite bemused about why he'd written the album, she made her way over to him to find out.

'We were given an introduction,' recollected Wendy in *Q*, 'and obviously I said thank you . . . He wished me luck and said have a good time. And that was the conversation. There really isn't any more to it than that. Strange. Strange but true.'[9] Costello and Pete Thomas recorded the demo material for Wendy James' album in Pathway Studios, in North London, the small eight-track recording facility where he made *My Aim Is True*. When Pete and he had completed the demo sessions, Costello was inspired to write and record several songs for his own needs. Hence began the route which led to the reformation of The Attractions.

The Pathway material had Costello playing all the instruments except the drums, which Pete Thomas looked after. Realizing that he and Pete could produce and make a whole album's worth of songs, the work continued. In the rock music equivalent of gathering the Magnificent Seven together for a final fling, Costello soon after bumped into Steve Nieve, who was working on a session for soul singer Sam Moore. Costello hadn't seen Nieve for some time (the keyboard player had been composing jingles and playing alongside Pete Thomas in Jonathan Ross' TV show house band for several seasons), but they got talking. The end result was a request by 'the Singer' for 'the Keyboard Player' to come down to Pathway Studios to add some piano to the freshly-written material.

More songs were written in such a way that Costello initially asked Nick Lowe to play bass on them, suited as they were to his particular style. Lowe professed to be uneasy with the shape of a couple of songs, dubbing those gathered there The Distractions, and leaving Costello to ponder whom he should ask to take over bass duties for those specific songs. By this time, Costello realised that he wasn't up for producing the album himself, so he contacted his old Costello Show chum Mitchell Froom to do the honours. Froom, who was working on recordings with his wife Suzanne Vega, was also working with Attractions bassist, Bruce Thomas. What happened next was a surprise to many.

Costello and Thomas had not been on talking terms for a couple of years. Bruce's book *The Big Wheel* was justifiably dismissed by Costello as petty, while Thomas himself had been on the end of a similarly stinging retort in 'How To Be Dumb'. Call it what you will – a show of maturity, a softening of the edges, a deliberate lapse in memory. However, Costello asked if Bruce would be interested in playing bass on the new material. The short and simple answer was yes.

The last time The Attractions had played on a record with Costello was *Blood & Chocolate*, a fraught affair ending up in a mess that, in theory at least, reflected the album title. Costello later admitted that he didn't handle the 'situation' very graciously. Without room for negotiation, he had announced he was leaving the set-up. Apparently, one of the main reasons was that he thought they were stagnating

167

musically. Two tours in a row, he reckoned, didn't show any pronounced signs of improvement. A tad arrogant, perhaps?

'Obviously there was tension with everybody,' he told *Record Collector*. 'We were always grumpy, and now we're older we're actually a little bit less grumpy than we used to be. We're quite different as people. There's this illusion that bands grew up together or lived in a house together. But we put the band together through auditions and connections with the business and it just happened to gel . . . We had no real reason to spend so much time together. We weren't naturally compatible socially and it was obviously forced on us that we spend this tremendous amount of time together. It was almost inevitable that we would end up falling out in some way. We probably fell out less dramatically than many other groups and consequently we've been able to just put it all to one side. We've never even really discussed the past and what anybody said about somebody else. It's irrelevant really and terribly boring for the people who weren't paying attention to every thing that you were doing along the way.'[10]

The Pathway Studios was a throwback to the old days of tape hiss and console noise. While his three previous studio albums had been sound orchestrated or 'scored' through use of twenty-four-track recording facilities (causing heated debate among the trainspotter element of his fans), Pathway's humble eighttrack suited and helped to define the consciously spontaneous sound of the demos. Having achieved the kind of sound they wanted, thirteen tracks for the subsequent record, now with the working title of *Brutal Youth*, were recorded at Olympia Studios. Two others, 'Kinder Murder' and '20% Amnesia' were remnants of the Pathway sound.

In the lead up to the record's release Warners pushed the Attractions angle, despite the fact that there had been no specific plan on Costello's part to regroup. Making the demos for the Wendy James album had given him the idea of an essentially back-to-basics, no-irony approach, and as that was the way the songs were developing, the logic of using The Attractions seemed right at the time. Warners, however, were conveniently juxtaposing the words 'Elvis Costello' and 'the Attractions' in its promotional material. After eight years apart they were together again! The 'comeback' had finally arrived! Costello was wise to the marketing trick . . .

'It's a common way of selling anything. How many times has Bob Dylan been back? If you have one period of your career that everybody points to and says, that's when they were hot, then the record companies will always try and associate you with that. It was a lazy way out I think everybody at the company recognizes that now. We were going through the beginnings of . . . upheaval, the corporate insanity at Warners, which affected everything at the company. It gave the troops of the company much less leeway to be creative. Therefore, they grabbed hold of the one thing they saw as a saleable feature, which was, hey, the band is back and they're rockin'! It's a bit of a simplification.'[10]

Irrespective of whether it was a simplification or not, or whether the marketing idea of Costello being with The Attractions worked (despite the band name not appearing on the album), *Brutal Youth* was released in March 1994 to huge acclaim. In the UK, it was Costello's most successful record and highest chart placing (No. 2) since *Get Happy!!* The selling point of The Attractions was irrelevant – the songs proved to be the ultimate litmus test. The fact that The Attractions were playing was merely an added bonus.

For a Costello fan raised on a diet of the first four furious platters, *Brutal Youth* was a long, strange trip back to the halcyon time of their thin years. For the more fickle Costello follower, who had begun to drift around the time of *Almost Blue*, but gave him the benefit of the doubt, who thought he had lost it with *Goodbye Cruel World*, and who had given up on him completely when *The Juliet Letters* came out, *Brutal Youth* was a head-on reaffirmation of his talents. Simply put, it was immeasurably more straightforward than his previous three experimental and ambitious records. It was also far more naturally enjoyable and accessible. Costello is of the opinion that one experimental record after another eventually led to *Brutal Youth*, an organic creative evolvement, in a sequence of which he was justly proud.

169

Brutal Youth's character was one of tart directness, a real live combo sound, and an example of what occurs when greater ambitions take second place to urgency. On this occasion there was no loss of quality control, rather a replacement of sophistication with immediate content. With the sounds achieved at Pathway and Olympic studios, the sparse instrumentation and the lack of Costello's penchant for sound 'scoring', all of the songs were frank and combustible examples of his craft. Less time than usual had gone into the material (he wrote six of the record's songs in one day) and not as much considered thought. Result? His best, best-loved and most vital collection of songs since *King Of America*. Using the basic fabrics of rock 'n' roll – bass, drums, guitars, and a curled lip – Costello harangued and hassled as well as he had always done. The beard and the violins were gone.

'The beard freaked people out,' he ruminated in *NME*. 'The beard was seen like, "Oh, he's lost his mind". It was also my turn. I was comparatively bulletproof until *Mighty Like A Rose*. Even *Spike*, when a lot of people freaked out and said it was overambitious or pretentious or whatever. Who cares? I like it! 750,000 people like it, so you can go fuck yourself, basically! But I do mean it quite literally, the beard did alarm people . . . Whether I like it or not, some people see me as representative of some time or attitude, that I've got to be angry or on the edge, and if I've got a beard . . . that represents something else. Are people as easily fooled as that? People always want their artist to be tortured. I'm harder on myself than anyone can be . . . It's this idea that I have to live up to something, it only comes from people that maybe worry a little bit too hard, 'cos they've been paying attention all along and they feel you owe them something. There's nothing in my contract anywhere with myself, with the devil that says I have to mean anything to anybody but myself.'[11]

Harking back to the method he and The Attractions used on their early records, effectively working by previous example, whereby a proven genre or a certain song serves as a common point of departure – sampling in its broadest sense

– the songs on *Brutal Youth* had particular reference points, some of which only the band and songwriter could connect with. Through these points The Attractions and Costello, who had never actually jotted down any musical ideas for each other, could communicate with each other. According to Costello, for instance, 'This Year's Girl' is based on the Rolling Stones' *Aftermath* track, 'Stupid Girl', not so much musically, but thematically. On *My Aim Is True*, there are songs similarly based on Velvet Underground, Byrds or Motown tunes. The references might not be obvious to most listeners, but in Costello's mind they're there. On *Brutal Youth*, the same applies. The Faces were in his mind for 'Just About Glad', while '20% Amnesia' is, according to an interview in *Pulse!*, meant to sound like 'a cross between Prokofiev and the Rolling Stones'.[12]

One of the treats of *Brutal Youth* is the lyrics, which work in a relatively logical way compared to previous records. Unlike the music, the stories they tell aren't necessarily direct (and he naturally leaves ambiguities and puns lying about like verbal land mines) but he has certainly outgrown his irritating habit of presenting to the listener an interesting idea only to drop it in mid-air. Costello never allowed wayward storylines to get in the way of a good song, and uses the jack the laddisms of 'Just About Glad' to explain why. 'It depends if people are really willing to give themselves over to it,' he continued in *Pulse!* 'If I wanted to put it all on a plate, then I wouldn't have written it like that. I'm always amazed when people criticize that kind of change of person speaking, or some obscure detail to the imagery that maybe is designed to be more evocative than directly communicating something. Do you not think that I knew I was doing that? It wasn't laziness or an accident. There are sections where things become vague, but they're calculated to be vague. More curious people respond to that as a stimulus to their imagination rather than an affront to their logic. I also got accused by the *New York Times* of not having a coherent world view. I thought, "What do you mean, like Hitler? Or George Bush?" '[13]

171

Brutal Youth put Costello back in favour with the critics, and his new-found admirers among the public gave him confidence that, once again, he could change direction and not have to worry about the critical fallout. Yet he still had to be marketed with an image of some kind. What irked Costello most about this process was that his changes of image were being misinterpreted as continuous and conscious reinventions, made in an effort to clinch new audiences. It was a fairly natural assumption to make, but wide of the mark nonetheless. A large number of rock stars other than Costello have been far more ruthless in following their commercial instincts. Costello has always been prepared to lose a section of his fanbase by releasing a record that doesn't find favour with them. There are millions of other folk out there, and he is sure in the knowledge that new fans will gradually emerge. Furthermore, some of those who fell by the wayside will grow to understand the thinking that leads him towards one style of music rather than another. This can always lead to the return of the prodigal admirer to the fold.

'The notion of reinventing yourself is just one of those pathetic journalistic words,' he said to the *Telegraph Magazine*. 'I first heard it applied to David Bowie and he very consciously invented theatrical characters. I don't see how it links with me, I'm just different, I get stuck on a certain kind of music and it becomes the overriding interest. That obviously influences the kind of life I'm living and in some cases it might influence the way I look. You don't necessarily go and get a new set of clothes because you're listening to a particular kind of music, but something about your frame of mind filters through to your dress.'[14]

It's quite likely that the majority of those who automatically buy the next Elvis Costello record are in their thirties and forties. Teenagers when Costello first came to prominence, they started leaving school and university in the years that CDs began to take over from vinyl, a time when their ideals were being challenged by real life. They have grown away from the mood of musical change that thrived in the late 1970s – not that everyone of that age was touched by the hand of punk rock – and they see in Costello a figure who has refused to change for the sake of a hit record. They see in him a person who, in the face of rock-music marketing, has, in an extremely singular way, stuck to the fundamental tenet of punk – do what you fucking well want to. The fact that Costello emerged alongside, rather than within, punk rock when he was in his early twenties, appropriating the attitude for his melodic songs, is irrelevant. The fact is, these admirers reckon, that Costello is still on their side. 'Only people of limited imagination would jump back with dismay at a change. It's not so radical,' Costello says.[15]

In September 1994, after seventeen years of a working relationship that could invariably be described as 'eventful', Costello split from his manager Jake Riviera, and started afresh with new management and a new company. He and Riviera remained connected in that Riviera was still a co-director of Demon Records, and he continued to manage Costello's friend Nick Lowe. But Costello clearly felt that he no longer needed someone to do his hustling for him. It was time to take stock, to move into a new era, and so a split became inevitable. It came at a time when Costello's confidence and record sales had been boosted by the success of *Brutal Youth*, and while there's probably no connection, one thing is for certain – in the eyes of the public, who more than likely didn't know who Jake Riviera was – Costello had grown up. From a Buddy Holly lookalike in clothes either too small or too big for him, to a post-punk renaissance man with a very neat line in smart suits, Costello had been seamlessly transformed into the 1990s equivalent of The Who's Pete Townshend: a supreme statesman of rock music, and a thinking person's idea of what a rock star shouldn't sound like. It is an irony, therefore, that Mr Smooth-Talking Guy had an album out that rubbed your nose in the dirt. Raw and rugged and pitiless, *Brutal Youth* was the sound of a man approaching his fortieth year with the bit between his teeth, refusing to let go, wanting to have a go. And as for the way he twice sings the word 'knickers' on the record, well, you should have been there.

173

'I couldn't have foreseen the jump,' Costello told *Pulse!* 'It wasn't a foregone conclusion, and there were times when it all seemed to be in jeopardy. My first two and a half years, every single I made was in the UK Top Thirty. When it stops, you think, "Hang on, this is the beginning of the end." But of course, all it meant was that the novelty had worn off and I was doing things too diverse for a broad market.'[16] Diversity, of course, is a double-edged sword for someone who wants a career in a commercially-creative environment. It is rewarded both by respect and moderate record sales, and so the very thing that saves an artist from creative boredom entraps them in a fiscal net. It was a balancing act that Costello proved to be adept at, for although his eclecticism thwarted even the best marketing strategists, it also helped to underpin the long-term approval of his audience.

In America, *Brutal Youth* reached No. 34 in the *Billboard* charts, a comparative disappointment. Warners no doubt cherished an artist such as Costello who was the epitome of a hard-working and extremely talented rock star who nevertheless didn't sell millions of records every time a record was released. And so it's strange to discover that at one point a Warners employee advised Costello for his music to be less Guns 'n' Roses and more *Juliet Letters*. Truly, the direction for Costello to take was to follow his own in-built bullshit-detector instinct, and forget about the marketing department's pie-chart plans for his future.

In the UK, people readily came to terms with the scope of the album. In Japan, *Brutal Youth* was the biggest-selling album of Costello's career. As for America . . . 'America is a country where you need your record company to understand what you're doing,' Costello told *Record Collector*. 'If they sell it the wrong way, they just confuse the hell out of people.'[17] A tour was most definitely in order, and before anyone could bark 'last orders' Elvis Costello and The Attractions were off. Of course, to those people who last saw Costello around the time of *Get Happy!!* and who had been too busy or lacked the interest to follow even the tiniest of his movements, a nostalgia tour was what was expected. Sure, they got the hits (he wrote the songs, after all) but nostalgia was a different thing. This was no once-more-round-the-block trip from a band hard up for some fish'n'chips money. The seven-month tour took in most parts of the world, and all was happy in the land of plenty.

'It doesn't sound like an oldies band,' Costello teased the *Montreal Gazette*. 'I couldn't believe it when they cranked up behind me. It was the most ungodly thing . . . very exciting. It was like being strapped on the front of a runaway train . . . People are going to be very surprised. I think it's a lot better group than it was eight years ago.'[18] Since they had not been on the road together for some years, Costello began the tour expecting everyone to get along just dandy. 'The whole thing has an air of mad humour, being together again,'[19] he was telling anyone who cared to listen, in this case the *Toronto Star*. It wasn't the sound of desperation, but already one could certainly detect little alarm bells beginning to ring.

The response to the first four gigs on the American leg of the tour was rapturous. Crowds were standing and screaming, especially when the band launched into an old favourite. Costello reckoned that at last, and not for want of him saying it in the past, The Attractions were being recognized as one of the greatest combos ever to come out of the UK. At home, this fact had been recognized by most listeners from the late 1970s on.

For the tour, the band and Costello specifically wanted to strike a balance between new material from *Brutal Youth* and the songs that pretty much everyone in the audience would know. They also played several songs from albums that they had never previously performed live. 'We didn't feel the necessity to come with radically new arrangements for the old songs, because during the eight years that we were together we'd been constantly updating and adorning the material with little things, little rhythms, that would keep them interesting to us,' Costello told the *Dallas Morning News*. 'For this tour, we decided to go back to the old records and play them like we did in the years that they were written.

175

In some ways that's much more inventive than for us to try to outsmart ourselves by doing a salsa version of 'Watching the Detectives' just to prove that we can. We're just having a great time so far, but it is only the first week. We could be killing each other by the time we get to Texas.'[20]

By the time the tour hit the UK, relationships were still apparently civil. To the band, the tour might not have been a sentimental retread through their back pages, but to the audience it was nostalgia nirvana a-go-go. For Costello it was not quite like the really old times, when the Attractions and he, fuelled up on their first mouth-rattling swirl of pills, would play a forty-five-minute set, go off back stage to 'freshen up', come back on ten minutes later abusing the audience, play one more song and then bugger off back to the hotel.

'We used to love baiting the audience then,' Costello admitted in *Record Collector*. 'We had thirty-five minutes of material, and after the first couple of tours and our first brush with amphetamines, we got that down to twenty-five minutes and we didn't have any more songs. Then it became a knee-jerk thing, that we didn't play encores. In the States, when we did shows that were being broadcast live on radio, we used to like leaving the radio DJ still talking, "Ahey, I think they're coming back to the stage," and we'd already be halfway back to the hotel. You can see how the mischief of that would appeal to a group on the road, who have this claustrophobic feeling of being holed up in a trench together.'[21]

There was more to the tour than just going out and playing the hits and near misses, however; Costello had a couple of points to prove. While the summer tour of the US had been conducted essentially to plug the album, a month-long November tour of the UK had been set up ostensibly to promote a new EP, featuring 'London's Brilliant Parade'. It didn't go according to plan, however, with record company reluctance and ill health augmenting the difficulties. Reports of Costello appearing somewhat tetchy on stage only added to the tension. 'I'd just split from my manager . . . and I decided the healthiest thing to do was to prove that I could still function professionally without him. Plus, I wanted to promote "London's Brilliant Parade" . . . The record company in England had released two singles in quick succession without much success. 'Sulky Girl' they'd managed to chart and we'd gone on *Top Of The Pops* but basically it was the usual major record company hocus pocus that got us into the charts, it didn't actually sell convincingly . . . Then came "13 Steps Lead Down", for no better reason than the fact there was a video made for it. But I knew it was never going to be a hit in England . . .

'"You Tripped At Every Step" was the real hit single, but there was no longer the willingness to find the budget for a video . . . Radio didn't seem to like it. I thought it sounded like an Abba record, but what do I know? So I became convinced that 'London's Brilliant Parade' should come out as a single, even if it wasn't a hit – much the same way that I wanted "Tramp the Dirt Down" to come off *Spike*, and was stopped by the record company because of the politics of it . . . The days of our consistent chart presence are long gone . . . If I seemed grumpy, it was just frustration, 'cos I'd planned the whole thing myself. If you get sick in the midst of that . . .'[22]

The tour ended with Costello and The Attractions back for as long as it would last. On some days they were lively and chirpy, on others the inter-band activity resembled particularly narky out-takes from *The Likely Lads*. Costello's future with The Attractions was, as ever, unsure but never unexciting. He finished 1994 having released one of the best albums of his career amidst apparent tom-foolery from Warners. Not being able to find the budget for a song he especially wanted to release as a single was ironic, to say the least, considering his earlier comment of the record company having enough pocket money to spare for him and his meagre requirements.

There are two sides to every story, though. You can be reasonably sure that Costello's philosophy of releasing records – 'certain songs should be singles just so they appear on the radio, however slight the probability that they'll chart'[23] – though profoundly and utterly correct in a creative context, was probably considered by record company executives to be the idealistic ramblings of a deranged person. Then again, maybe it was something else altogether . . . Perhaps Warner Brothers president, Lenny Waronker, just didn't find Costello's idea to release a specific song as a single 'interesting' enough.

Whatever way one looks at it, the end result was that *Brutal Youth* was Costello's last album of spontaneous original material for Warners. What was he playing at? And how long would the game last?

CHAPTER 10

'I like him, but I'm not a big fan. This is really hard to put, but I don't find him very natural. I'm not talking about his lyrics, because he has great insight into things, but there isn't grace there that I see in people who would be considered less in such elevated company. I feel terrible about it, but it's passed me by. I like to hear grace in music. Irving Berlin had it. Paul McCartney has it.'
Paddy McAloon discussing Elvis Costello,
The Irish Times, *August 1997[1]*

'I'm thinking of deleting my entire catalogue in the year 2000 . . . I think after a while you've got to get rid of them, throw them away. People must have them by now if they want them . . . I might get more sentimental by the year 2000. But what I'd really like to do is delete them and destroy them, so they could never come out again. That would be kind of cool. Ha! I'm sure I'll change my mind about it.'
Interview with Paul Du Noyer, Mojo, *June 1996*

'My commercial fortunes are very erratic in this country [UK]. People say to me, what do you do now? People whose view of music is formed by tabloids or Top Of The Pops, *they think you're retired. I started out with people thinking I was a fantasist and twenty years later they still do.'*
Interview with Stuart Maconie, Q, *June 1996*

The next step was that, early in 1995, Elvis Costello went out on the road with Bob Dylan. With just an acoustic guitar, he supported Dylan across Europe, playing most of the songs that would comprise his next studio record. The difference with these songs is that he had originally written them for other people to record. He wasn't exactly used to playing them live, and wanted to run through them, to know them, ready for when it came to record them.

In the meantime, Costello was grinning all over. On stage with Bob Dylan? Would somebody pinch him!?! While he hadn't been old enough to have faithfully bought Dylan's records as they came out, considering him to be merely part of the 1960s and a pop singer and little else by the early 1970s, he had nabbed a copy of *Blonde On Blonde*, slowly but surely collecting four or five other albums from that point onwards. He had managed to get the support slot through an agent he and Dylan shared in the US, who had been requested by Dylan to see if Costello would be interested in joining him. Well, why not? It gave him an opportunity to road test the songs and to become familiar with them in front of an audience that were, presumably, there to listen. Generally speaking, a Dylan audience is a wholly responsive one that listens intently and empathetically to everything, giving it more than a chance, though Sinead O'Connor will probably tell you otherwise.

'I had a naturally-disposed curious audience who were used to listening to words, either in new songs or, to use a horrible modern word, deconstructed versions of familiar material,' he told *NME*. 'They didn't seem to have any objections, they got it as a free bonus. Probably more than once, because he gets the same people coming to his shows night after night.'[2] On 23 May 1995, Elvis Costello collected the Most Outstanding Contemporary Song Collection trophy at the Fortieth annual Ivor Novello Awards at London's Grosvenor House Hotel. Around the same date, he released an album of cover versions. Once again, the irony clock was ticking away.

The album in question was *Kojak Variety*, a collection of fifteen songs that had been languishing in the Warners vaults for over four years. He had planned to release it into the shops unsuspectingly, without fuss or bother, but was prevented from doing so: his record company, with some justification, wanted to push it. Furthermore Costello had soon after become involved with the Brodsky Quartet, so he concentrated fully on that project instead.

Kojak Variety wasn't the first time Costello had put out a covers record – *Almost Blue* had been released some fourteen years earlier, but had concentrated on faithful renditions of country songs. Here, the net was cast wider, with material that trawled through decades across various genres, a veritable 'private jukebox,' was how he described it in *Q*.[3] He had first heard some of the songs in the early 1960s on the BBC Light Programme, which showcased about three hours of beat music per week. At that time, mainstream rock 'n' roll had lost its hold on youngsters, who were forced to hear Elvis Presley croon 'It's Now Or Never', 'Are You Lonesome Tonight?' and 'Wooden Heart' over the airwaves, and listen while their mums and dads sang along to them. Rhythm & blues was the favoured hip sound, an exciting, sexual and exotic style of music that was far more attractive to young rebellious souls than the music their parents liked. And as the kids well knew, the songs The Beatles weren't themselves writing were by the likes of Little Richard, Arthur Alexander and Smokey Robinson.

The cast list of songwriters that Costello included on *Kojak Variety* was impressive, if mostly obscure to the average listener: sandwiched in between the familiar (possibly Bob Dylan, definitely The Kinks) were lost gems from the likes of the Supremes, Screamin' Jay Hawkins, Little Richard, Jesse Winchester, Mose Allison, The Louvin Brothers and Randy Newman. The album was recorded over a two-week period in Barbados with musicians from the Costello Show and The Confederates (plus Pete Thomas). Costello specifically wanted (in every way) a record of his time with them, so the idea to relax in the studio whilst going over a series of favourite songs seemed like a good one. The 'youngest' song on the collection dated from 1970 – Jesse Winchester's 'Payday' – while the oldest, Ray Noble's 'The Very Thought Of You', dated from the 1930s.

Covers albums from major artists were nothing new, though. Perhaps the first few well-known and better examples of the form were David Bowie's *Pin Ups*, Bryan Ferry's *These Foolish Things* and John Lennon's *Rock 'N' Roll*. Come the 1980s, it seemed as if everyone was doing them. Most were stylish, overproduced exercises in musical redundancy, like Duran Duran's *Thank You*, which actually included a version of 'Watching the Detectives' – 'it sounds extraordinarily like Duran Duran playing "Watching the Detectives" . . . with everything that implies,' Costello cryptically noted in *NME*[4] – Jeff Healey's *Cover To Cover*, Annie Lennox's *Medusa* and, once more, the master of fifty-two-track spontaneity, Bryan Ferry with *Taxi*.

Costello was, of course, very comfortable covering songs, and has always been unusual in that he readily on stage and on record doffs his hat to acts who have influenced his own songwriting. Those with keen ears and a good record collection would have noticed Costello paying homage to any amount of pop stars through the course of his career. There's a hint of Dusty Springfield in the lyrics of both 'Accidents Will Happen' and 'Just A Memory', an influence of Aretha Franklin in 'I Want You', The Supremes in 'High Fidelity' and The Beatles in too many to mention. In the very early days of The Attractions, he was extremely unusual in the range of cover songs he performed (Rodgers and Hart's 'My Funny Valentine', Abba's 'Knowing Me Knowing You', Bacharach/David's 'I Just Don't Know What To Do With Myself'), something that his punk-rock counterparts just couldn't get a handle on. His breadth of covers even back then reflected his pre- and post-teenage years, his age (and parents) governing his tastes to a degree. But more importantly it was a wilful career-sneering acknowledgement that there was more to life than using The Stooges or MC5 as a blueprint for a credible punk-rock profile.

On records (not all his own), he had released about forty

cover versions, two of which were with The Attractions 'I Can't Stand Up For Falling Down' and 'A Good Year For The Roses' both reached the UK Top Ten. The reason why he covered so many songs (viewed by some as most curious when one considers his standing as the best British song-writer of the past two decades) was that he was a fan, and wanted to share his enthusiasms with his own fan clan. 'They're just some of my favourite songs,' he told *NME*. 'Everybody's got a favourite song they bet no one else has heard. Everybody likes to surprise, but there's nothing exasperating about this that I can see. What would be exasperating would be to do a whole record of songs that you can't possibly get out of the shadow of. What's the point?'[5]

There was a neat connection between Costello's solo shows with Bob Dylan and *Kojak Variety*. On his very first solo tour in 1984 he performed Dylan's 'I Threw It All Away'. Eleven years later it turned up on an album released in the same year that he performed with the song's writer. No wonder he was beaming. While supporting Dylan, Costello watched him play from the wings and in front of the stage, learning from him, encouraged by him, impressed at the work Dylan put into making his songs come across as constantly reactivated items of popular culture. The lessons learned were valued by Costello, proof positive that an audience/performer/songwriter parallel could be achieved way past middle age. It was something he had always known, of course, but here was concrete proof.

Costello had little time and patience for the theory beloved of blinkered rock fans that cover versions were not a suitable thing for their 'heroes' to be involved in. Apart from the consideration that great songs are precisely that, whoever sings them, the theory is shot down by the fact that so many 'original' songs are rubbish. For most people, Costello included (primarily because of the large amount of music his parents listened to), the success of a song was not so much down to its composer, as to the range of artists that covered it. Not that Costello was without prejudice. Nor indeed, was his new friend Bob Dylan, who criticized Elvis Presley's rendition of Clyde McPhatter's 'Money Honey', stating that originals were always the best. There was a time when he wouldn't buy records with electric guitars on them, an unnecessarily purist stance.

The fundamental idea behind *Kojak Variety* was simple: a pleasurable exercise for the love of it and not, as is the occasional case with covers albums from major artists, a contractual conceit. Yet Costello probably knew hundreds of songs that suffered from similar obscurity. How did he realistically make the choice? Simple, really he made up a list. 'If anyone ever asks you what your favourite record is, my mind goes blank usually,' he admitted in *FAD*. 'I can't think of any records I like. Over a period of time I was thinking of doing this record . . . I knew the musicians I had and I had an idea of some of the things we could do with some songs. Most of all I wanted to get away from songs that would be overly familiar to people. I wanted to avoid any song that was known. Admittedly, there will be somebody who knows every song on this record but not that many. I tried to pick songs that would be fresh. So that cut away a lot that have been my favourites as a listener. But I didn't really think I had anything to add to them as a performer. And then it was just how the mood takes you. If I were to go and do the same today I might have five of the same songs and ten different ones. Or I might have the same fifteen songs.'[6]

With the exception of The Kinks' 'Days' (Kirsty MacColl had a version out in 1989), Costello wasn't aware of any other recent covers of the songs on *Kojak Variety*. He knew of a couple of renditions of James Carr's 'Pouring Water On A Drowning Man', and connected with it first through a version he had heard by Bonnie Raitt. Similarly with Mose Allison's 'Everybody's Crying Mercy', which he knew through both Raitt and Georgie Fame, and The Louvin Brothers' 'Must You Throw Dirt In My Face' via The Byrds and Gram Parsons.

Likening his appreciation of a song through an intermediate artist to his own album *Almost Blue* and the song with the same title that Chet Baker covered, Costello realized that, like religion, all paths lead to the same place. Lighting the way for a voyage of discovery for the enthusiastic listener was something that had happened to him (hearing The Byrds, for example, had directed him to the music of Merle Haggard). If he could do something similar, then so much the better. Having a huge record collection was only half the pleasure. If a person didn't have it in their head and heart to seek out new songs, then what was the point?

'I don't have that big a collection,' he admitted. 'I've had more records in the past, and things happen, you don't always get to keep hold of all your possessions. You can get a little neurotic about the actual possession of objects – it's whether it's in your heart. I've never been too bothered about the rarity of a particular label or record as long as I could hear the music. Although some of the records invoke memories; like an album I picked up from my father when he was playing with a band. It's wonderful that I actually have that record. Just picking it up and looking at it reminds me of my dad sitting around the house and learning songs; I learned a lot through absorbing all of that and that's very personal to me.'[7]

Kojak Variety stiffed in the States, but reached a reasonable No. 21 in the UK. A more relaxed album in comparison to some of his self-penned records, the music is less aggressive, the sensual mood pretty much unvarying throughout. Unlike a large number of his own songs, there are no instrumental devices or conceits forged deliberately to startle or puzzle. The musical scope is simple to comprehend; there is no insistence on bedazzling, beguiling or bemusing the listener with Costello's regular compulsion for pun-laden lyrics and wilfully obscure phrases; the words of the songs are couched in a common tongue and can easily be appreciated. This was Costello and his musicians bowing at the feet of the great and the good, working with songs that might not be the most poetic but which utilized the primary principle of the very best pop music: keep it simple. Which Costello did most of the time. Now and again, Marc Ribot and his guitar went crazy, notably on Screamin' Jay Hawkins' 'Strange', where he freaks out in an instrumental wobble the likes of which hadn't been heard on a Costello record before. Similarly on Jesse Winchester's 'Payday'. Clearly the band were having fun in the studio, but the guitar grimacing on these two tracks is more wasteful than productive. These cavils aside, the album is a slow burning R&B treat, with particularly yearning treatments of The Supremes' 'Remove this Doubt', Mose Allison's 'Everybody's Crying Mercy' and Bacharach and David's 'Please Stay'. As a sidestep into yet more unexplored territory it was a moderate success, but then it wasn't recorded with a view to selling millions, but to give people certain reference points for their own musical adventures.

No sooner had he released and toured with *Kojak Variety* than he was on to something far more ambitious and quite the polar opposite of that record's low-key, haphazard, mostly sultry approach. But first, hold the front page: he had given up drinking alcohol, he had played before Prince Charles, he'd been managing a team for BBC2's *Fantasy Football League*, contributing to Channel Four's *Football Italia* and had been the first guest on Radio Three's classical music equivalent of *Desert Island Discs*.

'I've just lost the taste for alcohol,' he told a shocked nation via *The Big Issue*. 'I'm not afraid of it. I drank a lot and some of it inspired some very good songs and then I got tired of it. It's quite interesting to be the only sober person in the room at a party. You have the memory of all those unhinged things that people say at the top of their voices.'[8] Drink (or lack of it) notwithstanding, he still went to St James Palace to play a gig with Paul McCartney and the Brodsky Quartet. McCartney had been asked to put together an upmarket gig in order to raise money for the Royal College of Music. Taking place in the Palace's Picture Gallery, the gig by Royal decree was followed by a sumptuous dinner. 'You know how it is,' Costello explained in *NME*, 'they get someone famous like Paul, who's probably the most famous British composer of this century, to sort out a musical evening and a load of rich people come along and get fleeced. That's the way charity works.'[9]

If the atmosphere was lacking in earthiness, the music wasn't. Costello and the Brodsky Quartet treated the throng to a rendition of The Beach Boys' 'God Only Knows' and an arrangement of 'Shipbuilding'. Costello and McCartney then sang The Beatles' 'One After 909' and a co-composition, 'Mistress And Maid'. This was followed by McCartney and the Brodsky Quartet singing 'For No One', 'Lady Madonna', 'Yesterday' and 'Eleanor Rigby'. Then a young Russian pianist premiered McCartney's latest classical work, *A Leaf*. Costello, as much as anyone else, was suitably impressed. As was Prince Charles, whose thoughts during and after 'Mistress And Maid' sadly go unrecorded.

'He seemed like a bit of a sad bog, really,' Costello told *NME*. 'He must be aware of the fact by now that it's not like the old days anymore . . . the old Pathé newsreel where Princess Elizabeth and Princess Margaret are off on holiday and there'd be fucking 50,000 people on the streets of Southampton to see two little girls get on a ship. He must know that every room he goes in now there's at least 50 per cent of the people thinking, "What a prat" . . . There's people who want to meet him and it's a big deal to them, it ain't a big deal to me. I was there at Paul's invitation, not his. I mean, if you want to get political about it, his family could have done one important thing in the last twenty-five years. Never mind whether the IRA lay down their guns, any time there was a Loyalist outrage in the last twenty-five years, the Windsors could have said, "This is not an expression of Loyalism". That was the one good thing they could have done and never did, so I don't want to shake the Prince's hand.'[10]

Bang goes the knighthood, then. Footie fandom aside, there was something of a more intriguing nature taking place in Costello's mind around this time. When he had visited Dartington summer school with the Brodsky Quartet at the time of finalizing the release of *The Juliet Letters*, he was approached by the South Bank Centre to see if he would be interested in the one-off position of Artistic Director of Meltdown, a nine-day festival of serious eclecticism. Being the adventurous gentleman he is, he accepted. Little did the organizers realize how wide ranging Costello's selections would be.

Of course, the average attitude towards something such as Meltdown depended on how broad a person's taste was. People who grooved only to death metal would be sorely disappointed. People who frugged solely to pygmy toe-drumming would be exasperated beyond endurance. People who whistled along primarily to the sound of modern pop music would also be irked. In fact, any musical taste that stayed within narrow confines would not be catered for. The person, however, who liked to mix Radiohead with Gorecki with Emmylou Harris with Propellerheads with John Coltrane with All Saints with Cornershop with the occasional Prom night was the ideal candidate for Meltdown. Luckily for Costello, there were plenty of takers for his (not by any means exclusive) vision of how music for the people should be shaping up.

Of course, Costello realized that he risked being accused of pretentiousness with his chosen bill of musical fare over the nine days. His selections included the following: Jeff Buckley, Chick Corea, the London Philharmonic with the animated movie scores of Carl Stalling and Korngold's violin concerto, the Brodsky Quartet, the American gospel group The Fairfield Four, saxophonist/composer John Harle, the Composers Ensemble with a selection from Brahms along-side jazzman Billy Strayhorn and a version of The Kinks' 'Waterloo Sunset', guitarist Bill Frisell (with whom Costello would perform and release a subsequent album), former Blondie vocalist Debbie Harry fronting the New York jazz eccentrics The Jazz Passengers, and *Dinah And Nick's Love Song* by Harrison Birtwistle (whom Costello first heard of thanks to his score for Sidney Lumet's film *The Offence*).

A number of the concerts were grouped around melan-cholic themes, something that Costello recognized as being a subjective response to his brief. Some ideas, however, just had to go into the waste bin. One of his original plans for Meltdown had to be discarded for fear of distancing even the most liberal of consumer – a simultaneous broadcast on Radio Three of an open-air recital of recherché music on Waterloo Bridge.

'I know that some people are going to say, "Who does he think he is", or imagine that I'm looking for approval, or that I'm trying to act grown up by doing some worthy thing,' Costello told Robert Sandall for the *Sunday Times*. 'I know those thoughts are out there. But it's rather like when I started, then I had to be very aggressive because sometimes you have to clear the ground around you, to lean a certain way too far maybe to get your point out. You have to scare people up a bit . . . There is nothing evangelical about this festival; I'm not on a crusade and I have no big theory, this is just a series of possibilities.'[11]

Costello, naturally, loved the idea of being the arbiter of taste for such a prestigious festival. He felt queasy about the one-word umbrella title of it (he likened it to a junk-food item in a greasy American diner) but realized that, minor quibbles aside, the good far outweighed the bad. His name alone would be better known to the general public than most of the participants, and would therefore attract a broader audience, which in turn would 'sell' classical music composed not only by the better-known dead names, but also new modern works by contemporary, living, composers. He was right about the adverse comments, though, and the manner in which some sections of the media took him to task for what they considered to be a distinct showing off of his undoubted intellectual and musical muscle.

'That's the way some of the media talk, it's like a sneering form of Tourette's Syndrome,' he told *NME*. 'As for "arty farty", that's a phrase that should be forcibly removed from the dictionary with a pair of scissors. They can sneer as much as they want, but I don't think Meltdown is a chance for me to show off. Everything is being presented on a one-time basis . . . We don't know how anything is going to turn out. What is there to show off about?'[12]

In the end, Meltdown was a success, a virtual sellout for the first time in its three-year existence. In every way, it was a validation of not only Costello's belief in the persuasive manner in which a 'classical' musical change could be brought about, but also of an expansion of people's ideas as to what music should sound like. It was proof that the tribal-ism affecting most music scenes was slowly being resolved. The millions of record buyers who now had Vanessa Mae and Pavarotti records in their collections did not necessarily buy into the perceived ideology that supposedly informed classi-cal music fans. Like the hoary old cliché about the hand of God moving in mysterious ways, so does music. Costello knew that, and after his own specialist take on Meltdown so did thousands of other people.

Back with The Attractions for a short American tour (coin-ciding with the release of the subdued *Deep Dead Blue*, a mini album of Costello and Bill Frisell at Meltdown), he played for five nights at New York's Beacon Theatre, premiering his recent song co-written with Burt Bacharach via fax and answering machine, 'God Give Me Strength', as well as featuring slightly older material.

Already, further ideas were fermenting in his mind: a new album with The Attractions was taking up his time, a record that would gather together his own versions of songs he had specifically written for other people. He was writing with Burt Bacharach – 'God Give Me Strength' was just one of the results for a film called *Grace Of My Heart*. He was applying the final polish to *Three Distracted Women*, a work written especially for the Brodsky Quartet and Anne Sofie von Otter, and there were collaborations with John Harle and The Jazz Passengers. There were tentative plans for a tour of America with Steve Nieve. While other people slipped into first gear for a while, it seems as if Costello was in constant overdrive. His fans loved it, but the critics warned of his downfall if he didn't take it slowly but surely. Amused as he was by the occasional shouts of 'slow down, give your head a break' he was nonetheless irked at the way in which the number of his creative activities (none of which could be strictly defined as extra-curricular, unless some fool regarded Costello as being purely a 'rock' musician) in some way implied that he was frittering away his energies or spreading himself too thin, perhaps like a curled knob of butter over a whole loaf.

'That's a fundamental misunderstanding about the nature of what I do,' he told Liam Fay for *Hot Press*. 'I don't see any divisions in the different types of music I play. I come back from all these things completely refreshed. Those divisions exist only in the heads of reviewers who have to come up with absurd judgements which don't exist because of their deadlines. Occasionally, it's funny. I've had journalists say all sorts of stuff to me. Some of the theories I've heard are preposterous, particularly in Germany for some reason . . . I had one guy say to me, "You are trying to destroy pop music like Wagner destroyed symphonic music." The guy had a bee in his bonnet about something. I said he should go for a little lie down, he's worrying about this too much, it's a record. A record is always changing. It's changing while you're making it, writing it, mixing it and performing it. But the theory that someone has to have for a deadline, you're stuck with. Occasionally, you see somebody revise their opinion of something and admit they were wrong but very, very, occasionally.'[13]

In May 1996, Costello embarked on a short tour of America with Steve Nieve. He had completed the projected 'originals of his own covers' album, now titled *All This Useless Beauty*, and due for release in June. The duo had visited Los Angeles, San Francisco, Chicago, Boston and New York, recording the concerts as they went from city to city in association with local radio stations. Apart from the obvious practicalities of such a tour (two blokes, a piano and a guitar), there was method to the try-outs for the material from *All This Useless Beauty*. With assistance from Pete Thomas only at the Los Angeles Troubadour gig, the rest of the shows were essentially a thoroughly effective, back-pages-and-some-covers tour. Costello was visiting songs in a way that he had rarely done before. With the stripped-down backing, the songs spoke as much of the truth as before, but this time with the combined passion and subtlety of a well-written love letter. Throughout the shows, Costello chatted humorously, once more deflating the perceived public opinion of him as the archetypal Mr Grumpy, taking the audience along with him on an emotional journey from ardour to zeal. Steve Nieve's mastery at the piano, at times maniacally furious, mostly elegiacally understated, only served to highlight the songs in an even brighter light.

All This Useless Beauty might have had The Attractions on it, but not in the way that one might assume they would sound. This was because, occasionally, they didn't sound like The Attractions at all. Amidst the usual instrumentation were sprinklings of dance loops, sound editing, curious changes of tempo at unexpected moments, and samples. The overall feeling was unlike that of *Brutal Youth*, the previous album recorded with the Attractions, and a record where you can almost hear the members nervously getting to know each other again. On *All This Useless Beauty* that sense of friction had disappeared, leaving in its place a seamless sonic compliancy. It was great, but The Attractions, the best bunch of bruising musicians ever to form a band, surely weren't going soft on themselves, were they?

'The songs begged to be treated that way,' Costello observed in *Hot Press*. 'To Attractionize them wouldn't have worked. We don't think of our sound as a stylized sound but sometimes it goes that way. We were really up on not sounding like ourselves. What The Attractions do is most effective when it illuminates a song like it does on "You Bowed Down" or "It's Time". The sound is used in a more descriptive way. It's more visual.'[14] It had a spark to it, as well. While *Brutal Youth* was by turns fulminating and tender, there was also an overriding tension (imaginary or not) that informed it. *All This Useless Beauty* subverted the same tension by investing a degree of knotty craftsmanship and different ambient sound textures amidst its riffs. It was certainly very different from the typical sounds of 1978.

'That's the way it should be,' he told *Mojo*. 'We know how to make a noise, but I don't want to just make a noise, because we did all that. The thrill we all get from that kind of music is terrific and I hope I never tire of it completely. But I would have tired of it seriously if I'd been doing it nonstop for twenty years. Plus, I would have been deaf. We play very loud . . .'15

The songs on *All This Useless Beauty* had either been written with someone in mind, or had been given away. The most important aspect of the record in Costello's mind was that it wouldn't be misinterpreted as yet another covers album – hardly likely seeing as they were his own songs, but one never knows what goes through the minds of the public, or the critics come to that. Costello's rule of thumb was, it wasn't where the songs had been, it was where they were off to. Considering about thirty candidates, Costello settled on a dozen, the criterion for their inclusion being they were the ones he wanted to sing, irrespective of how good the covers had been. He had quite a time to mull over exactly what songs he wanted and what they meant to him, having put them aside because he wasn't able to find the right kind of environment for them to thrive. While he reckoned that some of them were the best he'd ever written (why give 'em away, then . . .) he also realized that there was a life to them beyond their original treatment. Most of the songs he writes for other people are requested, while various songs on previous records had been written with specific people in mind not that they would have known about it. He likes writing customized songs, but is aware of how some singers are uneasy at singing too many words over the space of three or four minutes. All the songs, then, on *All This Useless Beauty* were concise, with Costello keeping in mind the fact that not everyone fully appreciated his own singular logic nor the overall reflective quality that unsurprisingly showed through.

'There are many moments of self-doubt in these songs,' he said in *Hot Press*. 'I try not to make any of the songs too absolute anymore. I listen to some of the older songs and . . . they have the conviction of youth and of being drunk! I'm not saying that I think that was wrong . . . But you've got to look at yourself. It's all very well to be critical of other people but

[here] I'm asking, "Am I this vain person? Am I this hypocrite?" '[16] This is a collection of ostensibly separate songs written for individuals, but if there isn't exactly a theme running through it, then there is certainly a song that defines the record – the title track. The wording of the title is itself a paradox. Another irony is the fact that the song was inspired by a visit to Italy, the great repository of classical art. In the early 1990s he and Cait spent a month in Florence while she was on an extended studies trip.

'We'd go and sit in a gallery or a church every day, and look at something that was meant to be looked at for hours and hours or for a whole lifetime. I always knew that that was the way paintings are supposed to be looked at but, like everybody else, I never had the time. When I suddenly had this brief period in my life when I did have the time, it was quite frightening. There's so much beautiful stuff and we don't have time to enjoy it all. You realize exactly how fast everything is passing us by. No wonder nobody can put the right value on anything anymore. It's why everybody is shouting at the top of their lungs for attention in music. And it's why this record isn't doing that very often.'[17]

All This Useless Beauty ended with a song titled 'I Want To Vanish'. As anyone with an interest in Costello will know, this was not accidental. Throughout his career, album titles, song titles and track listings have been invested with a rigorous dedication for meaning. 'You want to be always able to leave,' he explained in *Mojo*. 'You should always have your fuck-off money, as they say. I was asked to produce a version of "Lone Pilgrim", an old Appalachian song. I found it went way back to the 1800s. There was a wave of singers who'd been successful like Robert Johnson and the blues guys, except that nobody bothered to rediscover them in the 1960s. They continued to live in the woods: "Oh, that guy at the sawmill up the road? He used to play the banjo twenty years ago." I got fascinated by the idea. What if a documentary film crew had come and said, "We want to tell the world your story, you're the real music!" and this guy had gone,

"Fuck off and leave me alone. I'm happy in my obscurity."
That parallels some of my own feelings.'[18]

Only to a small degree, though. Never one to sit still if
there was something interesting to be considered, Costello
forged ahead in a spirit of adventure and fun, the range of
possibilities in his head apparently never ending. His self-
termed 'pop-art' project just lay ahead – the release every
week for a month of a different single from *All This Useless
Beauty*, which included an original version of the song as
well as remixes and new versions by the likes of Lush, Tricky
and Sleeper. Dropping hints, that is exactly what these other
diversions were – sound trails deliberately and creatively left
at the side of the road to entice others to follow. Another trail
to follow in the future will be his songwriting collaboration
with Attraction Steve Nieve, very little of which, Costello
says, is for a band format.

All This Useless Beauty led up to the expiry of his
contract with Warners. He had one more record to do for
them, and then he would see what would happen. Having a
large enough degree of artistic control to decide to release
four singles in a month might have been great for Costello's
creatively fluctuating frame of mind, but it's quite possible
Warners viewed it as artistically self-indulgent and a bad
marketing move that bordered on the reckless. Sales of the
singles didn't prove them wrong, but at least the company's
marketing executives were kept on their toes. 'It's good for
them . . .,'[19] laughed Costello, no doubt reasonably safe in
the knowledge that not many at his record company agreed
with him. Nor indeed, the good old BBC.

'I was being told officially, in this building [Warner
Brothers, Kensington, London], from the most senior levels,
that I was wasting my time,' Costello fumed in the *Big Issue*.
'The head of all music at the BBC told me that I was wasting
my time. He said I would have more hits if I took all the
seventh chords and all the minor chords out of my songs. I'm
not trying to make myself sound like Mozart, but doesn't it
have a sort of "too many notes" feel to it? It's such a fright-
eningly ignorant statement.'[20]

While the singles died a cheery if ignominious death at the hands of the record-buying public, come early 1997 it was rumoured that he was, in fact, about to leave Warners. It came as little surprise, and with not one but two opportunities to buy his last releases on the label. The first was an American label import, *For The First Time In America*, a limited-edition, five-CD, singles box set that, officially anyway, was the first recorded 'live' Costello music deemed worthy of release. The second was the final contractual compilation album. Titled *Extreme Honey: The Very Best Of The Warner Bros Years*, it culled tracks from *Spike* to *All This Useless Beauty*. It was a solid enough kiss-off, with a pointer to one of the many possible musical futures for Costello, a new song called 'The Bridge I Burned'. This is a wonderfully strange hiphop ballad replete with samples, loops, stray choruses, sonic clangs, a background grunge riff, and easy listening loungecore drifting in and out of the mix. Prince was asked for a sample of 'Pop Life' for it, but he refused.

For Costello, it was time to go again. Happy once more about his varying and non-definable place in the music industry – a year previously he had informed chat-show host Jay Leno that he was seriously thinking of pulling the plug on both touring and recording – he still couldn't understand the stance he felt Warners had taken on the promotion of his records. This was despite the fact that *Spike*, *Mighty Like A Rose*, *The Juliet Letters* and *Brutal Youth* had sold very well. Perhaps he was still smarting from the reaction to the intellectual exercise of releasing four singles in one month. Or perhaps it was from his claim that the original marketing budget for *Extreme Honey* in America was a mere $1,000: 'a calculated insult.'[21]

Frankly, he had more things to concern and intrigue him, namely the batch of songs he was currently writing with Burt Bacharach, and a cunning plan to release a different verson of a 'best of . . .' collection. 'I have a large back catalogue of work I own it . . . We're going to promote a new record, the older "best of". We're going to kick their arse, is what we're going to do.'[22] While he was relishing the thought of that (lashings of revenge with no guilt on the side) there was always the ongoing songwriting with Burt Bacharach to consider. Bacharach, like Paul McCartney, is rightly regarded as one of the most important songwriters in contemporary pop music. Born in Kansas City in May 1928, but reared in New York, he was a jazz aficionado who played in various bands during the 1940s. Following musical theory and composition studies and a stint in the US army, he worked as a pianist, arranger and conductor for numerous artists, clinching the post of musical director for Marlene Dietrich from 1956 to 1958.

In the early 1960s Bacharach teamed up with Hal David to produce a startling number of hit songs for a range of American and UK artists, the songwriter's mellifluous style defined by the likes of Dionne Warwick and Dusty Springfield. With his training in composition leading him towards a breadth of vision other contemporary songwriters couldn't ever have imagined, Bacharach achieved a vast string of hits. Following an absence from the charts for most of the 1970s and several successes in the 1980s, the 1990s have revived his standing, with the likes of Oasis, Blur, Prefab Sprout and the easy-listening brigade happy to bow to his genuine greatness.

Costello first met Bacharach while recording 'Satellite' for the *Spike* album. Nothing further took place until the writing of 'God Give Me Strength' for *Grace Of My Heart*, a musical biopic loosely based on the life of Carole King. The partnership was suggested by the film's soundtrack producer Larry Klein and music supervisor Karyn Rachtman, who brought together a number of surviving Brill Building songwriters with contemporary songwriters they had influenced or inspired. Hence, there was Gerry Goffin, Los Lobos, Lesley Gore, David Baerwald, J Mascis of Dinosaur Jr and Sonic Youth. The collaboration between Costello and Bacharach, however, was effectively a 'virtual' one, the bridge between America and Ireland the only kind they didn't want to attempt to cross.

'He'd fax me some music and I'd play a demo into his phone,' he told *Mojo*. 'I was doing dates with Bob Dylan last year. After the show in Dublin I went out with Bob and his people, got home about two, got on the phone and finished the song. I couldn't believe this was happening. It's hard to get past who Bacharach is, but he's a very easy-going chap. He's a thorough musician, but not a muso – they're the people who go, "hey, these are my chops" and really that's all they've got, whereas he's got everything. He works just as hard as he ever did . . . It would be great to see what could happen if we did get in a room together.'[23]

By the end of 1997, after a few extensive brainstorming sessions, Costello and Bacharach had written up to twelve songs. The release date of the collaborative album is expected to be sometime before the end of 1998. Appearances on tribute albums for Gram Parsons and Joni Mitchell are on line, as are new records with the Brodsky Quartet and Steve Nieve. Apart from all these, Costello claims to have his next five records mapped out in his head. Thankfully, a recently-signed unique record contract is structured to encompass all his requirements. In theory, anyway. In February 1998, Costello signed a multi-label worldwide record contract with PolyGram, a deal created to maximize the company's varied label resources as well as providing multiple channels for his eclectic musical activities. The basic arrangement is that Costello's defined pop and rock output be released through Mercury Records, while his other, more diverse work be released via the numerous labels in PolyGram's jazz and classical division. Once again, Costello has pulled out a plum.

'All these works have some marvellous moments of which I'm proud,' he told Mike Gee. 'I've stopped worrying about things so much. I don't want to try and stop the world or move it off its axis with every record. It's good you can have some records that have more ambition than others, some of which are more modest in ambition but have a smaller beauty at the passing moment and fade in time: you buy a bunch a flowers, you don't expect them to last forever.'[24]

From 1977 onwards, Elvis Costello has continually shown an often neglectful public and regularly sneering media just how good, arrogant, and eminently quotable he is. While there have been times when his output was deemed to be that of a defensive, misunderstood artist, his grumpiness and dislike of journalists exceeded only by that of Van Morrison there are very few who could deny him his right as an artist to express himself in the way that he saw fit. His carping about record-label treatment could be seen to stem from the inevitable conflict with his own ideas about self-marketing. He'd have less of a point if he wasn't such a good songwriter. He's not one for selling himself short, that's for sure, although he would argue that that's precisely what some record companies have done.

With over twenty records out there in the market place, it's remarkable just how tight his quality control has been. He's never made a truly awful album. Some may have been dogged by his wilful experimentation, others may have been dragged down by over-elaborate production. The fact remains, however, that there has been no record released by him that hasn't had at very least three or our killer songs (most have had double that), and no record released by him hasn't been touched by an honest hand and an even more scrupulous heart. This doesn't mean to say he hasn't written songs that haven't achieved all he set out to do. He has many disappointing songs spread throughout his career. Critics mention this and Costello bristles. The critics? He continually and contemptuously claims to have no time for them (despite the fact that, more often than not, he is a critics' favourite), and while his protestations of their misunderstandings ring true they are harped upon far too often. He protests too much, which negates his creative aim and makes him come across as a gnarled curmudgeon.

Costello rightly defends his privacy. He plays the media game to his advantage, talking to journalists at his discretion. Sometimes he has given interviews only on the condition that they be for a specific publication in a specific country, not to be sold on or syndicated. Yet there is an irony here that

Costello is probably keenly aware of. For all his claims of wanting to keep his past to himself and to protect those closest to him, he has, through the past twenty-odd years, revealed enough about himself for anyone with a mind to do so to piece together an overall picture. While it is optimistic to concentrate on his lyrics for clues, it would also be foolhardy not to try. Reading between the lines is an occupational necessity for anyone with half an interest in Costello, because as the strapline for *The X-Files* has it, the truth is out there. Somewhere . . .

Costello arrives at the end of a millennium generally recognized as one of the best and most important songwriters in the vast plains of popular culture. He is the recipient of several prestigious international awards (two Ivor Novello Awards, a BAFTA, and a Nordoff-Robbins Silver Clef Award). Oasis fans can snigger, but when Noel Gallagher is able to write a song as witty and acerbic and knowing as an Elvis Costello lyric, then they can really start to sneer.

Aside from the fact that he has collaborated extensively with two of the giants of popular music (Paul McCartney and Burt Bacharach) he effectively stands alone in relation to the standards he has set for himself, and which other songwriters must follow. Simply put, there are very few songwriters, contemporary or otherwise, who can match his output on an album-to-album basis. Of his contemporaries from the late 1970s onwards there are none to match his depth of passion, his sense of purpose, his eclecticism, his eloquence and, most importantly of all, his directness of purpose.

Of other songwriters over the past forty years, the only one to match him in terms of lyrical deftness and conscious iconoclasm has been Bob Dylan. Not even Dylan, however, has the sense of purpose or the breadth of vision that Costello has. Somewhere, some time long ago he lost that (*Time Out Of Mind* is but a brilliant and worrying reminder of Dylan's loss of effervescence and vital spark, the brutally honest work of a man without hope). Of course, in terms of experience the two men differ tremendously, but as songwriters they share a common bond of expression. Only

Dylan's very best efforts come close to beating Costello's. But this isn't a game, and there are no winners, except in the enquiring minds of fans or the subjective analytical processes of critics.

Yet there is a fear that Costello's main creative strengths and the lack of a bolshy manager (he manages himself now) could be his commercial undoing. Certainly, when Jake Riviera was in his prime, each spike of commercial activity on Costello's career chart was somehow connected to a Riviera Extra Special Scam. One wonders what Riviera really thought of *The Juliet Letters*, and whether he would have ever foreseen such a record in Ye Olde Amphetamine days when he was bullying journos for pleasure. While there's no doubt that Costello's back catalogue is one of the strongest in rock, the songwriting that the majority of people remember him for is rooted in the classic tradition of either the humble folk song or the rock 'n' roll template. Inevitably this dates him, making his prospects for reaching out across age groups a much more difficult matter. I'd wager the Prodigy generation think their mums and dads soft for liking stuff like *Imperial Bedroom*. In some ways, Costello's Meltdown theories just don't fit the demographics.

There's always an upside, however. He can't have released records over the past twenty-plus years without influencing some people who have since grown up into Very Important Pop Stars themselves, can he? Through the likes of Radiohead's Thom Yorke and Tricky, who sampled 'Pills And Soap', Costello slowly filters down through the generations. And what did the prepubescent hordes think when they saw him for a microsecond in *Spiceworld*? Just another old geezer along for the ride? Probably if indeed they saw him at all as they searched for their fallen popcorn: 'Mummy, who's that silly looking man in the glasses?' Costello's a Spice Girl fan, by the way . . .

So what next? Well, it must be reassuring for him to know that his son, Matt, is also a musician, the fourth generation of McManus to choose music as a career. From *All This Useless Beauty* onwards Matt has been assisting his father in various ways, most notably on record with 'The Bridge I Burned', on which he played bass.

Bass? Now there's an interesting thought. Regrouping The Attractions for both *Brutal Youth* and *All This Useless Beauty* was a great idea, and it's no small irony that both album titles reflect perfectly how brilliant the band is at both ends of the rock 'n' roll spectrum. But let's face it, these things were never meant to last, were they? The Attractions are no more because, in Costello's own words in *Q*: 'It wasn't such a great idea as people, not all of us working together. There's bad blood.'[25]

Blood, of course, can be bad, but it's also thicker than water, which can be foul. It's a spurious notion, anyway, the son performing with the father, but one not without a certain twinge of intrigue. And yet the overnight success after five years of plugging away, the hits, the drugs, the drink, the women, the critics and the record companies have taken their toll. Elvis Costello might be one of the most successful pop stars of the last twenty years but is he happy inside himself? The prevalent image of a bitter Costello beavering away while all around the critics cavil is one that melts in the face of reality. The fact is that Costello has achieved far more than even he can have dreamed of back in the bedroom studio of his small suburban semi in Whitton, or on his nights traipsing around the folk clubs of Wallasey. In the early 1970s, he dreamed of writing songs that would stand the test of time, that would be compared with those of the pop song-writing greats, that would be covered by singers whose music he loved and respected. That all this has taken place is a testament to the man's irrepressible self-belief, his huge talent, and, no doubt, tremendous facility to tell people to bugger off. Is he happy? Well, what else could he possibly be?

Costello bores will tell you at length and in great detail exactly what the man has contributed to rock music and popular music in general throughout his career: a musical style that runs the gamut (and occasionally amok) from top to bottom and around the clock; a lyrical craftsmanship that regularly begs quotation marks (but unfortunately not in this book), and an unerring ability to fashion melodies that bring a nod to the head, a tear to the eyelash, and a jerk to the feet.

Elvis Costello will tell you something completely different and altogether more modest. As he once said to me: 'If nothing else, I've contributed a lot of headlines to journalism over the years.'[26]

Oh, Mr Costello . . . *really!*

Selected UK Discography

(All songs written by E. Costello/D. MacManus unless specified)

1977

March	(7" Single)	Less Than Zero/Radio Sweetheart (Stiff)	—
May	(7" Single)	Alison/Welcome To The Working Week	—
July	(7" Single)	(The Angels Wanna Wear My) Red Shoes/ Mystery Dance	—
July:	(Album)	**My Aim Is True** (Stiff)	*14*

Welcome To The Working Week/Miracle
Man/No Dancing/Blame It On Cain/
Alison/Sneaky Feelings/(The Angels Wanna
Wear My) Red Shoes/Less Than Zero/
Mystery Dance/Pay It Back/I'm Not Angry/
Waiting For The End Of The World

My Aim Is True was re-issued on CD in
July 1986 by Demon Records. It was re-
issued on CD again by Demon in March
1993 with the following extra tracks:
Radio Sweetheart/Stranger In The House/
Imagination (Is A Powerful Deceiver)/
Mystery Dance/Cheap Reward/Jump Up/

Wave A White Flag/Blame It On Cain/
Poison Moon

October	(7" Single)	Watching the Detectives/Blame It On Cain (live)/Mystery Dance (live)	*15*

1978

March	(7" Single)	(I Don't Want To Go To) Chelsea/ You Belong To Me (*Radar*)	*16*

March	(Album)	**This Year's Model** (*Radar*)	*4*

No Action/This Year's Girl/The Beat/
Pump It Up/Little Triggers/You Belong To
Me/Hand in Hand/(I Don't Want To Go To)
Chelsea/Lip Service/Living In Paradise/
Lipstick Vogue/Night Rally
A free 7" record was included with the
original album: Stranger In The House/Neat
Neat Neat (*Brian James*)

This Year's Model was re-issued on CD in
July 1986 by Demon Records. It was
re-issued on CD again by Demon in March
1993 with the following extra tracks:
Radio Radio/Big Tears/Crawling To The
USA/Running Out Of Angels/Green
Shirt/Big Boys

May	(7" Single)	Pump It Up/Big Tears	*24*
October	(7" Single)	Radio Radio/Tiny Steps	*29*

1979

January	(Album)	**Armed Forces** (*Radar*)	*2*

Senior Service/Oliver's Army/Big Boys/
Green Shirt/Party Girl/Goon Squad/Busy

Bodies/Sunday's Best/Moods For Moderns/
Chemistry Class/Two Little Hitlers/
Accidents Will Happen
A free 7" record was included with the
original album: Talking In The Dark/
Wednesday Week
A free EP, **Live At Hollywood High**,
was also released with the original album:
Watching The Detectives/Alison/Accidents
Will Happen

Armed Forces was re-issued on CD in
January 1986 by Demon Records. It was
re-issued on CD again by Demon in March
1993 with the following extra tracks:
My Funny Valentine (*Rodgers & Hart*)/
Tiny Steps/Clean Money/Talking In The
Dark/Wednesday Week/Watching The
Detectives/Alison/Accidents Will Happen
(Live At Hollywood High)

February	(7" Single)	Oliver's Army/My Funny Valentine	2
May	(7" Maxi single)	Accidents Will Happen/Talking In The Dark/Wednesday Week	28

1980
February	(7" Single)	I Can't Stand Up For Falling Down (*Homer Banks/Alan Jones*)/Girls Talk (*F-Beat*)	4
February	(Album)	**Get Happy!!** (*F-Beat*) Love For Tender/Opportunity/The Imposter/Secondary Modern/King Horse/Possession/Men Called Uncle/ Clowntime Is Over/New Amsterdam/High Fidelity/I Can't Stand Up For Falling	2

Down/Black & White World/5ive Gears in
Reverse/B Movie/Motel Matches/Human
Touch/Beaten to the Punch/Temptation/
I Stand Accused (*Colton/Smith*)/Riot Act

Get Happy!! was re-issued on CD in
January 1986 by Demon Records. It was
re-issued on CD again by Demon in May
1994 with the following extra tracks:
Girls Talk/Clowntime Is Over No.2/Getting
Mighty Crowded (*Van McCoy*)/So Young (*J.
Camilleri/T. Faehse/J. Burstin*)/Just A
Memory/Hoover Factory/Ghost Train/Dr
Luther's Assistant/Black & White World/
Riot Act

April	(7" Single)	High Fidelity/Getting Mighty Crowded	*30*
	(12" Single)	High Fidelity/Getting Mighty Crowded/ Clowntime Is Over (Version No. 2)	
June	(7" Single/ ep)	New Amsterdam/Dr Luther's Assistant/ Ghost Train/Just A Memory	*36*
December	(7" Maxi Single)	Clubland/Clean Money/Hoover Factory	*60*

1981

January	(Album)	**Trust** (*F-Beat*)	*9*

Clubland/Lovers' Walk/You'll Never Be
A Man/Pretty Words/Strict Time/
Luxembourg/Watch Your Step/New Lace
Sleeves/From A Whisper To A Scream/
Different Finger/White Knuckles/Shot
With His Own Gun/Fish'n'Chip Paper/
Big Sister's Clothes

Trust was re-issued on CD in January 1986
by Demon Records. It was re-issued on CD

again by Demon in May 1994 with the following extra tracks:
Black Sails In The Sunset/Big Sister/Sad About Girls (*Brain/Hart; Brain is a Steve Nieve pseudonym*)/Twenty-Five To Twelve/Love For Sale (*Cole Porter*)/ Weeper's Dream/Gloomy Sunday (*Sam Lewis/Rezso Seress*)/Boy With A Problem (*E. Costello/Chris Difford*)/Seconds Of Pleasure

February	(7" Single)	From A Whisper To A Scream/ Luxembourg	—
September	(7" Single)	Good Year For The Roses/Your Angel Steps Out Of Heaven (*Jack Ripley*)	6
October	(Album)	**Almost Blue** (*F-Beat*)	7

Why Don't You Love Me (Like You Used To Do) (*Hank Williams*)/Sweet Dreams (*Don Gibson*)/Success (*Mullins*)/I'm Your Toy (*Chris Ethridge/Gram Parsons*)/ Tonight The Bottle Let Me Down (*Merle Haggard*)/Brown To Blue (*Johnny Mathis*)/Good Year For The Roses (*Jerry Chestnut*)/Sittin' And Thinkin' (*Charlie Rich*)/Colour Of The Blues (*Williams/Jones*)/ Too Far Gone (*Billy Sherrill*)/Honey Hush (*Big Joe Turner*)/How Much I Lied (*Gram Parsons/Pam Rifkin*)

Almost Blue was re-issued on CD in January 1986 by Demon Records. It was re-issued on CD again by Demon in May 1994 with the following extra tracks:
He's Got You (*Hank Cochran*)/Cry, Cry, Cry (*Johnny Cash*)/There Won't Be Anymore (*Charlie Rich*)/Sittin' And

Thinkin'/Honey Hush/Psycho (*Leon Payne*)/Your Angel Steps Out of Heaven/ Darling, You Know I Wouldn't Lie (*Wayne Kemp/Red Lane*)/My Shoes Keep Walking Back To You (*L. Ross/B. Wills*)/Tears Before Bedtime/I'm Your Toy

December	(7" Single)	Sweet Dreams/Psycho (live)	*42*

1982

April	(7" Single)	I'm Your Toy (Live)/Cry Cry Cry/ Wondering (*Joe Werner*)	*51*
	(12" Single)	I'm Your Toy (Live)/My Shoes Keep Walkin' Back To You/Blues Keep Calling (*Janis Martin*)/Honky Tonk Girl (*Loretta Lynn*)	
June	(7" Single)	You Little Fool/Big Sister/The Stamping Ground (*third track credited to The Emotional Toothpaste aka E. Costello*)	*52*
July	(Album)	**Imperial Bedroom** (*F-Beat*) Beyond Belief/Tears Before Bedtime/ Shabby Doll/The Long Honeymoon/ Man Out Of Time/Almost Blue/. . . And In Every Home/The Loved Ones/Human Hands/Kid About It/Little Savage/ Boy With A Problem (*E. Costello/Chris Difford*)/Pidgin English/You Little Fool/ Town Cryer	*6*

Imperial Bedroom was re-issued on CD in January 1986 by Demon Records. It was re-issued on CD again by Demon in May 1994 with the following extra tracks: From Head To Toe (*Smokey Robinson*)/ The World Of Broken Hearts (*Doc Pomus/*

209

Mort Shuman)/Night Time (*Chambers*)/
Really Mystified (*Tony Crane/Johnny
Gustafson*)/I Turn Around/Seconds Of
Pleasure/The Stamping Ground/Shabby
Doll/Imperial Bedroom

July	(7" Single)	Man Out Of Time/Town Cryer	*58*
	(12" Single)	Man Out Of Time/Town Cryer/ Imperial Bedroom	
September	(7" Single)	From Head To Toe/The World Of Broken Hearts	*43*
November	(7" Single)	Party Party/Imperial Bedroom (A&M)	*48*

1983

May	(7" Single)	Pills And Soap/Pills And Soap (extended) (Imp-Demon) (*Tracks credited to The Imposter aka E. Costello*)	*16*
July	(7" Single)	Everyday I Write The Book/Heathen Town (F-Beat)	*28*
	(12" Single)	Everyday I Write The Book/Heathen Town/ Night Time	
July	(Album)	**Punch The Clock** (F-Beat) Let Them All Talk/Everyday I Write The Book/The Greatest Thing/The Element Within Her/Love Went Mad/Shipbuilding (*C. Langer/E.Costello*)/T.K.O. (Boxing Day)/Charm School/The Invisible Man/ Mouth Almighty/King Of Thieves/Pills And Soap/The World And His Wife	*3*

Punch the Clock was re-issued on CD in
January 1988 by Demon Records. It was

re-issued on CD again by Demon in
February 1995 with the following extra
tracks:
Heathen Town/The Flirting Kind/Walking
On Thin Ice (*Yoko One*)/Town Where Time
Stood Still/Shatterproof/The World And His
Wife (Live)/Everyday I Write The Book (Live)

September (7" Single)	Let Them All Talk/Keep It Confidential		*59*

1984

April	(7" Single)	Peace In Our Time/Withered and Died	*48*
		(*Richard Thompson*)	
		(A- & B-sides credited to The Imposter)	

June	(7" Single)	I Wanna Be Loved/Turning The Town Red	25

June	(Album)	**Goodbye Cruel World** (*F-Beat*)	10

The Only Flame In Town/Room With No
Number/Inch By Inch/Worthless Thing/
Love Field/I Wanna Be Loved (*Farnell/
Jenkins*)/The Comedians/Joe Porterhouse/
Sour Milk Cow Blues/The Great Unknown
(*E. Costello/C. Langer*)/The Deportees
Club/Peace In Our Time

Goodbye Cruel World was re-issued on
CD in March 1986 by Demon Records. It
was re-issued on CD again by Demon in
March 1995 with the following extra tracks:
Turning the Town Red/Baby It's You
(*M. David/B. Bacharach/B.Williams*)/Get
Yourself Another Fool (*Tucker/Hayward*)/I
Hope You're Happy Now/The Only Flame
In Town (Live)/Worthless Thing (Live)/Motel
Matches (Live)/Sleepless Nights (Live)
(*Felice & Boudleaux Bryant*)/Deportee

211

| August | (7" Single) | The Only Flame In Town/The Comedians | 71 |
| | (12" Single) | The Only Flame In Town/The Comedians/ Pump It Up (Dance Mix) | |

1985

| April | (7" Single) | Green Shirt/Beyond Belief | 68 |
| | | *(12" version had extended A-side)* | |

| July | (7" Single) | The People's Limousine (*Henry & Howard Coward aka T-Bone Burnette & E. Costello*)/They'll Never Take Her Love From Me (*Leon Payne*) (Imp-Demon) (credited as The Coward Brothers, with T-Bone Burnette) | — |

| November | (12" EP) | Watching The Detectives/Radio Sweetheart/Less Than Zero/Alison (*Stiff*) | — |

1986

| January | (7" Single) | Don't Let Me Be Misunderstood (*B. Benjamin/S. Marcus/G. Caldwell*)/Baby's Got A Brand New Hairdo (*F-Beat*) | 33 |
| | (12" Single) | Don't Let Me Be Misunderstood/Baby's Got A Brand New Hairdo/Get Yourself Another Fool | |

| February | (Album) | **King Of America** (Imp-Demon) | 11 |

Brilliant Mistake/Loveable (*C. O'Riordan/ D. MacManus*)/Our Little Angel/Don't Let Me Be Misunderstood/Glitter Gulch/Indoor Fireworks/Little Palaces/I'll Wear It Proudly/American Without Tears/ Eisenhower Blues (*J.B. Lenoir*)/Poisoned Rose/The Big Light/Jack Of All Parades/ Suit Of Lights/Sleep Of The Just

King Of America was re-issued on CD in March 1993 by Demon Records. It was

212

re-issued on CD again by Demon in
February 1995 with the following extra
tracks:
The People's Limousine/They'll Never Take
Her Love From Me/Suffering Face/Shoes
Without Heels/King Of Confidence
*A limited edition live CD was also issued
with the February 1995 re-issue. The tracks
are:
That's How You Got Killed Before
(*D. Bartholomew*)/The Big Light/It Tears
Me Up (*D. Penn/S. Oldham*)/The Only
Daddy That'll Walk The Line (*I. J. Bryant*)/
Your Mind Is On Vacation & Your Funeral
And My Trial (segue medley) (*M. Allison &
Sonny Boy Williamson*)/That's How You
Got Killed Before (Reprise)

August	(7" Single)	Tokyo Storm Warning/Tokyo Storm Warning, Pt Two (*D. MacManus/ C. O'Riordan*)	73
	(12" Single)	Tokyo Storm Warning/Tokyo Storm Warning, Pt Two/Black Sails In The Sunset	
September	(Album)	**Blood & Chocolate** (Imp-Demon) Uncomplicated/I Hope You're Happy Now/Tokyo Storm Warning/Home Is Anywhere You Hang Your Head/I Want You/Honey Are You Straight Or Are You Blind?/Blue Chair/Battered Old Bird/ Crimes Of Paris/Poor Napoleon/Next Time Around	16

Blood & Chocolate was re-issued on CD
in March '93 by Demon Records. It was
re-issued on CD again by Demon in
February 1995 with the following extra
tracks:

213

Seven Day Weekend (*E. Costello/Jimmy
Cliff*)/Forgive Her Anything/Blue Chair/
Baby's Got A Brand New Hairdo/
American Without Tears No. 2 (Twilight
Version)/A Town Called Big Nothing
(Really Big Nothing)

November	(7" Single)	I Want You/I Hope You're Happy Now (acoustic)	—
	(12" Single)	I Want You/ I Hope You're Happy Now (acoustic)/I Want You (Part 2)	

1987

January	(7" Single)	Blue Chair/American Without Tears No. 2	—
	(10" Single)	Blue Chair/American Without Tears No. 2/ I Want You	
	(12" Single)	Blue Chair/American Without Tears No. 2/ I Want You/Shoes Without Heels	
May	(7" Single)	A Town Called Big Nothing/Return To Big Nothing (*credited as The MacManus Gang*)	—

(All albums/singles released from now are on CD format)

1989

February	(Album)	**Spike** (Warners)	5

. . . This Town . . ./Let Him Dangle/Deep
Dark Truthful Mirror/Veronica (*P. McCartney/
D. MacManus*)/God's Comic/Chewing
Gum/Tramp The Dirt Down/Stalin Malone/
Satellite/Pads, Paws And Claws
(*P. McCartney/D. MacManus*) Baby Plays
Around (*C. O'Riordan/D. MacManus*)/
Miss Macbeth/Any King's Shilling/Last
Boat Leaving (CD version as above plus:
Coal Train Robberies)

214

February	(Single)	Veronica/You're No Good (*Swinging Blue Jeans*)/The Room Nobody Lives In/Coal Train Robberies	31
May	(Single)	Baby Plays Around/Poisoned Rose/ Almost Blue/My Funny Valentine/Point Of No Return (*G. Goffin/C. King*)	65

1991

April	(Single)	The Other Side Of Summer/Couldn't Call It Unexpected No. 4/The Ugly Things (*N.Lowe*)	43
May	(Album)	**Mighty Like a Rose** (Warners) The Other Side Of Summer/How To Be Dumb/All Grown Up/Invasion Hit Parade/ Harpie Bizarre/Hurry Down Doomsday (The Bugs Are Taking Over) (*E. Costello/ J. Keltner*)/After The Fall/Georgie And Her Rival/So Like Candy (*P. McCartney/ D. MacManus*)/Interlude: Couldn't Call It Unexpected No. 2/Playboy To A Man (*P. McCartney/D. MacManus*)/Sweet Pear/ Broken (*C. O'Riordan*)/Couldn't Call It Unexpected No. 4 (**Mighty Like a Rose** was re-issued in February 1995)	5
October	(Single)	So Like Candy/Veronica (demo version)/ Couldn't Call It Unexpected (live)/ Hurry Down Doomsday (The Bugs Are Taking Over)	—

1993

January	(Album)	**The Juliet Letters** (Warners) Deliver Us/For Other Eyes (*D. MacManus/*	18

215

P. *Cassidy/M.P. Thomas*)/Swine
(*D. MacManus/P. Cassidy*)/Expert Rites/
Dead Letter (*P. Cassidy*)/I Almost Had A
Weakness (*D. MacManus/M. Thomas*)/
Why? (*I. Belton/D. MacManus*)/Who Do
You Think You Are? (*D. MacManus/
M.P. Thomas/M. Thomas*)/Taking My Life
In Your Hands (*D. MacManus/J. Thomas/
M.P. Thomas/P. Cassidy*)/This Offer Is
Unrepeatable (*D. MacManus/P. Cassidy/
Brodsky Quartet*)/Dear Sweet Filthy World
(*D. MacManus/I. Belton/M.P. Thomas*)/
The Letter Home (*D. MacManus/P. Cassidy/
I. Belton*)/Jackson, Monk And Rowe
(*M. Thomas/J. Thomas/D. MacManus*)/
This Sad Burlesque (*D. MacManus/
P. Cassidy*)/Romeo's Seance (*M.P. Thomas/
(D. MacManus/M. Thomas*)/I Thought I'd
Write To Juliet /Last Post (*M. Thomas*)/The
First To Leave/Damnation's Cellar/The
Birds Will Still Be Singing

February	(Single)	Jackson, Monk And Rowe/This Sad Burlesque/Interview Excerpts	—

1994

March	(Single)	Sulky Girl/A Drunken Man's Praise Of Sobriety (W. B. Yeats)/Idiophone	22
March	(Album)	**Brutal Youth** (Warners) Pony St./Kinder Murder/13 Steps Lead Down/This Is Hell/Clown Strike/You Tripped At Every Step/Still Too Soon To Know/20% Amnesia/Sulky Girl/London's Brilliant Parade/My Science Fiction Twin/ Rocking Horse Road/Just About Glad/ All The Rage/Favourite Hour	2

| April | (Single) | 13 Steps Lead Down/Do You Know What | 59 |

I'm Saying?/Puppet Girl/Basement Kiss/
We Despise You (*Latter four by
E. Costello/C. O'Riordan*)

| July | (Single) | You Tripped At Every Step/You've Got To | — |

Hide Your Love Away (*Lennon &
McCartney*)/Step Inside Love (*P. McCartney*)/
Sticks & Stones (*R. Charles*)

| November | (Single) | London's Brilliant Parade/London's | 48 |

Brilliant/(Other issues of this single
included the following:
New Amsterdam/Beyond Belief/
Shipbuilding/From Head To Toe/The Loved
Ones/Sweet Dreams/My Resistance Is Low/
Congratulations (*P. Simon*)

1995

| May | (Album) | **Kojak Variety** (*Warners*) | 21 |

Strange (*W. Hawkins*)/Hidden Charms
(*W. Dixon*)/Remove This Doubt (*Holland/
Dozier/Holland*)/I Threw It All Away
(*B. Dylan*)/Leave My Kitten Alone (*Little
Willie John/T. Turner*)/Everybody's Cryin'
Mercy (*M. Allison*)/I've Been Wrong Before
(*R. Newman*) Bama Lama Bama Loo
(*R. W. Penniman*)/Must You Throw Dirt In
My Face (*B. Anderson*)/Pouring Water On
A Drowning Man (*D. Baker/D. McCormack*)
The Very Thought Of You (*R. Noble*)/Payday
(*J. Winchester*)/Please Stay (*B. Bacharach/
H. David*)/Running Out Of Fools (*K. Rogers/
R. Ahlert*)/Days (*R. Davies*)

| August | (Album) | **Deep Dead Blue** (With Bill Frisell) | — |

(*Nonesuch*)

217

Weird Nightmare/Love Field/Shamed Into
Love/Gigi (*Lerner & Loewe*)/Poor Napoleon/
Baby Plays Around/Deep Dead Blue

1996

April	(Single)	It's Time/Life Shrinks/Brilliant Disguise	*58*

June	(Album)	**All This Useless Beauty** (*Warners*)	*28*

The Other End Of The Telescope/Little
Atoms/All This Useless Beauty/Complicated
Shadows/Why Can't A Man Stand Alone?/
Distorted Angel/Shallow Grave/Poor
Fractured Atlas/Starting To Come To Me/You
Bowed Down/It's Time/I Want To Vanish

July	(Single)	Little Atoms/Why Can't A Man Stand Alone?/Almost Ideal Eyes/Just About Glad	—

July	(Single)	The Other End Of The Telescope/Almost Ideal Eyes/Basement Kiss (live)/Complicated Shadows (demo)	—

July	(Single)	Distorted Angel/Almost Ideal Eyes/Little Atoms (*DJ Food mix*)/All This Useless Beauty (*performed by Lush*)	—

July	(Single)	All This Useless Beauty/Almost Ideal Eyes/The Other End Of The Telescope (*performed by Sleeper*)/Distorted Angel (*Tricky mix*)	—

1997

March	(5CD Box Set)	**Costello & Nieve** (*Warners Import*)	—
	CD1	*Live at the Troubadour, Los Angeles*	

Temptation/Poor Fractured Atlas/I Just
Don't Know What To Do With Myself
(*B. Bacharach/H. David*)/It's Time/Man

Out Of Time/Shallow Grave (*P. McCartney/ E. Costello*)

CD2 *Live At The Fillmore, San Francisco*
Just About Glad/Why Can't A Man Stand Alone?/My Dark Life/All This Beauty/ Ship Of Fools (*J. Garcia/R. Hunter*)

CD3 *Live At The Park West, Chicago*
The Long Honeymoon/Starting To Come To Me/The Other End Of The Telescope (*E. Costello/A. Mann*)/All The Rage/ Watching The Detectives

CD4 *Live At The Paradise, Boston*
You Bowed Down/The Long Honeymoon/ Distorted Angel/(The Angels Wanna Wear My) Red Shoes/Little Atoms/My Funny Valentine (*Hart/Rogers*)

CD5 *Live At The Supper Club, New York*
Black Sails In The Sunset/You'll Never Be A Man/Just A Memory/I Want To Vanish/ *Medley*: Alison/Living A Little, Laughing A Little (*T. Bell/L. Creed*)/Tracks Of My Tears (*M. Tarplin/W. Moore/W. Robinson Jr*)/ Tears Of A Clown (*W. Robinson Jr/ S. Wonder/H. Cosby*)/No More Tearstained Make-Up (*W. Robinson Jr*)

Compilations

1980

March   (Album)   **Ten Bloody Marys & Ten How's Your**   —
Fathers (*Imp/Demon*)
Clean Money/Girls Talk/Talking In The Dark/Radio Sweetheart/Big Tears/ Crawling To The USA/Just A Memory/ Watching The Detectives/Stranger In The House/Clowntime Is Over/Getting Mighty Crowded/Hoover Factory/Tiny Steps/ (What's So Funny 'Bout) Peace, Love And

Understanding/Dr Luther's Assistant/
Radio Radio/Black And White World/
Wednesday Week/My Funny Valentine/
Ghost Train

1985

April   (Album)   **The Best Of Elvis Costello – The Man**   *8*
(*Telstar*)
Watching The Detectives/Oliver's Army/
Alison/Accidents Will Happen/Pump It
Up/High Fidelity/Pills And Soap/(I Don't
Want To Go To) Chelsea/New Lace
Sleeves/A Good Year For The Roses/I Can't
Stand Up For Falling Down/Clubland/
Beyond Belief/New Amsterdam/Green
Shirt/Everyday I Write The Book/I Wanna
Be Loved/ Shipbuilding

1987

October   (Album)   **Out Of Our Idiot** (*Imp/Demon*)   —
Seven Day Weekend/Turning The Town
Red/Heathen Town/The People's
Limousine/So Young/Little Goody Two
Shoes/American Without Tears No. 2
(Twilight Version)/Get Yourself Another
Fool/Walking On Thin Ice/Withered And
Died/Blue Chair/Baby It's You
(*B. Bacharach/M. David/B.
Williams*)/From Head To Toe/Shoes
Without Heels/Baby's Got A Brand New
Hairdo/The Flirting Kind/Black Sails In The
Sunset/A Town Called Big Nothing (Really
Big Nothing)/Big Sister/Imperial
Bedroom/The Stamping Ground

1989

October   (Album/2CD)   **Girls, Girls, Girls** (Imp/Demon)   *67*
Watching The Detectives/I Hope You're

Happy Now/This Year's Girl/Lover's
Walk/Pump It Up/Strict Time/
Temptation/(I Don't Want To Go To)
Chelsea/High Fidelity/Loveable/Mystery
Dance/Big Tears/Uncomplicated/Lipstick
Vogue/Man Out Of Time/Brilliant Mistake/
New Lace Sleeves/Accidents Will Happen/
Beyond Belief/Black And White World/
Green Shirt/The Loved Ones/New
Amsterdam/(The Angels Wanna Wear My)
Red Shoes/King Horse/Big Sister's
Clothes/Alison/Man Called Uncle/Party
Girl/Shabby Doll/Motel Matches/Tiny
Steps/Almost Blue/Riot Act/Love Field/
Possession/Poisoned Rose/Indoor
Fireworks/I Want You/Oliver's Army/Pills
And Soap/Sunday's Best/Watch Your
Step/Less Than Zero/Clubland/Tokyo
Storm Warning/Shipbuilding

1994

November (Album)   **The Very Best Of Elvis Costello**   57
(*Imp/Demon*)
Alison/Watching The Detectives/(I Don't
Want To Go To) Chelsea/Pump It Up/
Radio Radio/(What's So Funny 'Bout)
Peace, Love And Understanding/Oliver's
Army/Accidents Will Happen/I Can't Stand
Up For Falling Down/New
Amsterdam/High Fidelity/Clubland/
Watch Your Step/Good Year For The
Roses/Beyond Belief/Man Out Of
Time/Everyday I Write The Book/
Shipbuilding/Love Field/Brilliant Mistake/
Indoor Fireworks/I Want You

1997

October   (Album)   **Extreme Honey** (*Warner Brothers*)   —

The Bridge I Burned/Veronica/Sulky
Girl/So Like Candy/13 Steps Lead Down/
All This Useless Beauty/My Dark Life/The
Other Side Of Summer/Kinder Murder/
Deep Dark Truthful Mirror/Hurry Down
Doomsday (The Bugs Are Taking Over)/
Poor Fractured Atlas/The Birds Will Still Be
Singing/London's Brilliant Parade/
Tramp The Dirt Down/Couldn't Call It
Unexpected No. 4/I Want To Vanish/All
The Rage

Other Selected Material (a recommended guide)

Costello/MacManus songs recorded by other artists

1977
(Single) **Barry Christian**: Alison (*Mercury*)

1978
(Album) **Linda Ronstadt: Living In The USA** (*Asylum*)
Alison
(Album) **Rachel Sweet: Fool Around** (*Stiff*)
Stranger In The House

1979
(Single) **Linda Ronstadt**: Alison (*Asylum*)
(Single) **Dave Edmunds**: Girls Talk (*Swansong*)
(Album) **George Jones: My Very Special Guests** (*Epic*)
Stranger In The House (*Duet*)
(Album) **Carlene Carter: Two Sides To Every Woman**
(*Warner Bros*) Radio Sweetheart
(Album) **Georgie Fame: That's What Friends Are For** (Pye)
That's What Friends Are For

1980
(Album) **Linda Ronstadt: Mad Love** (*Asylum*)
Party Girl/Girls Talk/Talking In The Dark

(Single) **George Jones**: Stranger In The House (Duet) (*Epic*)

1982
(Album) **Robert Wyatt: Nothing Can Stop Us** (*Rough Trade*)
Shipbuilding (*Released as a single in August 1982*)
(Single) **The Shakin' Pyramids**: Just A Memory (*Virgin*)

1983
(Album) **Dusty Springfield: White Heat** (*Casablanca*)
Losing You (*Just A Memory – with extra lyrics written especially for the artist*)

1984
(Single) **Billy Bremner**: Shatterproof (*Arista*)
(Album) **Tracie: Far from the Hurting Kind** (*Respond*)
(I Love You) When You Sleep

1985
(Album) **Nick Lowe: The Rose of England** (*F-Beat/Demon*)
Indoor Fireworks

1986
(Single) **Hue & Cry**: Shipbuilding (*Circa*)
(*Extra track on* I Refuse *CD single*)
(Album) **Allen Mayes: Stumblin' In The Aisle** (*STC*)
Maureen & Sam (*E. Costello/A. Mayes*)

1987
(Album) **Johnny Cash: Johnny Cash Is Coming To Town** (*Mercury*)
The Big Light
(Single) **Paul McCartney**: *Back On My Feet* (*Parlophone*)
(*B-side to* Once Upon A Long Time Ago)

1988
(Album) **Was (Not Was): What Up, Dog?** (*Fontana*)
Shadow & Jimmy (*E. Costello & D. Weiss*)
(Album) **Ruben Blades: Nothing But The Truth** (*Elektra*)
The Miranda Syndrome/Shamed Into Love (both
E. Costello/R. Blades)

1989

(Album) **Roy Orbison: Mystery Girl** (*Virgin*)
The Comedians

(Album) **'Til Tuesday: Everything's Different Now** (*Epic*)
The Other End Of The Telescope (*E. Costello/A. Mann*)

(Album) **Paul McCartney: Flowers In The Dirt** (*Parlophone*)
My Brave Face/That Day Is Done/Don't Be Careless, Love/
You Want Her Too (*all P. McCartney/D. MacManus*)

(Single) **Kirsty MacColl**: Clubland (*Virgin*) (*B-side of* Innocence)

(Album) **Roy Orbison & Friends – A Black And White Night** (*Virgin*)
The Comedians

(Album) **Christy Moore: The Voyag**e (*WEA*)
The Deportees Club

1990

(Album) **Johnny Cash: Boom ChickaBoom** (*Mercury*)
Hidden Shame

1991

(Album) **Various: Peace Together** (*Island*)
Blur: Oliver's Army

(Album) **Roger McGuinn: Back from Rio** (*Arista*)
You Bowed Down (*E. Costello/R. McGuinn*)

1992

(EP) **Everything But The Girl: The Covers EP** (*Blanco Y Negro*)
Alison

(Album) **June Tabor: Angel Tiger** (*Cooking Vinyl*)
All This Useless Beauty

(Album) **Charlie Brown: Someone To Love** (*Munich Records*)
I Wonder How She Knows (*E. Costello/C. Brown*)

(Album) **T-Bone Burnette: The Criminal Under My Own Hat**
(*Columbia*)
It's Not Too Late (*E. Costello/T-Bone Burnette/B. Neuwirth*)

1993

(Album) **Paul McCartney: Off The Ground** (*Parlophone*)
Mistress And Maid/The Lovers That Never Were (*both songs
E. Costello & P. McCartney*)

(Album) **Wendy James: Now Ain't the Time For Your Tears** (*MCA*)
This Is A Test/London Brilliant/Basement Kiss/Puppet Girl/
Earthbound/Do You Know What I'm Saying/We Despise You/
Fill In the Blanks/ The Nameless One/I Want To Stand Forever
(*All tracks by E. Costello & C. O'Riordan*)

(Album) **Mary Coughlan: Love For Sale** (*Demon*)
Baby Plays Around/Upon A Veil Of Midnight Blue (*The
original version of the E. Costello/C. Brown* I Wonder How
She Knows)

(Album) **Zucchero: Miserere** (*Polygram*)
Miss Mary (*E. Costello/Z. Fornaciari*)

1994

(Single) **Tasmin Archer**: Shipbuilding/Deep Dark Truthful Mirror/
All Grown Up/New Amsterdam (*EMI*)

(Album) **June Tabor: Against The Streams** (*Cooking Vinyl*)
I Want To Vanish

(Single) **Skin**: Pump It Up (*Parlophone*)
(*Extra track on* Look But Don't Touch *CD release*)

1995

(Album) **Duran Duran: Thank You** (*Parlophone*)
Watching The Detectives

(Album) **Ronnie Drew: Dirty Rotten Shame** (*Sony Ireland*)
Dirty Rotten Shame

(Single) **Wet Wet Wet**: Town Crier (*Precious/Polygram*)
(*extra track on* She's All On My Mind *CD release*)

1996

(Album) **Norma Waterson: Norma Waterson** (*Rykodisc*)
The Birds Will Still Be Singing

1997

(Album) **The Jazz Passengers: Individually Twisted** (*32 Records*)
Aubergine (*E. Costello also duets with singer Debbie Harry
on* Don'cha Go Away Mad)

(Album) **Anúna: Deep Dead Blue** (*Danu*)
Deep Dead Blue

(Album) The Fairfield Four: Couldn't Hear Nobody Pray (*Elektra*)
That Day Is Done

1998
(Album) Various: Unknown Pleasures (*Demon*)
Mary Coughlan: Baby Plays Around (Compilation CD, free with
UnCut magazine)

**(Album) Bespoke Songs, Lost Dogs, Detours & Rendevous:
Songwriting By Elvis Costello** (*Rhino*)
Girls Talk (*Dave Edmunds*)/Unwanted Number (*For Real*)/My
Brave Face (*Paul McCartney*)/Hidden Shame (*Johnny Cash*)/
All Grown Up (*Tasmin Archer*)/Miss Mary (*Zucchero*)/Shadow
Jimmy (*Was (Not Was)*)/Upon A Veil Of Midnight Blue
(*Mary Coughlan*)/Deep Dead Blue (*Anúna*)/The Comedians
(*Roy Orbison*)/The Deportees Club (*Christy Moore*)/Punishing
Kiss (*Annie Ross & The Low Note Quintet*)/Shamed Into Love
(*Ruben Blades*)/Shatterproof (*Billy Bremner*)/Dirty Rotten
Shame (*Ronnie Drew*)/Shipbuilding (*Robert Wyatt*)/The Birds
Will Still Be Singing (*Norma Waterson*)/I Want To Vanish (June
Tabor)/The Other End Of The Telescope (*'Til Tuesday*)/Indoor
Fireworks (*Nick Lowe & His Cowboy Outfit*)/Almost Blue
(*Chet Baker*)

*Costello/MacManus songs (sung by Costello/MacManus)
and featured on other artists'/various artists' albums*

1978
(Album) Live Stiffs (*Stiff*)
Miracle Man

1981
(Album) Various: Concert For The People Of Kampuchea (*Atlantic*)
The Imposter
(Album) Rock Against Racism's Greatest Hits (*Virgin*)
Goon Squad

1991
(Album) Various: Bringing It All Back Home (*Hummingbird*)

Mischevious Ghost (*duet with Mary Coughlan*)

(Album) **The Chieftains: The Bells Of Dublin** (*RCA*)
St Stephen's Murders

1996

(Album) **Various: Songs In The Key Of X – Music From And Inspired By The X-Files** (*Warners*)
My Dark Life

1997

(Album) **Various: A Hard Nights Day** (*MCA*)
Watching The Detectives/Alison

(Album) **The Bridge School Concerts, Volume 1** (*WEA*)
Alison (Live)

1998

(Album) **The Chieftains: Long Journey Home** (*Unisphere*)
Long Journey Home

(Album) **Various: Unknown Pleasures** (*Demon*)
Tokyo Storm Warning (*Compilation CD free with* Uncut *magazine*)

Cover versions featured on records other than his own (songwriter/s in brackets)

1978

(Album) **Various: Live Stiffs** (*Stiff*)
I Just Don't Know What To Do With Myself (*Bacharach/David*)

1981

(Album) **Various: Rock Against Racism's Greatest Hits** (*Virgin*)
White Man In Hammersmith Palais (*Strummer/Jones*)

1987

(Album) **Various: Live For Ireland** (*International Version*) (*MCA*)
Many Rivers To Cross (*Jimmy Cliff*)
Various: Live For Ireland (*Irish Version*) (*MCA*)
Leave My Kitten Alone (*Little Willie John/Titus Turner*)

1991
(Album) **Various: Deadicated** (*Arista*)
Ship Of Fools (*J. Garcia/R. Hunter*)

1994
(Album) **Various: Adios Amigo** (*Demon*)
Sally Sue Brown (*Arthur Alexander*)
(Album) **Various: No Prima Donna** (*Exile*)
Full Force Gale (*Van Morrison*)
(Album) **The Brodsky Quartet: Lament** (*Silva Classics*)
She Moved Through The Fair (*Trad arr*)

1996
(Album) **Various: Volume 17** (*5th Anniversary CD*) (*Volume*)
What Do I Do Now? (*L. Wener*)
(Album) **Various: Common Ground** (*EMI Premier*)
The Night Before Larry Was Stretched (*Trad Arr*)

1997
(Album) **September Songs: The Music Of Kurt Weill**
(*Sony Classical*)
Lost In The Stars
(Album) **Various: The Ray Davies Songbook** (*Connoisseur*)
Days (*R. Davies*)

Soundtracks (all songs/music performed by E. Costello
unless otherwise specified)

1979
(Album) **Americathon OST** (*CBS*)
(I Don't Want To Go To) Chelsea
(Album) **That Summer OST** (*Arista*)
(I Don't Want To Go To) Chelsea/Watching The Detectives

1983
(Album) **Party Party OST** (*A&M*)
Party Party

228

1987

(Album) **The Courier** (*Virgin*)
Mad Dog/Painted Villain/Stalking/Furinal Music (Piano)/Rat
Poison/Furinal Music (Sax)/Unpainted Villain/Last Boat Leaving

1989

(Album) **Chet Baker: Let's Get Lost** (*OST*) (*BMG*)
Almost Blue

1991

(Album) **GBH** (*Demon*) (*Original music from the Channel 4 series,
composed by Elvis Costello and Richard Harvey*)
Life And Times Of Michael Murray/It Wasn't Me/Men Of
Alloy/Lambs To The Slaughter/Bubbles/Goldilock's Theme/
Perfume The Odour Of Money/Assassin/Pursuit Suite/
Roaring Boy/So I Used Five/Love From A Cold Land/In A
Cemetery Garden/Smack 'Im/Woodlands – Oh Joy/It's Cold
Up There/Going Home Service/Grave Music/Puppet Masters'
Work/He's So Easy/Another Time, Another Place/Closing
Titles

1993

(Album) **Various: Short Cuts OST** (*Imago/BMG*)
Punishing Kiss (*performed by Annie Ross & The Low Note
Quintet*) (*D. MacManus/C. O'Riordan*)

1995

(Album) **Jake's Progress** (*Demon*) (*Original music from the Channel
4 series, composed by Elvis Costello and Richard Harvey*)
Jake's Progress Opening Sequence/Map Of Africa/Julie's
Pregnant Pause/Monica's Fortune Telling/'Cisco Kid/Graveyard
Waltz/Housewarming/Moving In/Howling At The Moon/
Unhappy Home Service/Ursine Variations/Mrs Rampton
Reminisces/A Friend In Need/Death Of Alex & Closing Titles/
Remembering Alex/Leaving Home/Eliot's Heartbreak And
Flashback/Kate's Abuse/Grave Dance/Banquo/Fall From
Grace/Play With Me, Mummy

229

1996

(Album) **Grace Of My Heart OST** (*MCA*)

Unwanted Number (*performed by For Real*) God Give Me Strength (*co-written by B. Bacharach and E. Costello. Performed by Kristen Vigard and For Real*) God Give Me Strength (*written and performed by B. Bacharach and E. Costello*)

1998

(Album) **The Big Lebowski OST** (*Mercury*)

My Mood Swings (*E. Costello and C. O'Riordan*)

(Album) **The Wedding Singer OST (Maverick)**

Everday I Write The Book

Classical/orchestral work

1994

Edge Of Ugly

A brief orchestral work written for The London Philharmonic Orchestra, conducted by Gunther Schuller. Premiered in June.

1995

Put Away Forbidden Things

A composition for the viol group Fretwork and counter tenor, Michael Chance. Premiered at Meltdown in March.

1996

John Harle: Terror And Magnificence (*Argo*) (Album)

O Mistress Mine/Come Away, Death/When That I Was A Little Tiny Boy (three song settings from Shakespeare's *Twelfth Night*).

Three Distracted Women

Three song composition for Anne Sofie von Otter and the Brodsky Quartet. Premiered in Paris in November.

1997

Tom Thumb

A concert performance for small orchestra (violin, viola, cello, double bass, flute, bassoon, two French horns, trumpet and percussion). Premiered in London at the Academy of St Martin in the Fields, July.

* * * *

Aside from independent research by the author, the above discography was compiled from the following excellent sources:

1) Great Rock Discography, Third/Fourth Editions, by M.C. Strong, (Canongate Books)
2) Paul Hosken, Kirchstrasse 23, 82284 Grafrath, Germany (paul.hosken@dlr.de)

The discography is, as far as the author knows, the most comprehensive and fully documented list of Elvis Costello songs/work (written and performed by him and other people), and cover versions he has performed on *record*. Songs (original and cover versions) – with the exception of orchestral/classical pieces – he has performed in a live context have not been included.

Songs – either originals or cover versions – not documented will be included in further editions of the book. If anyone knows of omissions or errors they think should be included in the discography, they can contact the author via the publisher.

Bibliography

I am greatly indebted to the writers and publishers of all the material I used as research tools during the course of writing this book. Books consulted include the following:

Aizlewood, John; Collins, Andrew; and Prince, Bill, (Co-compilers, in association with Guinness Publishing), The Q Book of Punk Legends (*Free with Q 116, 1996*)

Clarke, Donald (Editor) – The Penguin Encyclopedia of Popular Music (*1990*)

Carlin, Richard – The Big Book of Country Music (*Penguin, 1995*)

Gouldstone, David – Elvis Costello: God's Comic (*St. Martin's Press, 1989*)

Kent, Nick – The Dark Stuff: Selected Writings, 1972–1993 (*Penguin, 1994*)

Larkin, Colin (Editor) – Guinness Encyclopedia of Popular Music (*Guinness Publishing, 1993*)

McDonald, Ian – Revolution In The Head (*Fourth Estate, 1994*)

O'Connor, Nuala – Bringing It All Back Home (*BBC Books, 1991*)

Parkyn, Geoff – Elvis Costello: The Illustrated Disco/ Biography (*Omnibus, 1984*)

Pym, John (Editor) – Time Out Film Guide, 6th Edition (*Penguin, 1997*)

Reese, Krista – Elvis Costello: A Completely False Biography Based On Rumour, Innuendo And Lies (*Proteus, 1981*)

Rockett, Kevin & Finn, Eugene – Still Irish (*Red Mountain Press, 1995*)

Stambler, Irwin – The Encyclopedia of Pop, Rock & Soul (*Papermac, 1992*)

Strong, M.C. – The Great Rock Discography, 3rd Edition (*Canongate, 1996*)

Thomas, Bruce – The Big Wheel (*Viking, 1990*)

Williams, Richard – Dylan: A Man Called Alias (*Bloomsbury, 1992*)

Also:

The Guinness Book of British Hit Albums, 7th Edition (*1996*)

The Guinness Book of British Hit Singles, 11th Edition (*1997*)

Sources

Chapter 1

1 Cheers! The Story of Pub Rock, by Will Birch, *Mojo*, May 1996
2 *ibid*
3 *ibid*
4 *ibid*
5 Relative Values, by Markie Robson-Scott, *The Sunday Times*, 1994
6 *ibid*
7 Interview with Paul Du Noyer, *Q*, March 1989
8 Interview with Paul Rambali, *The Face*, August 1983
9 Cheers! The Story of Pub Rock, by Will Birch, *Mojo*, May 1996
10 Interview with Paul Rambali, *The Face*, August 1983
11 Interview with Stuart Maconie, *Q*, June 1996
12 Interview with Paul Rambali, *The Face*, August 1983
13 Cheers! The Story of Pub Rock, by Will Birch, *Mojo*, May 1996
14 Interview with Greil Marcus, *Rolling Stone*, 1982
15 I Fought The Law, by Dave Schulps, *Trouser Press*, December 1977
16 Interview with Allan Jones, *Melody Maker*, 1978
17 I Fought The Law, by Dave Schulps, *Trouser Press*, December 1977
18 Interview with Nick Kent, *NME*, 27 August 1977
19 *ibid*
20 Cheers! The Story of Pub Rock, by Will Birch, *Mojo*, May 1996

21 Interview with Greil Marcus, *Rolling Stone*, 1982
22 Charles Shaar Murray, *NME*, 26 March 1977
23 Interview with Paul Rambali, *The Face*, August 1983
24 Interview with David Wild, *Rolling Stone*, June 1989
25 I Fought The Law, by Dave Schulps, *Trouser Press*, December 1977
26 Interview with Nick Kent, *NME*, 27 August 1977

Chapter 2

1 Elvis Costello: I Fought The Law, by Dave Schulps, *Trouser Press*, December 1977
2 On The Town review, by Roy Carr, *NME*, 17 September 1977
3 Stiff's Greatest Stiffs Live! by Will Birch, *Mojo*, October 1997
4 *ibid*
5 *ibid*
6 *ibid*
7 *ibid*
8 *ibid*
9 Interview with Nick Kent, *Creem*, May 1979
10 Can Elvis Costello Cure Acne? by Patrick Goldstein, *Creem*, May 1978
11 Stiff's Greatest Stiffs Live! by Will Birch, *Mojo*, October 1997
12 Can Elvis Costello Cure Acne? by Patrick Goldstein, *Creem*, May 1978
13 *ibid*
14 Man Out Of Time, by Paul Rambali, *The Face*, August 1983
15 Interview with Nick Kent, *NME*, March 1978
16 *ibid*
17 Interview with David Wild, *Rolling Stone*, June 1989
18 Singles Review, by Charles Shaar Murray, *NME*, 4 March 1978
19 Interview with Nick Kent, *NME*, March 1978

20 Can Elvis Costello Cure Acne? by Patrick Goldstein, *Creem*, May 1978
21 Interview with Nick Kent, *NME*, March 1978
22 Can Elvis Costello Cure Acne? by Patrick Goldstein, *Creem*, May 1978
23 *ibid*
24 Interview with Nick Kent, *NME*, March 1978
25 Interview with Tony Schwartz, *Newsweek*, May 1978
26 The It Girl, by Mat Snow, *Mojo*, October 1997
27 *ibid*
28 *ibid*
29 *ibid*
30 Interview with Nick Kent, *NME*, March 1978
31 Singles Reviews, by Tony Parsons, *NME*, October 1978
32 Ross MacManus, *Sunday Times Magazine*, March 1994

Chapter 3

1 Interview with Nick Kent, *Creem*, May 1979
2 *ibid*
3 What'd I Say: Elvis Costello Puts His Foot In His Mouth, *Rolling Stone*, May 1979
4 Armed Force, by Allan Jones, *Uncut*, July 1997
5 Random Notes, *Rolling Stone*, April 1979
6 Armed Force, by Allan Jones, *Uncut*, July 1997
7 In an exchange with Nick Kent, *NME*, 9 June, 1979
8 *ibid*
9 *ibid*
10 *ibid*
11 Elvis Costello: A Completely False Biography Based On Rumour, Innuendo And Lies, by Krista Reese (Proteus, 1981)
12 *ibid*
13 Excerpt from interview with Bebe Buell, *Oui* magazine, May 1980

14 Interview with Robert Palmer, *New York Times*, June 1982
15 Interview with Greil Marcus, *Rolling Stone*, July 1982
16 In an exchange with Nick Kent, *NME*, 9 June 1979
17 Armed Force, by Allan Jones, *Uncut*, July 1997
18 Interview with David Wild, *Rolling Stone*, June 1989
19 Interview with Neil Spencer, *NME*, 30 October 1982
20 Elvis – What Happened? by Scott Isler, *Trouser Press*, April 1980
21 *ibid*
22 *ibid*
23 *ibid*

Chapter 4

1 Man Out Of Time, by Paul Rambali, *The Face*, August 1983
2 *ibid*
3 Interview with *Record Collector*, October 1995
4 Live review by Richard Grabel, *NME*, 6 September 1980
5 *ibid*
6 Interview with *Record Collector*, October 1995
7 *ibid*
8 *ibid*
9 Elvis Costello: A Completely False Biography Based On Rumour, Innuendo And Lies, by Krista Reese (Proteus, 1981)
10 Live review by Richard Grabel, *NME*, 14 February 1981
11 Man Out Of Time, by Paul Rambali, *The Face*, August 1983
12 Interview with Neil Spencer, *NME*, 30 October 1982
13 Interview with *Record Collector*, October 1995
14 Interview with Neil Spencer, *NME*, 30 October 1982
15 *ibid*
16 *ibid*
17 Interview with *Record Collector*, October 1995

Chapter 5

1 The It Girl, by Mat Snow, *Mojo*, October, 1997
2 *ibid*
3 Interview with *Record Collector*, October, 1995
4 Transcript from *Talking In The Dark*, by Nick Kent, NME, 21 August 1982
5 *ibid*
6 *ibid*
7 Interview with *Record Collector*, October 1995
8 *ibid*
9 Man Out Of Time, by Paul Rambali, *The Face*, August 1983
10 *ibid*
11 Interview with Neil Spencer, *NME*, 30 October 1982
12 *ibid*
13 *ibid*
14 *ibid*
15 Interview with *Record Collector*, October, 1995
16 News report, *NME*, 20 August 1983
17 In conversation with Gareth O'Callaghan, *Upbeat*, RTE Radio One, 26 August 1997

Chapter 6

1 Interview with Barney Hoskyns, *NME*, 8 October 1983
2 *ibid*
3 *ibid*
4 *ibid*
5 Interview with *Record Collector*, October, 1995
6 *ibid*
7 From *The Dark Stuff*, by Nick Kent, Penguin, 1994
8 *ibid*
9 Interview with David Fricke, *Rolling Stone*, April 1986
10 Interview with Paul Du Noyer, *Q*, March 1989
11 Interview with Mat Snow, *NME*, 11 May 1985
12 *ibid*

13 *ibid*
14 Interview with Danny Kelly, *NME*, 1 March 1986
15 Interview with *Record Collector*, October, 1995
16 Interview with Danny Kelly, *NME*, 1 March 1986
17 Interview with David Fricke, *Rolling Stone*, April 1986
18 *ibid*
19 Interview with *Record Collector*, October, 1995
20 *ibid*
21 Interview with David Wild, *Rolling Stone*, June 1989
22 Interview with *Record Collector*, October, 1995

Chapter 7

1 Interview with David Wild, *Rolling Stone*, June 1989
2 *ibid*
3 From *The Dark Stuff*, by Nick Kent, Penguin, 1994
4 Interview with Roy Carr, *NME*, 29 April 1978
5 Interview with David Wild, *Rolling Stone*, June 1989
6 From *The Dark Stuff*, by Nick Kent, Penguin, 1994
7 Interview with Paul Du Noyer, *Q*, March 1989
8 Interview with David Wild, *Rolling Stone*, June 1989
9 The Amazing World of Fred Dellar, *NME*, August 1987
10 Interview with Paul Du Noyer, *Q*, March 1989
11 From *Penguin Encyclopaedia of Popular Music*, 1990
12 Interview with the author for *In Dublin*, 6 June 1991
13 Interview with Paul Du Noyer, *Q*, March 1989
14 Interview with *Record Collector*, November, 1995
15 Interview with David Wild, *Rolling Stone*, June 1989
16 *ibid*
17 Interview with Paul Du Noyer, *Q*, March 1989
18 Interview with Nick Coleman, *Time Out*, 8 February 1989
19 Interview with Paul Du Noyer, *Q*, March 1989
20 *ibid*
21 Interview with David Wild, *Rolling Stone*, June 1989
22 *ibid*
23 *ibid*

24 *The Big Wheel* by Bruce Thomas, Viking, 1990
25 Interview with Simon Rogers, *Big Issue*, 1 December 1997
26 Interview with *Record Collector*, November, 1995

Chapter 8

1 Interview with David Burke, *Evening Herald*, 22 November 1994
2 Interview with *Record Collector*, November 1995
3 Interview with Dermott Hayes, *Irish Press*, 23 May 1991
4 Interview with the author for *In Dublin*, 6 June 1991
5 Barbara Ellen, *NME*, 18 May 1991
6 Interview with the author for *In Dublin*, 6 June 1991
7 *ibid*
8 *ibid*
9 From *Bringing It All Back Home*, by Nuala O'Connor, BBC Books, 1991
10 *ibid*
11 *ibid*
12 Interview with Paul Du Noyer, *Q*, March 1993
13 Interview with Joe Jackson, *Irish Times*, 8 January 1993
14 Interview with *Record Collector*, November 1995
15 Interview in *Rolling Stone*, March 1993
16 Interview with Adam Sweeting, *Guardian*, 15 January 1993
17 Interview with David Sheppard, *Q*, October 1997
18 Interview with Joe Jackson, *Irish Times*, 8 January 1993
19 Interview with Paul Du Noyer, *Q*, March 1993
20 Interview with John Mulvey, *NME*, 26 February 1994
21 Interview with *Record Collector*, November 1995
22 *ibid*
23 Interview with Claudia Buonaiuto, *Musician*, February 1993

Chapter 9

1 Interview with the author for the *Sunday Tribune*, 7 March 1993
2 Interview with Giles Smith, *Q*, March 1993
3 *ibid*
4 Interview with the author for the *Sunday Tribune*, 7 March 1993
5 Interview with *Record Collector*, November 1995
6 Interview with Giles Smith, *Q*, March 1993
7 Interview with *Record Collector*, November 1995
8 Interview with George Byrne, *Hot Press*, October 1993
9 Interview with Giles Smith, *Q*, March 1993
10 Interview with *Record Collector*, November 1995
11 Interview with John Mulvey, *NME*, 26 February 1994
12 Interview with Jeffrey Stock, *Pulse!*, April 1994
13 *ibid*
14 Interview with John Whitley, *Telegraph Magazine*, February 1994
15 *ibid*
16 Interview with Jeffrey Stock, *Pulse!*, April 1994
17 Interview with *Record Collector*, November 1995
18 Interview with Brendan Kelly, *Montreal Gazette*, 5 June 1994
19 Interview with Peter Howell, *Toronto Star*, 3 June 1994
20 Interview with Michael Corcoran, *Dallas Morning News*, 19 May 1994
21 Interview with *Record Collector*, November 1995
22 *ibid*
23 *ibid*

Chapter 10

1 From an article by the author, *Elvis: The Next 20 Years, Irish Times*, August 1997
2 Interview with Terry Staunton, *NME*, 20 May 1995
3 Interview with Stuart Maconie, *Q*, June 1995

4 Interview with Terry Staunton, *NME*, 20 May 1995
5 *ibid*
6 Interview with James Cury, *FAD*, May 1995
7 *ibid*
8 Interview with Simon Rogers, *Big Issue*, 1 December 1997
9 Interview with Terry Staunton, *NME*, 20 May 1995
10 *ibid*
11 Interview with Robert Sandall, *Sunday Times*, 11 June 1995
12 Interview with Terry Staunton, *NME*, 20 May 1995
13 Interview with Liam Fay, *Hot Press*, June 1996
14 *ibid*
15 Interview with Paul Du Noyer, *Mojo*, June 1996
16 Interview with Liam Fay, *Hot Press*, June 1996
17 *ibid*
18 Interview with Paul Du Noyer, *Mojo*, June 1996
19 Interview with Eamon Carr, *Evening Herald*, 25 June 1996
20 Interview with Simon Rogers, *Big Issue*, 1 December 1997
21 *ibid*
22 *ibid*
23 Interview with Paul Du Noyer, *Mojo*, June 1996
24 Interview with Mike Gee: *Reverberation Home Page*
25 Questions For Cash, *Q*, February 1998
26 Interview with the author, *In Dublin*, 6 June 1991

Picture Credits